P9-DUK-630

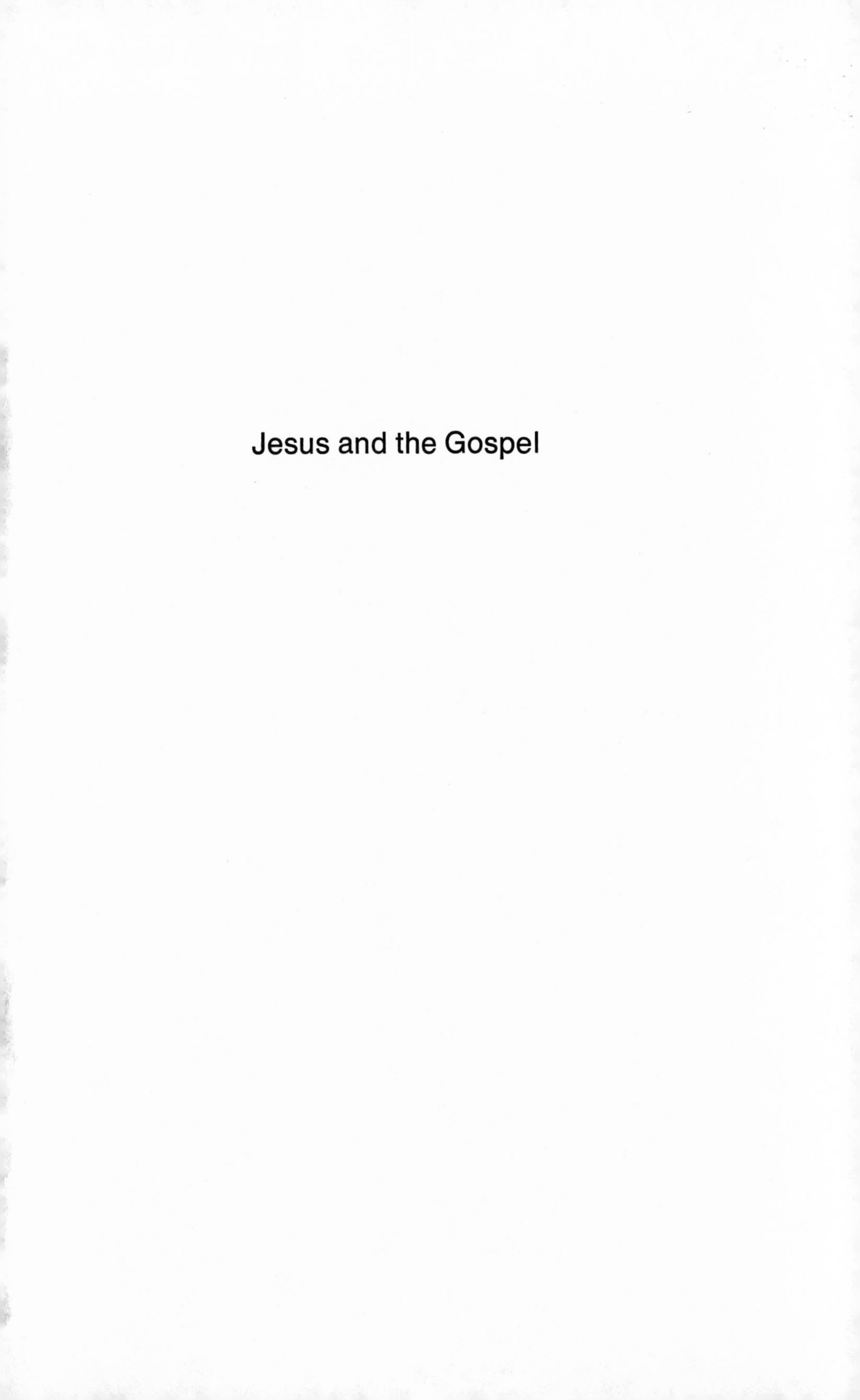

Jesus and the Gospel

Jesus and the Gospel

TRADITION, SCRIPTURE, AND CANON

WILLIAM R. FARMER

FORTRESS PRESS
Philadelphia

Library of Congress Cataloging in Publication Data

Farmer, William Reuben.
Jesus and the gospel.

Includes bibliographical references and index.
1. Jesus Christ–History of doctrines–Early church, ca. 30-600. 2. Bible. N.T. Gospels–Criticism, interpretation, etc. 3. Bible. N.T.–Canon. 4. Jesus Christ–Historicity. I. Title.
BT198.F34 226′.012 81–43078
ISBN 0–8006–0666–3 AACR

8555J81 Printed in the United States of America 1–666

To my Mother
Elsie L. Farmer
and
To my wife
Nell C. Farmer

Contents

PART III
The Development of the New Testament Canon

Preface

I am convinced that the history of scriptural exegesis from Luther to Pope John XXIII constitutes one exegetical era, and that following Vatican Council II we have entered a new era of exegesis. The era from Luther to John XXIII was essentially shaped by the needs of the Reformation and was characterized by polemics and a preoccupation with European and Western problems. The new era is yet to be defined, but it is characterized by a nonpolemical ethos in which exegetes aspire to be authentically ecumenical and seek to do their work within a global context.

In 1964, while Vatican Council II was still in session, I published *The Synoptic Problem: A Critical Review of the Problem of the Literary Relationships Between Matthew, Mark and Luke.* In this study I set forth reasons for the view that the first three Gospels were written in the sequence Matthew, Luke, and Mark. Since this contradicts the widely held two-document hypothesis, I was obliged to write the history of the development of the consensus favoring Marcan priority and the existence of Q, to show how this consensus arose in the absence of convincing evidence and in spite of still unresolved difficulties standing in the path of its critical acceptance. Since then, a second study of the history of the Marcan hypothesis has been published which supplements and complements my findings in important ways, and essentially strengthens the case against the two-document hypothesis (see Hans-Herbert Stoldt, *History and Criticism of the Marcan Hypothesis,* trans. Donald L. Niewyk [Macon: Mercer University Press, 1980]).

Moreover, in *The Synoptic Problem* I offered a fifty-page discussion of the gospel tradition under the heading of "Notes for a History of the Redaction of Synoptic Tradition in Mark."

It was one year later, in 1965, that I received an invitation to contribute an essay to *The Universal Bible* on the theme "The Gospel Tradition and the Gospels." By 1967 I had completed the assignment, and for several years I made extensive use of my manuscript in classes in New Testament. Plans for *The Universal Bible,* however, were abandoned. Therefore, in 1975, this manuscript was published in a modified form in the *Perkins School of Theology Journal* under the title "Jesus and the Gospels: An Historical and Theological Essay." This essay has been extensively modified and expanded for use in this book.

Since 1975 my research interests have focused on Christology and canon. This has made it possible to expand the scope of my study and to devote a major section of this book to the topic of the development of the New Testament canon.

Thus, the overall purpose of this book is to give a credible account of how we can document the essential lines of development which lead from Jesus to Eusebius and Constantine. The book falls into three parts: (1) an account of how the traditions concerning Jesus originated and developed; (2) an account of how the literary and theological framework of the Gospels was developed out of Jewish and Hellenistic literature, and the way in which the Jesus tradition was incorporated into this framework and influenced its shape and meaning; and (3) an account of how the New Testament canon developed, showing the decisive role of the Jesus tradition and the Gospels in relation to Pauline concerns, and the normative influence of persecution and heresy in the early church.

There is little if anything assumed in this book that is problematic which has not been discussed to my satisfaction in the extant critical literature. Where there have been gaps in that literature, I have attempted to supply critical essays of my own. This explains why at several points the reader is referred to other books and scholarly journals containing methodological and exegetical essays in which I have treated certain disputed matters at length.

The present volume covers important ground presently neglected in existing literature. It helps the reader to understand the message of Jesus within the context of his own environment and sets Paul and the Gospels within the context of the history of the Christian church. In all these matters it breaks new ground insofar as it remains abreast of the critical results of contemporary Gospel research and proceeds on the assumption that the first Gospel to be written was Matthew, followed by Luke and Mark, in that order. Finally, it recognizes the importance of studying the Gospels with reference to their place in the canon and suggests the apostolic basis for what subsequently developed into mainline Christianity.

This book has been written within the context of a particular crisis in modern theology, that is, a crisis regarding the relation of Christian faith to history. Modern theology, in part, has arisen in response to the determination of the church to expose its Scriptures to the full and untrammeled inspection of historical inquiry.

The crisis with which this essay contends exploded in Germany during the first half of the nineteenth century, and from there spread throughout Europe and into the Western Protestant world. It has not yet made massive headway into the consciousness of Orthodox Christianity, but is presently making serious inroads into the thinking of contemporary Roman Catholic theologians.

The crisis may be stated this way: the Christian church, which for centuries depended upon the Gospels as reliable witnesses to the life, teaching, passion, and resurrection of Jesus Christ, must now adjust to a situation in which its theologians recognize that the Gospels were not written by authors who participated in the events they recount, but by later figures in the early churches who belonged to the generation that lived after the eyewitness period so clearly revealed in Paul's authentic letters.

For those who are convinced that the Gospels were written earlier (for example, by contemporaries of the apostles Peter and Paul), much of this book is otiose. For those who, like Lessing, are convinced that Christian faith cannot in any case be dependent upon historical judgments concerning Jesus or the Gospels, this study can only be of historical interest and can have little theological importance. But for the remainder—and this certainly includes many modern theologians, the vast majority of questioning lay persons in the church, and some conscientious and morally sensitive persons who have no direct contact with organized church life—this book possesses more than historical interest. It possesses potential theological importance, for it offers for thoughtful consideration a credible account of the development from Jesus to the Gospels of the church. More particularly, it demonstrates how it is possible to get from Jesus, as he is accessible through historical inquiry, to the Gospels, which are Scripture for the church. Those who are intellectually alienated from and morally disenchanted with the church, but who are attracted to Jesus, have in this study a basis for responsible conversation with the church.

In no sense can the church justly appeal to Jesus in defense of avoiding controversy over matters vital to God. The gospel tradition and the churches' Gospels make that abundantly clear. The peace that Jesus came to bring is the peace that comes when one is embraced by the sovereign love of God. It is not "ease in Zion."

It is important to recognize the decisive role of Jesus as martyr in the church which formed the New Testament. That eschatological Jesus once enlisted for the defense of Christendom is now breaking old forms and making all things new. By faith we lay claim on the scriptural promises of God and live in hope.

WILLIAM R. FARMER
DALLAS
NEW YEAR'S DAY 1982

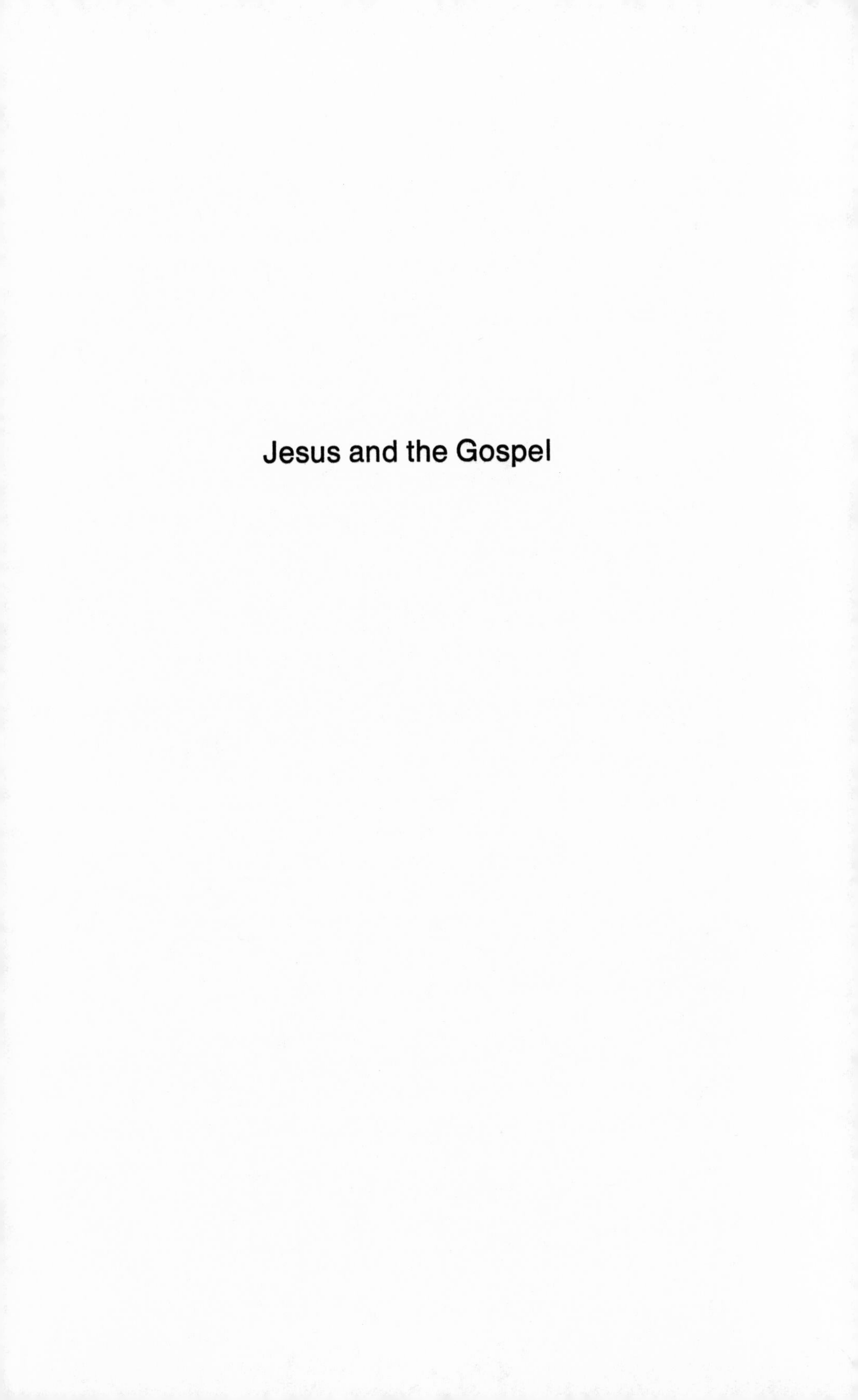

Jesus and the Gospel

Introduction

THE INADEQUACIES OF THE MARCAN HYPOTHESIS

One point of departure for this book is the synoptic problem. The chief argument flows, though not inevitably, from the recognition that Mark was not our first Gospel. Due respect for the tradition of Marcan priority requires that reasons be given for departing from this generally accepted research paradigm. The problem we face was defined by Thomas Huxley eighty-four years ago as "that of the origin of the synoptic gospels and that of the historical value of the narratives which they contain."[1]

Which of these Gospels was written first, which second, and which third? What was the relationship between them? Did the evangelist who wrote first use all the sources at his disposal? Did the one who wrote second know the first? If so, what use did the second make of the first? Did the second, in addition to the first, make use of another source or sources? Did the one who wrote third have knowledge of either one or both of the other two? If so, what use did the third make of the first and/or the second, and did the third have, in addition, other sources? Are all three of the synoptic Gospels, or are any two of them, completely independent of one or both of the other two? Could all three be dependent upon an earlier gospel that is not now known? Or could one, two, or all three have used a source referred to by one or more ancient witnesses which has not come down to us? If so, was this source oral or written?

These are the kinds of questions that scholars have posed in their effort to understand what, since the creation of the modern synopsis by Johann Jakob Griesbach in 1776, has been called "the synoptic problem." Our task is not to consider this problem comprehensively, nor shall we attempt to set forth in detail a case for the most adequate solution to the problem. All that is required at this point is that we consider seriously the most important "inadequacies" of today's generally accepted solution, which by now has become almost commonplace in church literature. Simply stated, the solution is that Mark was written first, that Matthew and Luke independently copied Mark, and that Matthew and Luke also independently copied a collection of the sayings of Jesus called Q.

An ancient tradition that can be traced back as early as Origen supports the view that Mark was written after Matthew, but before Luke. Another ancient tradition, resting upon the testimony of Irenaeus and Clement of Alexandria and going back to the testimony of Papias, assures us that Matthew and John, disciples of Jesus, wrote the Gospels that bear their names, and that Mark and Luke were written by apostolic men. Mark assisted Peter, and Luke was a traveling companion of Paul. According to this stream of tradition, Mark actually heard Peter preach in Rome, and his Gospel is based on Peter's preaching.

Griesbach (1745–1812) stood solidly within this ancient double tradition. He accepted the tradition that Mark had been written after Matthew as well as the tradition that Mark had committed to writing what he had heard from Peter. These two traditions did not seem mutually exclusive to him. But Griesbach also knew that this ancient tradition had been recently challenged from different directions. (We are talking about the situation in Germany during the last quarter of the eighteenth century.) The two most important challenges he mentions are (1) signs had been noted indicating that Mark had Luke before him as he wrote his Gospel, and (2) it had been noted that there were difficulties with the generally held view that Mark had abbreviated Matthew.

Some scholars in Griesbach's day were suggesting not only that Mark did not copy Matthew, but also that Mark came before Matthew. Others were suggesting that Mark came after Luke. Thus, Mark was being dislodged from its traditional place between Matthew and Luke from two directions—one lever moving Mark before Matthew and the other after Luke.

In this situation, standing firmly within the tradition that had come to him but aware of new observations that were being made, Griesbach discovered something about Mark in relationship to Matthew and Luke that he regarded as very important.

Mark's Selection of Items in Relation to Matthew and Luke

It will require some historical imagination to put ourselves in Griesbach's place and reexperience with him the shocking realization that Mark must have known both Matthew and Luke. Griesbach reasoned that if Luke and John included many things which Matthew had not mentioned at all, and if the evangelists themselves hinted that for the sake of brevity they had passed over many wonderful and illustrious deeds of Jesus Christ and omitted numerous of his discourses, then how did it happen that Mark did not use more of the enormous quantity of those omitted items, but largely confined himself to the *same* items Matthew and Luke took from the *same* source?

If we object that Mark does indeed have some items not found in Matthew and Luke, Griesbach is right in coming back with the answer, "Yes, but altogether these few items do not total more than twenty-four verses in the entire Gospel of Mark!" Thus, for Griesbach the problem remained. For this reason and others, Griesbach concluded that "Mark's purpose was to select from the Gospels of Matthew and Luke the items most useful for his intended readers, and to narrate them in the manner appropriate to them."[2] Griesbach claimed that in this view everything was clear and simple. Otherwise we seem to run into a blank wall.

Why Mark would have thought the items he selected from Matthew and Luke were more useful than certain items he omitted (for example, the Sermon on the Mount, including the Lord's Prayer) is a secondary question for Griesbach. He is prepared to discuss this. But at the fundamental level of initial insight it is the shock of realizing that there seems to be no other way to explain the overall pattern of selection Mark has made from the enormous store of tradition presumably available to him that presses in upon Griesbach and helps convince him that Mark could not be first or second, but must be third and must have known Matthew and Luke.

The first inadequacy in the hypothesis of Marcan priority, then, is its failure to account for Mark's selection of items in relation to Matthew and Luke from the presumably rich storehouse of tradition available to him.

The Order and Chronology of Mark's Gospel

A second inadequacy is closely bound up with the above. If Mark had been written first, there would be no way to explain the fact that the Gospel has no independent chronology. Every evangelist but Mark has chronology both in common with the others and independent from them. But not Mark! This is best explained by recognizing that Mark drew upon the chronologies of Matthew and Luke and had no other authority for his chronology.

Moreover, ever since Bishop Butler refuted the argument for Marcan priority based upon the phenomenon of order (Butler proved that this argument did not support Marcan priority, only that Mark's order is in some sense a middle term between that of Matthew and Luke), it has become fashionable to say that the phenomenon of order prove nothing.[3] Butler to the contrary, however, the phenomenon of order clearly indicates more than that Mark is a middle term. It also indicates that Mark is third, a point that Butler overlooked.

Of course, a great deal depends upon how one begins. One may begin with the recognition that the fundamental fact constituting the synoptic problem is the agreement and disagreement in order and content of *all three* synoptic Gospels *considered together*. If so, then the synthetic judgment is to be preferred. The evangelist who wrote second used the work of the first, the one who wrote third used the work of both of his predecessors, and the evangelist who wrote third was the evangelist who wrote Mark. It is to be preferred because it can best explain the pattern of Mark's selection of items and the order in which these items are presented. Moreover, both the selection of items and their order of presentation can be explained if Mark knew and drew upon Matthew and Luke in composing his own Gospel.

In summary, it is an inadequacy of the view of Marcan priority that it can explain neither the pattern of selection Mark has made from the rich storehouse of items presumably available to him in composing his Gospel nor the pattern of order Mark gives to the items he selects *in relation to the pattern of selection and of order* that we find in Matthew and Luke. I emphasize these last words because they are decisive. We must never lose sight of the fact that we need a solution for the synoptic problem that can explain the relationship of agreement and disagreement in order and content of *all three Gospels considered together*.

The Relationship of Matthew and Luke

A third inadequacy of the generally accepted solution to the synoptic problem is that it requires us to believe that Matthew and Luke are independent of one another. Such a view, however, does not permit explanation of two very important sets of facts.

The first set consists of the numerous agreements between Matthew and Luke in passages where they are supposed to be independently copying Mark. If Matthew and Luke are independently copying Mark, there ought not to be as much agreement between them and against Mark as in fact there is. Efforts have been made at various times to explain away this embarrassment for the two-document hypothesis, but all such efforts have failed to convince most experts. This has led in some cases to a modification of the two-document hypothesis, as, for example, with Morgenthaler, who concluded that Luke must have known Matthew at a later stage after he had composed the main text of his Gospel, using Mark and Q. In other cases, as with Austin Farrer, it has led to giving up belief in Q entirely and to positing Luke's extensive use of both Matthew and Mark. This latter path really leads to the abandonment of the two-source hypothesis, though it still leaves room for belief in Marcan priority.

A second set of facts working against the independence of Matthew and Luke is constituted by the overall agreement in literary form between these two Gospels. Each is more like the other than either is like any other document. There are at least twenty topics that Matthew and Luke have in common.[4] These cannot be explained through a dependence upon Mark, because Mark does not contain several of these topics. For example, Mark does not have birth narratives, a genealogy, a temptation story, the Sermon on the Mount, or large collections of parables. The parables, genealogies, and birth narratives contained in Matthew and Luke differ from one another, but a topical agreement remains which cannot be explained by the generally accepted solution to the synoptic problem. In addition, Matthew has seven distinguishable discourses, all of which are represented in Luke, generally by the opening sayings in each discourse. This is a remarkable concatenation of compositional agreement, especially since these seven discourses occur (except for one displacement) in exactly the same sequence in both Matthew and Luke. This adds to the evidence that there was some compositional dependence between Matthew and Luke.

Thus, it is an inadequacy of the two-document hypothesis that it affords no satisfactory explanation for the very extensive agreement between Matthew and Luke.

The Testimony of External Evidence

Fourthly, an inadequacy of the generally accepted solution to the synoptic problem is that it goes contrary to the external evidence, which points consistently to Matthean priority. For example, when 2 Peter cites the gospel story of the Transfiguration, the textual affinity is closer to Matthew than to Mark. While the text of Matthew is known to Ignatius, the first clear use of Mark does not come until the middle of the second century with Justin Martyr. Moreover, all the church fathers who mention the sequence in which the Gospels were written indicate that Matthew came first. The earliest statement regarding sequence was made by Clement of Alexandria who indicated that both Matthew and Luke were written before Mark.

A commonplace of sound historiography is for the historian to balance internal with external evidence. An inadequacy of the theory of Marcan priority is that it does not maintain such a balance. Those who defend Marcan priority ignore their responsibility to account for the fact that there is little or no support for it from external evidence.

The Testimony of History

Finally, there is the historical question. Can historians give a credible account of the origin and development of the Christian church on the basis of Marcan priority? This question can be made quite specific in terms of contemporary scholarship. For example, can Grillmeier in his highly regarded treatment of the history of Christology give a credible account of the development of Christology in the biblical period, assuming the priority of Mark and the existence of Q?[5] The reader of this otherwise masterful study can quickly see how little help Grillmeier is able to derive from Mark by regarding it as the earliest Gospel. Or we can ask, can von Campenhausen in his discussion of the formation of the Christian Bible[6] show how the priority of Mark and/or the existence of Q contributes to our understanding of the development of the New Testament canon? Though accepting Q, von Campenhausen finds no place for it and devotes only one five-sentence paragraph to Mark!

Leaving aside the matter of a hypothetical Q, do Grillmeier's and von Campenhausen's virtual neglect of Mark mean that the Gospel is relatively unimportant in the development of Christian doctrine and the New Testament canon? Not necessarily; it could mean in fact that scholars have rendered Mark a great disservice by placing his Gospel at the beginning of the gospel genre instead of where it actually belongs in the synoptic sequence.

Let us put the matter another way. Jesus and his disciples were Jews living in Palestine. In due time the community that began with Jesus and his disciples spread out into the Mediterranean world. As the extra-Palestinian expansion of the community took place, more and more gentiles sought membership in it until finally it developed into a community that was predominantly gentile.

How does this affect our view of the Gospels? All would agree, of course, that Matthew is the most Jewish Gospel in the canon. It is also the Gospel that best reflects the Palestinian origins of the Christian church. Luke too is very Jewish, but there are many passages where, by comparison, this Gospel is better adapted for use by gentiles outside of Palestine. While unmistakably retaining traditions of Jewish and Palestinian origin, Mark is the best adapted of the three for gentile readers who are not acquainted with Palestinian culture. Thus, in terms of historical development, we can begin easily enough with Matthew and go on to Luke and/or Mark. But historically speaking, it is difficult to reverse the process and to place Matthew after either one or both of the others.

Here is a concrete example that illustrates this point. Jesus opposed people carrying out their religious duties in an ostentatious manner. He in fact pointed out the practices of some of the religious authorities as examples *not* to follow.

In Matt. 23:5, Jesus notes that these people "make their phylacteries broad and their fringes long." All of Jesus' hearers understood very well what he was referring to by phylacteries and fringes (*kraspeda*). In predominantly gentile circles outside Palestine, however, these terms were much less intelligible. Luke, therefore, in a parallel passage (20:46), has selected the ostentatious dress of legal authorities, which was known to his readers, and simply refers to scribes wearing stoles or long robes. A good deal is lost in this modification of the tradition because the ostentatious dress of lawyers in gentile circles does not necessarily carry with it the force of Jesus' teaching, which was specifically aimed at religious ostentatiousness. However, what was intelligible to Jewish and Palestinian hearers needed to be modified and put into a form that was intelligible to gentile readers living outside of Palestine. This explains the text of Luke. The text of Mark (12:38) is the same as that of Luke in this instance, so that if Mark wrote this passage after Matthew and Luke, he simply chose to follow that form of the tradition best suited for gentile readers (in Luke) over what was for his purposes a comparatively less intelligible Jewish and Palestinian text (in Matthew).

Here is another example. In Matt. 15:1–20 (see also Mark 7:1–23) we have a story about Pharisees and scribes coming to Jesus, asking why his disciples do not wash their hands when they eat. The issue in question is clearly understandable in circles well acquainted with Jewish concern for observance of Mosaic purity laws. But for gentile readers far removed from Palestine and presumably from Jewish society, it might require a word of explanation. Therefore, Mark clarifies the matter by noting that unwashed hands are defiled. Then he adds the following remarkable explanatory gloss:

> For the Pharisees, and all the Jews, do not eat unless they wash their hands, observing the tradition of the elders; and when they come from the market place, they do not eat unless they purify themselves; and there are many other traditions which they observe, the washing of cups and pots and vessels of bronze (Mark 7:3–4).

Luke has chosen to omit this Matthean story possibly because he does not often allow himself the literary license of using an explanatory gloss, which would have been necessary in this case. On the other hand, Mark often resorts to explanatory glosses even though never as extensively in other instances as in this one. Therefore, assuming for the moment that Mark is third, this time he has chosen not to follow Luke in omitting the story. Instead, he follows Matthew, but only as was appropriate for his readers and with the addition of fitting words of explanation. Here again it is possible to understand how the tradition that assumes the sequence Matthew, Luke, Mark developed in passages where the text of Mark seems to be clearly secondary to the parallel text of Matthew.[7]

The fifth inadequacy of the Marcan hypothesis, then, is that it offers no explanation for its requirement that the more Jewish and Palestinian Gospel, Matthew, must be perceived as coming after and as dependent upon the less Jewish and less Palestinian Mark. This is a historical difficulty of very great consequence.

We may conclude with the following observations. Combinations of any two or three of these five alleged inadequacies would seem to constitute a damaging case against the two-document hypothesis. This means that if any one or two of these alleged inadequacies could be answered, the case against Marcan priority and the existence of Q would still seem formidable.

Why, then, do scholars continue to hold to the two-document hypothesis? Any one of these alleged inadequacies would normally be accepted as grounds for disbelief in any other hypothesis. Does this mean that these alleged inadequacies are merely "alleged," but of no real substance?

Let me assure you that the inadequacies discussed above are genuine and not just phantoms in the minds of disgruntled critics. They are inadequacies that are grounded in the facts of the case. The academic literature on this subject supplies ample supporting evidence for these allegations.

Why, then, do competent critics continue to hold to such a discredited hypothesis? First, they are loathe to grant that it has been all that discredited. Marcan priority still has worthy defenders. The very staying power of the two-document hypothesis seems to lend credence to its validity. But from where does this staying power come?

To be sure, there is a great body of data that fits the two-document hypothesis, and such data may be construed as evidence for that hypothesis *in a broad sense*. But unless there is data that can be said to fit *only* the two-document hypothesis and *no other* hypothesis equally well, that data can hardly be counted as proof. As far as I am aware, there is very little evidence that can be said to fit *only* the two-document hypothesis.

We must look elsewhere for the great confidence that many scholars have in this generally accepted solution. Therefore we repeat the question, From where does the remarkable staying power of the two-document hypothesis come? Has it any source other than its seemingly infinite capacity for being modified? Few experts continue to hold to the two-document hypothesis without contending that it needs some modification. How many modifications is the expert who holds to Marcan priority and the existence of Q willing to consider? "As many as the evidence may require" seems to be the answer.

How, then, do those who continue to hold to the generally accepted solution distinguish themselves in principle from the medieval defenders of the Ptolemaic theory? The discovery of every new heavenly body that constituted an anomaly for that theory was met by hypothesizing some new epicycle to account for the apparent discrepancy in the theory. No number of epicycles seemed to be so great as to cause universal doubt in the theory itself.

The important thing about the Ptolemaic theory was that it seemed to work. One could account for the data as long as one continued to believe in the basic truth of the paradigm and as long as one's belief in the essential adequacy of that paradigm was strong enough to sustain faith in its truth in the face of the expanding body of data that called for an increasingly complex series of epicycles. As long as one could account for the data, no matter how many epicycles were required, one could continue to rest assured that the Ptolemaic theory, which had been so useful over such a long period of time, was the correct theory after all.

It is the human capacity for credulity that helps explain why, in spite of the fact that no hypothesis has been more thoroughly falsified over a period of many years in learned books, in articles in scholarly journals, and in scientific monographs published by university presses, the two-document hypothesis continues as the generally accepted solution to the synoptic problem. In any case, this hypothesis appears to be incapable of being falsified because of its infinite capacity for modification.

How, then, can we make progress? It seems to me that progress can be made only when an alternate hypothesis is set forth that explains all the data equally well and that does not place too great a strain on our credulity. To me that hypothesis appears to be the one that Matthew and Luke were written before Mark, and that Mark was composed with Matthew and Luke in view. Luke apparently had access to Matthew and other written and oral source material. The key to opening up the subject of Christian faith and history, therefore, is to understand the origins of the Gospel of Matthew.

MATTHEW AND THE BIBLE

When one approaches Matthew afresh on its own terms, it is easy to see why this Gospel has been accorded the priority it enjoys in the New Testament canon. In addition, when we consider the shape of Scripture as a whole, it is remarkable how well the shape of Matthew suits the function it fills in the canon of the Christian church.

The Shape of Matthew

Matthew was profoundly immersed in Jewish scriptures. Isaiah, and interestingly enough, the Wisdom of Solomon, seem to have exercised the greatest influence upon the way he formed his Gospel. The fact that the Wisdom of Solomon must be included among the writings that have obviously influenced our author takes on added interest when we remember that it is this book which, scholars tell us, Paul at some time in his life must have given a considerable amount of study. Paul and Matthew stand in the same exegetical tradition and in a closely related theological and ecclesiastical tradition—Matthew coming a generation later than Paul and after certain cataclysmic developments in Judaism and in the church.

The writings of Isaiah dominate the exegetical tradition in which Paul and Matthew stand. The Book of Genesis, the Book of Job, the Psalms, and the Wisdom of Solomon also stand within the conceptual compass of this Isaianic exegetical tradition.

As for the Wisdom of Solomon, Matthew concentrates his attention on the first and second chapters where the author develops for his Hellenistic readers Isaiah's concept of the suffering servant in terms of the righteous man. This man is "God's son" (2:18), professing to "have knowledge of God, and calls himself a child of the Lord" (2:13), and "boasts that God is his father" (2:16). The ungodly mock him and say:

> Let us see if his words are true, and let us test what will happen at the end of his life; for if the righteous man is God's son, he will help him, and will deliver him from the hand of his adversaries. Let us test him with insult and torture, that we may find out how gentle he is and make trial of his forbearance. Let us condemn him to a shameful death. . . . (2:17–20).

The influence of this particular Isaianic exegetical tradition upon the formation of the text of the Gospel account is unmistakable. It is important to recognize, however, that Matthew tells the story of what happens to the righteous servant of God in terms of the life of Jesus. The life of Jesus *transforms* the story of the righteous servant of God as we might have expected it to be told by our reading the Psalms, Isaiah, and the Wisdom of Solomon. In the Gospel those who oppose Jesus are not the ungodly, the unrighteous, the sinners, and those who transgress the law. Jesus' opponents are the righteous, those who do not transgress but who uphold the law. They oppose Jesus above all because he is a friend of those who transgress the law, a friend of tax collectors and sinners. Central to this story of theological reversal is the claim that Jesus came to save "not . . . the righteous, but sinners" (Matt. 9:13). Jesus represents a new or different kind of righteousness—a righteousness that "exceeds that of the scribes and Pharisees" (Matt. 5:20).

Matthew's revelation that the righteous servant of God will be opposed not by the wicked, but by the righteous gives power to the Gospels. Those who thirst after righteousness and are grasped by this truth are freed to give themselves to the service of God without suffering illusions as to the realities of their situations. They certainly will not place their ultimate trust in the "righteousness of men," but rather, as Paul teaches us, in the "righteousness of God."

The idea of a written gospel probably never entered the head of mortal man before the Book of Isaiah was written and handed on to the Hellenistic world. Somewhere in the Hellenistic world after the time of the apostle Paul, someone standing in the apostle's tradition and reading Isa. 53:7–12 in the Greek version preserved for us in the Septuagint came to the words:

> And he, because of his affliction, opens not his mouth: he was led as a sheep to the slaughter, and as a lamb before the shearer is dumb, so he opens not his mouth. In his humiliation his judgment was taken away: *who will set out in detail* (or describe) *his generation*? For his life is taken away from the earth: because of the transgressions (or lawlessness) of my people, he was led to death. And I will give the wicked for his burial, and the rich for his death; for he practiced no iniquity, nor craft with his mouth. The Lord also is pleased to cleanse him of his bruise. If you can give an offering for sin, your soul shall see a long-lived seed: the Lord also is pleased to take away from the travail of his soul, to shew him light,

and to form him with understanding; to justify the Righteous One who serves many well; and he shall bear their sins. Therefore he shall inherit many, and he shall divide the spoils of the mighty; because his soul was handed over to death, and he was reckoned with the lawless ones (or transgressors or sinners); and he bore the sins of many, and was handed over because of their lawlessness (or transgressions).

There is no mistaking the striking similarities between the prescriptions of this passage and the detailed account we find in Matthew. Nor is it surprising that traditional Christian piety since the second century has combined the descriptions of the servant in Isaiah with the gospel descriptions of Jesus. One need only think of Handel's *Messiah* to see one form of this conflation taking place.

This conceptional, theological, and christological kinship between Isaiah and Matthew is closer than that between Isaiah and any other Gospel. Yet there are modern critics who deny the existence of any clear evidence that the servant songs have significantly influenced the thinking of Matthew. Such purists overlook the nature of influence, which is seldom either direct or explicit in literature. More often lines of influence, while obvious to the mind's eye, are difficult to trace in provable terms. So it is with Isaiah and Matthew. Between them stands the Wisdom of Solomon, and between Isaiah and the Wisdom of Solomon on the one hand and Matthew on the other stands the towering figure of the apostle Paul. The point is that Matthew never read Isaiah in a context where the prophet's meaning was understood without reference to what we think of as apochryphal writings or tradition.

Matthew stood in an exegetical tradition in which the servant songs of Isaiah were considered together not only with messianic passages in the Psalms, but also with the portrait of the righteous one as the Son of God in the Wisdom of Solomon. This portrait of the righteous one is close enough to Isaiah's portrait of the servant of the Lord to warrant the assumption that Matthew perceived the two sources in some relationship to one another. In any case, it would appear that both have markedly influenced his portrait of Jesus, which immediately tells us that he was not woodenly following one to the exclusion of the other.

In addition to the visual images in Isaiah and other prophetic books (possibly Job, certainly Psalm 22, and the Wisdom of Solomon), the chief source at the evangelist's disposal for his composition of Matthew was what is called the "Jesus tradition." Or perhaps we can even speak of the public career of Jesus as it left its imprint on the memory of the Christian community and was preserved in the Jesus tradition. In any case, this tradition was rich and variegated, including (1) material in relatively fixed written form (as, for example, parables, wisdom sayings, *chreiae,* beatitudes, apocalyptic sayings, woes, birth stories, healing stories, legends, mythological accounts, genealogies, and so forth) and (2) an undefinable body of lore, largely oral in nature, and varying and developing differently in different communities.

Against this background, consider one moment in the formation of the Bible in the following way. Imagine that under the influence of a call from God the evangelist has responded to the question, "Who will set out in detail (or describe) his generation?" by saying in effect, "Here am I, Lord." No one can prove this happened, but it affords a plausible explanation for the origin of the idea of composing the Gospel of Matthew. It also provides an explanation for the tradition that must have developed from some source that this composition was of the same order as Scripture, that is, that it was inspired by the same God of Abraham, Isaac, and Jacob who had inspired the prophets and who, to paraphrase the author of the Book of Hebrews, in these latter days has spoken to us in his Son.[8]

What I mean to suggest (and I mean this as literally as metaphorical language can express the thought) is that the Gospel of Matthew was conceived in the mind of the evangelist by the active agency of the Holy Spirit as that mind was devoutly engaged in probing the Scriptures to find the purpose and meaning of God for his own existence. Or, to use the language of Paul, though not quite in a Pauline way, "God's spirit spoke to his spirit." Thus was set in motion something very distinctive in what we call our Bible. Until then there were letters of Paul, a vast amount of corresponding Christian correspondence, multifarious religious writings of the Jews, and the Jesus tradition, *but there was no distinctively Christian Bible.*

The Bible eventually emerged as a canon of Scripture which included letters of Paul, religious writings of the Jews, the Gospel of Matthew (with three others like it), and an assorted collection of other Christian writings (Acts, Hebrews, Revelation, and so forth). It did not emerge simply as an unorganized collection of books. The Bible emerged as a sacred book with a fixed beginning and end and with a particular arrangement of the contents.

Such a notion cannot be accounted for simply on the basis of Hebraic or Jewish antecedents. Arthur Jeffery, after surveying the matter of the Hebrew scriptures, concludes:

> In all of this there is no hint of a canon of scripture, but there are some elements out of which such a canon could arise. We find writings considered as sacred and tending to be collected, though there was no fixed body of them, since the Chronicler made use of some which were not preserved in the final collection. We find the sense of writings being authoritative as a *regula*. We find official pronouncement of certain writings as authoritative, though what Ezra is said to have "canonized" was a body of laws, and so not the Pentateuch as we have it, which contains much besides law and, indeed, includes material from a time later than that of Ezra. The canon of scripture had not yet come into existence.[9]

The Challenge of Hellenism

Consider the possibility that our notion of Bible may have been incipiently present in Alexander's determination to carry a copy of Homer wherever his campaigns took him, and to keep these scriptures at his bedside. Cities that had been founded by Alexander established schools in which the Greek classics were studied. Elias Bickerman, in a memorable lecture at Columbia University almost a quarter of a century ago, developed the thesis that the Jewish synagogue came into existence as the definable institution we know in response to these Hellenistic schools, which emerged all over the *oikoumene* in the wake of Alexander's conquests. The very term *synagogue* is a Hellenistic expression and is often simply transliterated as a lone word from Greek in the Hebrew and Aramaic texts of rabbinic Judaism. The technical exegetical rules and vocabulary developed by the rabbis are largely taken over from the rhetorical usage and terminology of the contemporary Hellenistic schools.

As Homer and other writings were to be studied in these Hellenistic schools, so the Torah (until then in custody of the priests), the Prophets, and other Jewish writings were to be read and studied in the synagogues. When developing a curriculum, of course, decisions have to be made concerning which books are to be read and by implication which are not worth reading. In the ancient world the latter eventually meant not worth copying. Aristotle obviously had to make some such decisions when tutoring Alexander; thus may have been born a conceptual basis for the core of the subsequent Alexandrian canon of Greek classics. Moreover, we have a hint of the vast amount of "not worth copying" Jewish religious literature that was floating around in antiquity whenever archaeologists uncover for us something like the Qumran library or the Cairo *Genizah*.

How it was decided which books were to be read and studied in the synagogues we may never know, unless it was a selection made at least in part over against or in response to the challenge of the Hellenistic (Alexandrian) canon of Greek classics. There are indications that the Book of Isaiah played a central role in this process. We see this symbolized in the fact that both in the scriptures of the Christian church and in the library of Qumran, at present our two most extensive and reliable indices on this matter, Isaiah stands out in importance over all other Jewish scriptures.

It would be interesting to probe why this is so. Perhaps the universal vision of Isaiah, developing presumably out of the Yahwist tradition in the Pentateuch and envisioning the nations as a family with God as Father, offered the pundits of the synagogues and other Jewish religious centers like Qumran the least inadequate conceptual basis for coping with the cosmopolitanism, universalism, and syncretism of the Hellenistic schools. Certainly the problem of the Gentiles and how the Jews were to relate to them dominated theological speculation in Judaism after Daniel. This also appears to be the period in which the Judeo-Christian concept of Bible began to take shape. Moreover, no recognition of the threefold canon of Jewish scripture (Torah, Prophets, and Writings) recognized in Luke-Acts seems to have occurred before ben Sirach. In fact we might ask whether this grouping of similar literary materials is not akin to the Aristotelian task of categorizing, cataloging, and systematizing for purposes of study and research. At a later period, is not also the separation of the Gospel of Luke from the more original two-volume work Luke-Acts and the inclusion of this Gospel with three others to form a fourfold Gospel canon a theological development with distinctive Aristotelian connotations? In any event, it seems clear that the collection of Paul's letters into a Pauline corpus would have been perceived at the time as in keeping with the spirit of the Alexandrian school.

The Challenge of Marcion

Marcion's canon of "Gospel and Apostle [Paul's letters]" differs from our Bible in that it omits many books included in the New Testament. These omissions, however, basically supplement the books contained in Marcion's canon: four Gospels instead of one; other letters attributed to the apostle Paul; letters attributed to other apostles; an Acts of the Apostles, and the Revelation of John.

The greatest difference between the Christian canon and Marcion's canon is found in the latter's omission of any Jewish scriptures. Therefore, the retention of the Old Testament books in the Christian canon is of greater theological consequence for the church than the addition of Christian writings not found in Marcion's canon. The union of a collection of distinctively and self-consciously Christian writings with a collection of Jewish scriptures is the fundamental fact about the shape of our Bible, theologically conceived. Of all the books of the Bible, Matthew bespeaks this shape most clearly. No other book in our Bible could have served so well as the logical link between the two collections. As full of Jesus Christ and Christian doctrine as Matthew is, no author of our Bible is as concerned as the author of Matthew to preserve theological and exegetical continuity with older Jewish scriptures and to perceive the new as fulfillment of the old.

The Shape of the Bible

Though it may seem paradoxical, Paul was more Jewish and less Christian than Matthew. This is true primarily because Paul came earlier in the development of that particular Jewish religious community that has come to be identified as "Christian." Paul was willing, for a time at least, to accommodate a twofold church mission: one to the Jews and one to the Gentiles. In this sense his Jewish ties were more substantial than those of Matthew, for whom there was really only a single mission to the Gentiles. Both Paul and Matthew accepted the authority of the Jewish scriptures and perceived the God of Abraham, Isaac, and Jacob as the God and Father of Jesus Christ. Most Christians, that is, the great majority of those who accept the authority of the Christian Bible, are Gentiles and have been since the end of the first century. Now that is a fact worth pondering, that gentile Christians should have a canon of Scripture so full of Jewish writings. This undoubtedly has to do with the fact that Jesus was a Jew, as were the disciples and the apostle Paul. The God whom gentile Christians worship is also the God whom Jews worship. However, God has given the church in Jesus Christ a world-shaking and restructuring revelation of himself, a revelation about which there are more than mere echoes in the prophets of old.

The letters of Paul could hardly have provided the nexus or logical link between the Jewish scriptures and Christian writings in a Christian canon. Regardless of Paul's respect for legal precedents from the Old Testament and his Christocentrism, his letters are dominated by his own personal experience and fate and the inseparable problems of his churches. Yet these very personal letters remain at the theological heart of the New Testament, in whose overall shaping they have found a corresponding place of real and symbolic importance. (I say this understanding very well how Acts and the pastorals in our canon control the church's understanding of these letters.)

Matthew, at the beginning of our New Testament, is transitional. This Gospel points back to the prophets who stand at the heart of the Old Testament, and forward to Paul, who stands at the heart of the New Testament, and bridges the two with the prophetic story of Jesus proclaimed as publicly crucified.

The public proclamation of Jesus Christ, crucified, is presupposed in Paul's letters. By themselves, however, Paul's letters could never be an adequate theological or documentary substitute for this public proclamation. In the economy of our Bible, shaped to serve as an *oikos* of the Spirit (an organized dwelling place of the Spirit and a place where the Spirit is alive and well), the Gospels function as developed fixed textual forms of the proclamation of Jesus Christ and him crucified. The Gospels state in Pauline form the premise of the Isaianic *pro nobis* argument for Christian life and faith.

Obviously, Matthew did not position his Gospel in the Bible. Others have seen to the construction of the argument about Matthew's position by the shape they have given our Bible, with its presuppositions laid out in full in the Jewish scriptures and its conclusion in the Book of Revelation and its heavenly Jerusalem: "I am the Alpha and the Omega, the first and the last, the beginning and the end" (22:13). We find that much of this same argument has been telescoped through the use of dramatic license into the life of Jesus and presented in a unique way in Matthew's Gospel. But the argument itself is older than Matthew and at least as old as Paul.

Conclusion

Reflecting on Matthew from the point of view of its place in the canon opens up a number of interesting historical and theological lines of investigation. Moreover, it tends to correct extreme formulations of the discontinuity between the Old and the New Testaments. At the same time it helps us to avoid the danger of falsely exaggerating the acknowledged discontinuities between Paul and the Gospel writers.

We have seen that to understand the Gospel of Matthew, it is not enough to note the motif of the fulfillment of Scripture. To account for the theological reversal we find in the Gospels, it is necessary to recognize that the actual life of Jesus has *transformed* the story of the righteous servant of God as we might have expected that story to be told by our reading the Psalms, Isaiah, and the Wisdom of Solomon. That Jesus ate with tax collectors and sinners, for example, cannot be explained in terms of fulfillment of Scripture.

But this presupposes that we can know in fact that Jesus did eat with tax collectors and sinners, and that we can reconstruct a reliable account of the essential outlines of his ministry. Can we know beyond a reasonable doubt such things about Jesus, and can we attempt a reliable account of his public ministry?

THE PUBLIC CAREER OF JESUS

Categories of Evidence

The story of the Bible is intrinsically mythical because it purports to tell us about God's activity among mortals, and myth is the chief mode of communicating about such divine-human activity. The Christian church has always denied attempts to reduce, translate, or even to elevate its faith to a philosophy that might bypass or obviate serious engagement with this story.

Since the nineteenth century's insistence on "history without myth," Christian theologians have expressed an interest in critical (that is, credible) reconstructions of the biblical story. Such reconstructions are not substitutes for the original biblical writings or for theology itself. Instead they serve a history-conscious age as theological aids to reflection, which can be used to focus attention upon themes of the biblical story that are of central concern to the historian. Since the historian is a contemporary who shares life in the present age with the theologian, his reconstructions afford theology one avenue to meaning for faith. Moreover, since the biblical story, including the story of Jesus as the Son of God, is intrinsically mythical, it is methodologically correct to ask whether the Gospels preserve reliable evidence that would enable the historian to reconstruct the public career of the actual Jesus, even if only in outline form.

The answer to this question might be as follows. If a commission of well-trained historians were to be transported back to the days immediately after the end of Jesus' public career, they would face this situation:

1. They would have opportunity to collect the correspondence of Jesus, including letters he sent and letters he received (for example, the letters of bar Cochba that have recently been recovered from the caves of the Judean desert).
2. They would be able to preserve all kinds of physical evidence important for understanding Jesus' lifestyle, that is, the clothing he wore, the tools he used as a carpenter, the copies of the scriptures he studied, the cross on which he died, and so forth.
3. They would have access to any public records that may have been kept of the hearings Jesus had before the authorities.
4. Through Jesus' disciples they would have access to the words he created to make clear what he had to say about God, peoples' relationship to God, and peoples' relationship to one another.

These and other categories of evidence would all be important to the historian, to one degree or another. But suppose these historians had to choose one category of evidence at the expense of all others. If their task was to preserve the evidence that would be most useful to historians in answering the question of what Jesus did and said, and that would account for the character and purpose of the movement that developed in his name, they would be remiss if they did not choose to preserve the words he created. This is precisely the category of evidence that has been preserved abundantly in Matthew and Luke. Unlike the case of Abraham Lincoln, where we have chiefly two of his public utterances (his Gettysburg address and his second inaugural speech) to live by, in the case of Jesus his followers have well over forty of his most memorable words by which to norm their faith and life.

It may be regrettable that we have no letters of Jesus' and no access to public records concerning his activities in Palestine. It would be even more regrettable if we allowed our methodological skepticism to distort the realities of the situation historians face in writing about Jesus. We have access to a large body of first-rate historical evidence that is decisive in answering important questions about Jesus, especially questions that are central for Christian faith and life. This evidence constitutes the nucleus of what is sometimes called the Jesus tradition. The Jesus tradition in turn is central to what is more broadly called the gospel tradition. How are we to think of the gospel tradition in relationship to the words of Jesus, and how can it be used in reconstructing an outline of Jesus' public career?

The chief methodological problem in writing about the historical Jesus is chronology. Since the turn of the century, critical theology has been aware of the historical uncertainty of the gospel chronologies. This has led to a virtual moratorium on writing "lives of Jesus" according to the nineteenth-century mode. The classic twentieth-century reconstruction by Bultmann in his *Jesus and the Word* is largely restricted to the reconstruction of Jesus' message. Bornkamm's *Jesus of Nazareth* is an improvement on Bultmann, primarily by taking into account the intervening parable research of Dodd (*The Parables of the Kingdom*) and Jeremias (*The Parables of Jesus*).

A peculiar merit of the present book is that it goes beyond the simple reconstruction of Jesus' message. Without uncritical dependence upon the gospel chronologies, it attempts to explicate Jesus' teachings within the context of an intrinsic development in his public career. To this extent it serves in a modest way to demonstrate the possibility of a "story of Jesus" acceptable to historians, a story which is not essentially different from the story of Jesus familiar to us from the Gospels.

Preliminary Methodological Considerations

The gospel tradition originated with Jesus and those who worked with him and experienced his saving influence. It developed in the earliest Christian communities where Jesus was remembered and worshiped as the crucified and resurrected Lord. The tradition's canonical function in the church calls for theological and historical reflection upon the way it developed into the forms given to it in the Gospels and upon the relationship of these Gospels to one another and to Scripture as a whole.

The Gospels embody tradition concerning Jesus. Between Jesus and the Gospels stands the traditioning process, by which the Gospel stories and sayings of Jesus were handed on. These traditions were oral and written and included sayings both of Jesus and of early Christian prophets speaking in the name of Jesus. They also included accounts of eyewitnesses concerning the actions and character of Jesus and later modifications of this tradition made to meet the changing needs of different Christian communities.

This traditioning process has never ceased. It flourished up to and through the period when the Gospels were written and achieved manifold expression during the second and third centuries. It was normed with the adoption of the fourfold Gospel canon, which in turn has enhanced the traditioning process through its influence upon the visual arts, music, literature, and preaching.

The canonical Gospels afford us our best access to the earliest traditions concerning Jesus. From a form-critical study of the Gospels, it is clear that the Jesus tradition was already richly developed by the time the Gospels were written. A study of this developed tradition is rewarding because it helps clarify the character of Jesus and improves our understanding of the evangelists' purpose in writing the Gospels.

The Gospels represent Jesus as he was remembered and worshiped in certain Christian communities a generation after the beginning of the church. This is clear from the traditions concerning Jesus that the evangelists used, which include not only traditions that originated with Jesus himself and his first associates, but also many which reflect the needs of later Christian communities.

Christianity as a religious movement began with Jesus and his disciples in Palestine, a meeting place for diverse cultural influences. This does not mean, however, that no viable distinctions can be made between the environment of Jesus and that of the evangelists. The environment of Jesus of Nazareth was physically Palestinian and temporally pre-Pauline. Therefore, whatever he did and said, however distinctive or even unique it may have been, would have been accommodated to those who shared this environment.

Presumably tradition concerning Jesus' words and actions, which achieved stable form at a very early date, would tend to reflect this environment both conceptually and pictorially.

On the other hand, the environment of the evangelists was extra-Palestinian and post-Pauline. We can assume that what the evangelists wrote was accommodated accordingly. The other New Testament writings make clear that the social and theological forces set in motion by Jesus and his disciples broke out of the original Palestinian environment at an early period. The Acts of the Apostles views this transition in retrospect. More importantly, however, the transition is seen firsthand in the letters of Paul. Thus, Paul's writings are an important control in distinguishing between the environment of Jesus and that of the evangelists.

In his letters it is clear that Paul considered carrying the gospel to the Gentiles his special vocation. This vocation committed him to lengthy journeys among people far removed from Palestine. Therefore Paul himself reflects the transitional situation, not simply because he was a Jew engaged in a mission to gentiles, but also because he met in Jerusalem with those who were apostles before him. He was concerned that these leaders understand that such changes in missionary policy as he had introduced in his efforts to expedite the spread of the gospel did not affect its saving truth. In fact, Paul was prepared to question the integrity of these apostles when they conducted themselves in a manner he perceived as prejudicial to the truth of this gospel.

Basically, then, what is seen in Paul's letters is one way in which it was possible to adapt the gospel so that it was viable for predominantly gentile churches in Asia Minor and points west.[10]

The works of the Jewish historian Josephus serve not only as background material to the letters of Paul and the rest of the New Testament writings, but also provide a basis for observing the contrast between the environments of Jesus and the evangelists. Like Paul, Josephus was basically of the pharisaic persuasion. Unlike Paul and most other New Testament writers, however, Josephus reflects first-century Judaism unchanged by Christian belief. Similarly, the manuscripts from the caves of the Judean desert, Jewish writings from the intertestamental period, and some Mishnaic and other rabbinic materials all afford access to first-century Palestinian Judaism unaffected by Christian belief. These Jewish writings together with the works of Josephus provide a reliable control in determining the nature of the religious, social, economic, and political environment of Jesus. In other words, in the effort to delineate the environment of Jesus, the modern historian is not confined to the limited and selective circle of New Testament writings.

When a tradition concerning Jesus or a saying attributed to him comes alive against the background of his environment as it is known through a study of the topography, geography, and climate of Palestine and the history of Palestinian Judaism prior to A.D. 70, then an element in the tradition is isolated or identified which may be early. If this tradition would be unintelligible outside Palestine or unfamiliar in gentile-oriented circles, then the probabilities increase that such a saying or story belongs to an early stage in the development of the tradition. Material in the Gospels which presupposes the death and resurrection of Jesus and reflects a situation where he is remembered and worshiped as a transcendent being represents tradition which probably originated in some post-Easter Christian community. Such tradition could have developed either early or late, either in Jewish or gentile circles. Paul's letters preserve evidence that mythopoeic tendencies were at work at a very early date in some Christian communities, producing powerful christological statements about Jesus.

There are four major turning points in the development of the tradition leading from Jesus to the Gospels: (1) Jesus' baptism by John followed by the arrest, imprisonment, and death of the Baptist; (2) the arrest, trial, death, and resurrection of Jesus and the emergence of a post-Easter messianic community; (3) sectarian conflict and division within the Jewish messianic community over the manner by which Gentiles were to be admitted to full membership; and (4) the inspiring rediscovery and renewal of ecumenical unity in the aftermath of the catastrophic Roman-Jewish military conflict. From this outline it may be seen that the crucial matter is not where a tradition belongs in some temporal progression conceived chronologically in decades, but in one conceived in periods marked off by decisive moments in a developmental sequence. The public career of Jesus falls between the first and second of these decisive moments and took place in Palestine. The Gospels were written during or following the fourth and are extra-Palestinian in provenance.[11] Paul's letters provide us with an indispensable control for understanding how the Jesus tradition developed between the second and fourth turning points by illuminating the third. Paul himself was intimately acquainted with both the Jewish-Palestinian environment of Jesus and with the extra-Palestinian, gentile-oriented environment of the evangelists, and his life and work provide an indispensable bridge between the two.

Because of both the historical uncertainty concerning the gospel chronologies and the mythopoeic character of much of Jesus' "life and ministry," it is best to focus our attention on sayings of Jesus which originated during the period of his earthly ministry if we wish to reflect on the actual Jesus.

Within the corpus of the tradition which originated during the period of Jesus' earthly ministry, the parables afford the best key for understanding his career and character. However, the following points concerning the parables merit consideration: (1) the parables are not to be interpreted allegorically (Jülicher); (2) in his parables Jesus proclaims that the eschatological Kingdom of God has already broken into reality (Dodd); (3) form criticism enables the critic to identify the parables of Jesus as belonging to the genre of rabbinic parables, while as a whole presenting theologically distinctive content (Jeremias); and (4) form criticism enables the critic to distinguish the original form of Jesus' parables from the additions that were made by the early church (Jeremias). Once these matters concerning the parables become clear, it is possible to recapture the most adequate image of Jesus' career and character.

To do this it is also necessary to meet minimal chronological requirements,[12] without, however, depending upon the historically questionable chronology of the evangelists. One need only recognize that Jesus' public ministry began with his baptism at the hands of John, whose identity is established by the historian Josephus; that Jesus' ministry ended in crucifixion in response to the fateful decisions of the procurator Pontius Pilate and the high priest Caiaphas, whose identities are also established by Josephus; and that between the beginning and end of Jesus' ministry a twofold and compound crisis occurred.[13] Central to this crisis was opposition to Jesus by the religious authorities, who felt challenged by his practice of eating with tax collectors and sinners. Recognizing this fact makes it possible to perceive a credible relationship between Jesus' ministry and his death and to develop an intrinsic chronology for his earthly career.

This can be accomplished by arranging the sayings of Jesus and particularly his parables in relationship to this twofold and compound crisis. For example, a parable in which Jesus rebukes the self-righteousness of those who resent God's mercy toward repentant sinners would have been prompted by his decision to defend his action of eating with tax collectors and sinners against the criticism of the Pharisees. This is a decision, however, that could not have come until after a decision by the Pharisees to criticize such conduct, which decision could not have been made before some tax collectors and sinners had decided to accept Jesus' invitation to table fellowship. This decision in turn could not have taken place until after Jesus' decision to invite repentant tax collectors and sinners into the intimacy of his table fellowship. And Jesus' decision could not have taken place until some of these persons had decided to respond to his gracious call to repentance, which could not have come until after Jesus' decision to issue this call—and so on right back to Jesus' decision to leave the sparsely settled regions of the wilderness of Judea where he had been with John and to carry his gracious call to repentance into the more densely populated urban areas of Israel.

With this necessary sequence of decisive moments in Jesus' public career, it is possible to reconstruct in outline form the essential development of his message. The ability to do this rests on the premise that the parables and other sayings of Jesus were not conceived all at once, but like the letters of Paul, were composed in response to particular situations. The essential outlines of this development are as follows:

1. Jesus followed John the Baptist, proclaiming the imminent coming of the kingdom of God.
2. His initial message issued in—
    a. A gracious call to repentance.
    b. A positive response from "tax collectors and sinners."
    c. The acceptance of sinners into table fellowship, which created a new community that existed in anticipation of the coming kingdom.
3. Jesus' ministry was beset by two separate crises, and a third occurred which was compounded by interaction between the other two.
    a. An internal crisis developed among Jesus' followers because of uncertainty concerning the coming of the kingdom.

b. An external crisis developed because of the Pharisees' resistance to Jesus' message and his table fellowship with sinners. Jesus rebuked the Pharisees and declared that it was better to be a repentant sinner than a self-righteous keeper of the law. The attitude of the Pharisees toward Jesus became increasingly hostile, and they plotted his death. Even in the face of death, Jesus reaffirmed the truth of his message.
c. The external conflict with the Pharisees compounded the internal uncertainty among the faithful, raising the question, Should we really allow sinners in our fellowship? Jesus assured his disciples that God would separate the just from the unjust. God alone, not some ritual, would decide who is justified and who is not.

On the basis of this analysis of Jesus' ministry and message, the image of Jesus is that of one who in the face of God's imminent destruction of the wicked issued God's gracious call to repentance, and with compassion and joy received sinners into his fellowship. Moreover, it is the image of one who defended this action in the face of criticism and rebuked the self-righteous attitude of those authorities who resented God's mercy toward repentant sinners.

The significance of this image of Jesus' life style is both theological and existential. There is in the parables of Jesus a theology of grace, a theology which is ethically and morally concerned with the little ones—those who are disadvantaged and victimized by the social and religious structures of their existence. This is a theology out of which comes a call to repentance and a promise of God's salvation to all who respond. In short, Jesus' parables demonstrate beyond a doubt that the one who communicated these parables and their message provides the primal historical and theological context within which to reflect on the meaning of the cross and resurrection.

If a critic takes each parable of Jesus and considers its theology in relation to the total corpus of Jesus' teaching, it will be seen that most fall into one or the other of two groups: (1) those that coalesce around the theme of "the folly of postponing repentance" and (2) those that coalesce around the theme of "rebuking self-righteousness." Both groups of parables reflect a theology of grace. It is precisely these parables of grace that are found neither in the

Gospel of Mark nor in the hypothetical source Q. The gospel criticism in which contemporary theologians have been schooled presupposes the priority of Mark and Q which in effect shunts the parables of grace to the side and into a critical limbo.

The reconstruction which follows develops out of the pioneering parable research of Dodd and Jeremias, but it is completely free from any dependence upon the very problematic notions of Marcan priority and the existence of Q. Any scholar who suspends judgment on the question of whether Mark is our earliest Gospel can take this reconstruction seriously, knowing that it rests on a critical basis that has been fully presented in the essay on the humanity of Jesus Christ in the John Knox *festschrift*.[14]

In that essay, the parables of Jesus preserved in the Gospel of Matthew are analyzed theologically and compared to the parables of Jesus preserved in the Gospel of Luke. In every case the theology of the parables in Matthew can be matched by the theology of one or more of the parables in Luke. Moreover, the theology of Jesus' parables is essentially the same as the theology of Paul. Since we learn from Paul himself that he preached the faith of the church he once persecuted, it follows that Paul preached a pre-Pauline faith. The historian has no alternative but to conclude that the theology common to Paul and to the two streams of parable tradition preserved separately in Matthew and Luke goes back to Jesus. To imagine that these three streams of tradition converge in some unidentified pre-Pauline theologian would only serve to create an unnecessary set of historical and theological problems.

It is important to clarify one further point. There is solid textual basis for making a fundamental theological distinction between Jesus and John the Baptist. Liberation theologies can be strengthened if they are careful not to blur this distinction and if they do not wrongly conclude that the polarizing effect of John's preaching should be attributed also to Jesus and identified as the cause for Jesus' execution at the hands of the political establishment.

Such a conclusion would be a vast oversimplification of a complex question and would leave important evidence unexplained—evidence both from the parables in Luke and Matthew and from Paul's account of his pre-Christian persecution of the church. This evidence indicates that the religious authorities, who were drawn from the righteous elements within the established world of Jewish piety, were opposed to Jesus' message and conduct. The woes of

Jesus (which, to be sure, were added to in the bitterest of terms during the persecution of the church in which Paul the Pharisee took part) and his cleansing of the Temple polarized his relationship with the religious authorities and sealed his fate. Jesus' fate was not in the first instance sealed by direct confrontation with Pilate and his political authority or with Roman military forces stationed in the capitol. Thus, while the words of the psalmist "zeal for thy house has consumed me" (Ps. 69:9) have been cited in Scripture in connection with Jesus' cleansing of the Temple (John 2:17), Jesus was certainly more than a zealot or a political activist.

Jesus is best perceived as a religious reformer. He certainly taught his disciples to love their enemies. Any reconstruction that stumbles on that fact will not stand up to criticism. The reconstruction offered here clarifies the relationship between religion and politics in Jesus' environment and focuses attention on what is truly liberating in Christianity.

The theology which comes to expression in the words and actions of Jesus is a theology which works against every form of oppression and exploitation and binds together all persons who love God and thirst after righteousness. It is a theology which calls for reformation and renewal in the life of the church and for political involvement in the struggle for justice in society—for self-sacrifice and a readiness for martyrdom as exemplified in the lives of Mahatma Gandhi, Martin Luther King, Jr., and Archbishop Oscar Romero. Jesus' prophetic power to unmask hypocrisy and self-righteousness is absolutely central to this theology and very distinctive of it.

PART I

The Origin and Development of the Gospel Tradition

THE HISTORICAL SETTING OF JESUS' PUBLIC MINISTRY

Jesus was a Jew who lived in Palestine during the period of Roman occupation. The climax of his ministry came while the procurator of Judea was Pontius Pilate, whose responsibilities included obtaining supplies and funds from the local populace to defray the costs of military occupation. Pilate did this by engaging Jewish tax collectors. As procurator, he had at his disposal sufficient forces to support the incumbent collaborating Jewish regime, to see that taxes were collected, and to police the normal rash of political discontent. Seldom was it necessary to call for help from the Roman provincial governor, who resided in Syria, and in whose hands rested ultimate military power.

Rome recognized the Law of Moses as the law of the land. The "established world of Jewish piety" was based upon that law. The Temple in Jerusalem, where the Sanhedrin sat, and the synagogues in the land were the chief institutions of that establishment. Key figures in the established world of Jewish piety were the Pharisees; they sat in Moses' seat and were recognized by the Romans as legal authorities whose power over the people in the cities and towns of Galilee was their best hope for maintaining social stability in the area. It is important in understanding the life situation of Jesus to realize that though the Pharisees sat in Moses' seat, their acceptance or toleration of the Herodian concordat, which had been worked out with Rome, gave that seat earthly stability.

The Romans found influence within high priestly families in Jerusalem to be their most direct key to effective control over the Jewish population. Because of the strong place of the Temple cultus in Jewish law and piety, offering security to the Temple authorities made it possible for Rome to maintain a basis of control over the nation as a whole. Only such Jewish groups as rejected the authority of the incumbent high priestly families were free from some measure of effective collaboration with Rome, and the price required for complete freedom was withdrawal from public life. A relatively small percentage of the population was either willing or able to pay this price. This included such groups as the Qumran community living in the wilderness of Judea and such paramilitary resistance elements as the Zealots. The Pharisees, by way of contrast, collaborated with the Jerusalem oligarchy and thus, at least indirectly, with Rome.

The benefits of the Pax Romana were felt by the educated and privileged classes and by the general populace. The Jews, however, could not enjoy these benefits without suffering a far greater degree of domestic disruption than did some other ethnic groups within the empire. This was because of the peculiar heritage of the Jews, many of whose customs and laws needed to be interpreted liberally wherever and whenever the inevitable need for close contact with gentiles arose. Alongside of the laws governing Jewish life and practice and inextricably bound up with them in the scriptures of the Jews were certain promises of God bearing upon the welfare of his covenanted people. These promises were conditional, depending upon obedience to the law. On the basis of these promises, therefore, the less privileged classes were always capable of envisioning a relative improvement in their welfare, if only more effective ways could be found to keep the law.

This situation also created conflict and tension within the common life. On the one hand there existed the need to minimize or set aside the requirements of the law in order to facilitate conditions favorable to more effective integration within the empire. On the other hand there existed the need to maximize and strictly enforce these requirements in order to meet conditions requisite for the fulfillment of divine promise.

Out of this conflict and tension and feeding upon heterogeneous messianic prophecies preserved in Jewish writings, came eschatological and apocalyptical hopes. These excited the populace whenever signs of the times indicated that God was about to redeem his people and especially when an eschatological prophet like John the Baptist began to preach.

Collaborating elements of the Jewish populace (whose close cooperation was essential to the effectiveness of the Roman occupation) included those, like the Pharisees, who sought conscientiously to observe the Mosaic law and those who were more or less lax in this respect. Those willing to be somewhat lax, especially in their attitude toward the dietary regulations and other levitical cleanliness rules, were sometimes preferred by persons in authority for certain of the more important, lucrative positions in the complex fabric of Roman hegemony over Jewish life. In the parlance of those Jews who strictly observed the Law of Moses, these nonobservant compatriots were sometimes referred to derogatorily as "tax collectors and sinners." Jesus called them "lost sheep of the house of Israel." To the degree that they were not observant, these Jews were regarded by observant Jews as having abandoned the covenant, as having sold their heritage for a mess of pottage, and as dead in trespasses. Observant Jews, on the other hand, were dependent upon the guidance of legal experts like the scribes and Pharisees, who could tell them what the law did and did not require under every varying circumstance.

Therefore, when apocalyptic hopes were at a fever pitch, nonobservant Jews, because of their fear of divine retribution, would seek in great numbers to return to the covenant. In principle this always presented a problem for Jews who were already righteous before the law. They questioned last-minute repentance and objected to any immediate, easy acceptance of sinners. Even if the eschatological fulfillment of God's longstanding promises were at last to be realized for *all* Israel, justice required recognition of a difference between those who had suffered because of their faithfulness to the law and those who, having disregarded God's law, had profited thereby. The basic problem conditioning the life of Jews in Palestine, therefore, was the law and its adequacy as a norm by which they could find a satisfying mode of existence within a life-affirming cosmopolitan culture that constantly called the separatist character of Jewish communal life into question.

JESUS AND THE GOSPEL TRADITION

There are numerous sayings of Jesus which make it clear that after his baptism by John, he shared the apocalyptic expectation of an imminent day of judgment when the wicked would be destroyed.

> As it was in the days of Noah, so will it be in the days of the Son of man. They ate, they drank, they married, they were given in marriage, until the day when Noah entered the ark, and the flood came and destroyed them all. Likewise as it was in the days of Lot —they ate, they drank, they bought, they sold, they planted, they built, but on the day Lot went out from Sodom fire and sulphur rained from heaven and destroyed them all (Luke 17:26–29).

This common expectation of the impending manifestation of God's power and righteousness united Jesus and John with all those who came out into the wilderness to hear John preach. It provided the theological and existential context of Jesus' public ministry. It was Jesus' conviction that he could see "Satan fall like lightning from heaven" that empowered him to give others "authority . . . over all the power of the enemy" (Luke 10:18–19).

Such sayings of Jesus which bespeak a peaceful, tranquil, and even idyllic life within a world where human existence is fraught with personal anxiety, therefore, presumably put us in touch with Jesus' earthly reflections on life *prior* to his eschatological baptism by John and reveal a sensitive detachment from the allurements of mammon.

> Do not be anxious about your life, what you shall eat or what you shall drink, nor about your body, what you shall put on. Is not life more than food, and the body more than clothing? Look at the birds of the air: they neither sow nor reap nor gather into barns, and yet your heavenly Father feeds them. Are you not of more value than they? . . . Consider the lilies of the field, how they grow; they neither toil nor spin; yet I tell you, even Solomon in all his glory was not arrayed like one of these. . . . Therefore do not be anxious, saying, "What shall we eat?" or "What shall we drink?" or "What shall we wear?" . . . your heavenly Father knows that you need them all (Matt. 6:25–32).

A saying like "Do not think that I have come to bring peace on earth; I have not come to bring peace, but a sword" (Matt. 10:34) seems, on the other hand, to reflect a situation in which Jesus has made sharp-edged eschatological commitments and is calling upon others to do the same. These kinds of sayings seem more likely to have originated in relation to Jesus' acceptance of John's baptism and/or after his decision to continue a public ministry following John's arrest, imprisonment, and death.

Such teachings as, "Do not be anxious. . . . Let the day's own trouble be sufficient for the day" (Matt. 6:25,34) or "Blessed are the peacemakers, for they shall be called sons of God" (Matt. 5:9) are not necessarily discordant or inconsistent with sayings that have a sharper cutting edge. In fact, these philosophical and irenic sayings undoubtedly were useful in sustaining commitment among the faithful during the arduous eschatological mission in which Jesus and his disciples engaged during that relatively brief period of preaching following the death of John and culminating in the journey to Jerusalem.

To be sure, irenic and philosophical observations on life can be born in the midst of active engagement and conflict. But unless it is believed that Jesus came to John without previous experience or reflection, there is no reason to imagine that such wise sayings originated only in the final period of his life. Their arresting beauty and usefulness, which assured their transmission in the early church, would also have been sufficient reason for their use by Jesus during and after his discipleship with John. Once Jesus became a disciple of John, it is unlikely that he rejected everything from his former mode of existence and began *de novo* to develop his theology, as if by baptism his mind had been washed clean (like a tabula rasa) of all that he had formerly believed and advocated.

Where certain parables of Jesus are interpreted within the context of initial developments in his ministry and specifically within the context of his gracious call for repentance, they enable the historian to make informed suggestions about the intention of Jesus as he responded to the exigencies and difficulties he encountered. How was one to understand the delay in the coming of the kingdom which John had pronounced to be at hand, especially after John's arrest and execution? And if one were to undertake to continue proclaiming the coming of the kingdom, how should he or she perceive this ministry? Was it to be understood as the work of God to be carried out during an extension of the period of grace in the face of the coming judgment? If so, was it not reasonable to expect that in due season, failing the fruits of repentance, this period of grace would come to a sudden and just end (Luke 13:6–9)? As for those who would mistakenly hold back because of their fear that the cost of repentance might be too great, was it not important for their sake to emphasize the joy of the kingdom (Matt. 13:44,45)? Should not those who were delinquent in setting their house in order be reminded of the inevitability of judgment (Matt. 21:33–41; Luke 20:9–16), the appropriateness of radical action in the face of certain change (Luke 16:1–7), the folly of not trusting God (Matt. 25:14–30; Luke 19:11–27), and the suddenness and unexpectedness of God's judgment (Matt. 24:45–51; Luke 12: 42–46; 13:1–5)?

Certainly parables which dramatically illustrate the folly of postponing repentance (Matt. 22:1–10, 25:1–13; Luke 13:6–9) and which teach the wisdom of living in ready expectation of God's gracious judgment (Luke 12:35–38) most likely would have originated in situations where such expectations would be enlivened and heightened—in the period of Jesus' active ministry after his baptism into the movement of John and his decision to continue proclaiming the imminence of the kingdom following John's arrest and death.

Even within this period it is possible to postulate development. Presumably Jesus would have understood the lesson the authorities intended by John's execution: "A disciple is not above his teacher" (Matt. 10:24). Jesus' decision to carry on would have been realistic only if he understood that he did so at great risk. Although John had been beheaded, a more usual form of execution was crucifixion. For Jesus to say "Take up (your) cross and follow me" (Matt. 16:24) was his way of making clear that he had placed himself outside the discipline and protection of the established world of Jewish piety, and was calling upon others to do the same. This established world of Jewish piety derived its earthly jurisdiction from Rome. Thus, in coming into conflict with the religious authorities, Jesus was risking the ultimate wrath of Roman power. To speak in this way was a determined response to a policy of oppression which had been calculated to discourage dangerous rhetoric associated with messianic activity. But Jesus was not intimidated by what the authorities did to John. He continued to preach. "No one can serve two masters. . . . You cannot serve God and mammon. . . . Repent, and engage in the service of God . . . for the kingdom of heaven is at hand" (Matt. 6:24; 3:2).

When Jesus said, "Take up (your) cross and follow me" (Matt. 16:24) or "Leave the dead to bury their own dead" (Matt. 8:22), he took upon himself the full measure of messianic leadership. With such startling statements Jesus challenged others to free themselves from a paralyzing fear of human authorities, both those who sat in Moses' seat and those who represented the emperor. In the former saying, Jesus unobtrusively clarified the all-important question of whether he was naively calling men into a course of action where the sacrifices being risked might be greater than he himself was prepared to bear.

"What will it profit a man, if he gains the whole world and forfeits his life?" (Matt. 16:26). "Whoever would save his life will lose it" (Matt. 16:25). Such brave and bold words staved off the disintegrating effects of temptation to abandon hope for the kingdom's coming, once news of John's arrest and imprisonment was followed by confirmation of his death. Even so, such sayings do not seem to carry one to the heart of Jesus' message. They simply show that Jesus gave expression to qualities of leadership that help account for his emergence as a contender for the mantle of John.

If we are to trust the earliest and most reliable tradition, Jesus saw himself in prophetic continuity with John in commitment to the call for national repentance in the face of the imminent coming of the kingdom (Matt. 11:7b–19). But Jesus saw himself in radical discontinuity with John regarding the basis for admission into the kingdom (Matt. 21:28–32). John's strictures against the moral laxities of the people were uncompromising, and the ostensible cause for his death was his denunciation of immorality in high places. With Jesus it was otherwise. The misdeeds of the wealthy and powerful did not seem to preoccupy him, though he was not unmindful of the plight of the rich (Matt. 19:23–24; Luke 16: 19–31). Jesus came to save sinners, not to condemn them. As children of their Father in heaven, they in turn were counseled to love their enemies even as God loved his (Matt. 5:43–48). They were admonished not to put forgiveness on any calculated basis, but to forgive freely, boldly, unconditionally, and from the heart—not seven times, but seventy times seven (Matt. 18:21–35).

The fellowship of such a community of forgiven and forgiving sinners was poignant and joyful. "There will be more joy in heaven over one sinner who repents than over ninety-nine righteous persons who need no repentance" (Luke 15:7). Therefore, Jesus ate with sinners and celebrated their repentance (Luke 15:1–10). Such radical doctrine and practice was difficult to justify by legal precedent from Jewish scriptures. So revolutionary an attitude on the part of Jesus could only irritate authorities whose social importance rested upon their mastery of the exegetical intricacies of a life-encompassing legal system.

In this respect, the relationship of Jesus to the Pharisees calls for some clarification. Their opposition to his practice of admitting tax collectors and sinners into the intimacy of table fellowship was rooted in two distinguishable legal concerns. First, there were the explicit food laws, called *kashrut,* which forbade eating pork, a kid seethed in its mother's milk, meat with the blood still in it, and the like. These laws had governed the diet of Jews for centuries and served to keep them from eating with gentiles or other Jews who lived and ate like gentiles. Second, there was the purity code which, when applied to the laity, separated Jew from Jew socially. Such social separation was going on in the time of Jesus when some groups of Jews were applying the priestly purity code to the laity. The Jews who did this, called *haberim* in rabbinic sources, were eventually followed by the rabbis, who attempted to extend the provisions of the purity code to all Israelites.[15]

Since gentiles were present in the Holy Land, righteous Jews were affected in different ways as far as eating was concerned. They sometimes found it helpful to band together to see that the *kashrut* laws were fully observed (and the purity code, too, when that was of concern to them). A common table where proper precautions regarding these laws were observed was in order among righteous Jews who, when away from home, could not depend upon this service being rendered by members of their respective families.

The admission of unrighteous Jews (those lax in their observance of the *kashrut* laws) into the table fellowship of those who were righteous was permitted at the discretion of the leaders of the group. Such admissions were defended on the grounds of *hesed* (covenantal love) and justified as a means of recruiting new members for the fellowship or for the renewal movement, as the case might be.

The Pharisees as righteous Jews, that is, as observants of the Law of Moses, including the *kashrut* laws, had no particular grounds for objecting to this practical way of facilitating the observance of the law within the wider community. To the extent that the Pharisees were looked to by the authorities, that is, the Roman-backed high priestly oligarchy, as the party best able to police the land in terms of observing the law, or to the extent that they were recognized by the people (and so perceived themselves) to be authorized by God to police the land, the Pharisees were nervous about any situation where the righteousness of those observing the law was being dangerously imputed to the unrighteous. (This is precisely what Jesus' acceptance of sinners at table fellowship implied.) Such nervousness could best be allayed by requiring a probationary period during which anyone seeking admission to an eating group could give evidence of a sincere intent to become truly and enduringly observant.

A scandalous feature of Jesus' admitting unrighteous Jews into the intimacy of his table fellowship was the absence of any fixed probationary period. The most liberal of the *haberim* required one month (Tosefta Demai 2:10–12) and the Essenes required two or three years.

Compared to the more established religious groups, then, Jesus' fellowship appeared dangerously subversive of that law upon whose strict observance the Pharisees placed such great importance. In any case, simple prudence dictated that the Pharisees take the precautionary step of warning righteous Jews who were most likely to heed their warnings. (Because of political restraints placed upon them that curtailed their zeal for the law, there was generally little the Pharisees could do against tax collectors and others who lived like gentiles, except to excommunicate them from their table fellowship.)

The Pharisees were certainly not the only righteous Jews in Palestine. The Qumran community constituted a haven for those who wanted to be right with God according to the Law of Moses. Doubtless there were other such righteous communities. But the special status of the Pharisees in the eyes of the people and their role in the power structure of the established world of Jewish piety, attested by Josephus, justify regarding some of the New Testament evidence about them as valid.

First, Paul was a Pharisee, and he was granted police power by Jewish authorities. He was not granted those powers because he was a Pharisee, but since he was a Pharisee he had credentials that stood him in good stead in carrying out his police duties. The local people present at the arrests Paul made, whose cooperation with the arresting authorities was important, knew that Paul was a Pharisee. Therefore they assented to his authority as derived from God, not from Rome. Second, Jesus recognized the Pharisees as righteous and alluded to them when his teaching required the example of a righteous person (for example, the parable of the tax collector and the Pharisee in the Temple). Third, Jesus perceived a difference between the righteousness practiced by the Pharisees and the obedience he taught his disciples to render to God. Fourth,

Jesus at times came into conflict with the Pharisees, for example, over Sabbath observance and over his practice of admitting sinners into the intimacy of his table fellowship. This latter opposition possibly arose only in those cases where the sinners were guilty of notorious transgression, as with tax collectors. Finally, Jesus recognized that the Pharisees possessed authority to rule on the interpretation of the Law of Moses. Taken as a legal guild, however, their example discredited their ultimate authority as reliable exponents of God's requirements of his sons and daughters.

Whether Jesus is responsible for the woes against the Pharisees is a historical question affected by the source paradigm that is applied. According to the two-document hypothesis, Matthew 23 can be understood as an expanded Matthean construction representing development of tradition from Q, some of which was also known to Mark. On form-critical grounds, however, even assuming the two-document hypothesis, there is much against this view. The tradition preserved in Matthew 23 reflects the influence of oral tradition, Jewish and Palestinian in provenance. Regarding Matthew as the earliest of the extant Gospels removes all doubt about the Jewish-Christian and Palestinian origin of most if not all of the tradition in Matthew 23.

It is possible on form-critical grounds to reconstruct the more original form of the woes and to separate the tradition that has been added. Paul's own testimony of his attack upon the church fits the historical requirement of a kind of violent persecution which, when inflicted by some Pharisees upon some Christians, would explain these bitter additions. The woes themselves, however, may well be authentic to Jesus. They certainly are profoundly consonant with the best-attested sayings of Jesus.

Thus, it is clear that one can give a credible account of the importance of the Pharisees for understanding the New Testament, especially the importance of their opposition to Jesus' table fellowship with tax collectors and sinners, without settling the question as to the extent the purity code was being applied to all Israelites in the time of Jesus. Depending upon the extent that the purity code was applied and whether the Pharisees had any interest at all in gaining wide acceptance of it among the laity, Jesus' table fellowship with tax collectors and sinners could have been of added concern to the Pharisees. A concern would have been there in any case, based simply on the *kashrut* laws. It would not have been only the Pharisees' concern, but one shared by all righteous Jews, to one degree or another.

It was normative that righteous Jews not eat with sinners. As one who came in the way of righteousness, John had not eaten with sinners. But Jesus did. This marks a profound theological difference between John and Jesus (Matt. 11:16–19).[16]

The objection of scribes and Pharisees to Jesus' practice of eating with tax collectors and sinners led to a major crisis for Jesus. Succumbing to pressure to abandon this practice would possibly have brought Jesus favor; instead, he struck at an important root of the problem—the self-righteousness of a scrupulous religious establishment.

Jesus represented the legal authorities' emphasis on minutia of the law and their neglect of justice, mercy, and faith as the counsel of "blind guides" (Matt. 23:23–24). This, however, may be a caricature. In any case, Jesus himself came from a religious background so akin to Pharisaism as to command the respect of the Pharisees. Their anxiety over what he was doing may have been rooted in the perception that one of their own kind was endangering the interests of "the righteous." Jesus openly said that he did not come to call the righteous (Matt. 9:9–13). Although he himself was known as a righteous man, in eating with sinners Jesus was breaking down the barriers by which many righteous Jews maintained an inner group strength. This group strength was necessary to withstand external pressures to compromise religious scruples in the interests of achieving an improved economy and a more cosmopolitan society.

Jesus' table fellowship with tax collectors and sinners may not have been in the first instance the nucleus of a new community. Nevertheless, it was based upon the recognition that God is the father of all. Indeed, if a man has a hundred sheep and one goes astray, will he not leave the ninety-nine to search for the one that is lost? And having found it, will he not put it on his shoulder and bring it back rejoicing, and call to his friends, "Rejoice with me, for I have found my sheep which was lost" (Luke 15:3–6; cf. Matt. 18:10–14)? How much more will our heavenly Father rejoice over the return of a lost son (Luke 15:11–24)? Therefore, how appropriate that we celebrate the repentance of those lost sons of Abraham who, once dead in trespasses, are now alive through God's merciful judgment (Luke 15:25–32, 19:1–10).

By such forceful imagery as this, Jesus defended his practice of table fellowship with tax collectors and sinners. Parables like the one about the lost son and his elder brother (Luke 15:11–32) or the laborers in the vineyard (Matt. 20:1–16) were first created in response to this crisis in Jesus' ministry. They were used to defend the gospel of God's unmerited and unconditional acceptance of the repentant sinner. Similarly, the parable about the great banquet (Matt. 22:1–10; Luke 14:16–24) served to remind the righteous that they had no ground for complaint over the eschatological acceptance of sinners since they themselves had turned their backs on the kingdom (cf. Matt. 23:13).

These parables in themselves were probably not intended to alienate the scribes and Pharisees, but to forestall their inquisitorial activity among the disciples. Nor is a parable like that of the Pharisee and the tax collector in the Temple (Luke 18:9–14) designed to hurt rather than to heal. The Pharisee in the parable does not represent all Pharisees and certainly not the ideal Pharisee. But to make his point that goodness can become demonic and destructive when it leads good men to isolate themselves from others, Jesus chose a man from the most virtuous circle of Jewish society. If such a man, no matter how moral, places his trust in his own righteousness and despises others, he goes from the house of God to his own house in a wrong relationship to God. However, a sinner who places his or her trust in the mercy of God goes home in a right relationship to God.

The love God has for the sinner shows no lack of love for the righteous. "All that is mine is yours," says the father to his elder son, but "it was fitting to make merry and be glad, for this your brother was dead, and is alive; he was lost, and is found" (Luke 15:31–32). This noble and heartfelt sentiment did not go completely unheeded, but lodged itself within the collective unconscious of the Pharisaic community, there to work its way inexorably against every tendency toward hardheartedness within the ranks of the righteous. Subsequently, one elder brother, a strict Pharisee, while persecuting the church, was won over by the powerful reality of God's love. He became the staunch defender of what Jesus' brother, James the Righteous, regarded as an illicit table fellowship, but which he himself saw as being at the heart of the gospel for which Jesus had died (Gal. 2:11–21).

In spite of the cogency of Jesus' defense of the gospel of God's mercy toward repentant sinners, opposition from the religious establishment stiffened. In this period of opposition by religious authorities responsible for upholding the law in the towns and cities outside Jerusalem, Jesus formulated his woes against the "scribes and Pharisees." These utterances are uncompromising. By this time the issue had become clear; Israel was at the crossroads. The people could either follow those whom Jesus characterized as "blind guides," who hypocritically held in their hands the keys of the kingdom but who neither entered themselves nor allowed others to enter (Matt. 23:13), or they could follow Jesus. Irony turned to bitter sarcasm in the judgment: "Woe to you, scribes and Pharisees, hypocrites! for you build the tombs of the prophets and adorn the monuments of the righteous, saying, 'If we had lived in the days of our fathers, we would not have taken part with them in shedding the blood of the prophets'" (Matt. 23:29–30). You hypocrites, Jesus said, because in so speaking you condemn yourselves as among those who murder prophets. For as you disassociate yourselves from those who have done evil and vainly imagine that had you been in their place you would not have committed the sins they committed, you show yourselves to be the very kind of self-righteous persons who will condone the killing of those God sends as his messengers.

Uncompromising words like these sealed the fate of Jesus. By their use he unmasked what many in positions of privilege and power could not bear to have unmasked. Jesus penetrated the facade of goodness behind which persons hid their lust for power. He represented them to be like "whitewashed tombs, which outwardly appear beautiful, but within . . . are full of dead men's bones" (Matt. 23:27).

After invective like this, the legal authorities were beside themselves to find some charge on which to get rid of Jesus. The compliance of high priestly circles and the rest of the Jerusalem oligarchy was assured once Jesus made it clear that he called for changes not only in men's hearts, but in the institutions of Zion—specifically within the central institution, the Temple itself (Matt. 21:12–13).

With the Pharisees, the high priests, and the elders of the people in concert, the Roman authorities, had they insisted on due process, would have risked a tear in the delicately woven fabric of political collaboration. This collaboration enabled Rome to maintain viable control over a key sector in the defensive perimeter of its frontier with the Parthians, who were an ever-present threat to the stability of the eastern provinces. Ostensibly, in the interest of maintaining Jewish law and Roman order, Jesus was executed. This was done in spite of the fact that Jesus programmatically insisted that he came "not to destroy the law, but to fulfill it" (Matt. 5:17). Moreover, Jesus taught his disciples that unless their righteousness exceeded that of the scribes and Pharisees, they would never enter the Kingdom of Heaven (Matt. 5:20). Yet it can hardly be doubted that in fulfilling the "law and the prophets," Jesus ran afoul of the scribes and Pharisees. This occurred not only when he ate with tax collectors and sinners, but also in regard to other matters as, for example, the Sabbath observance (Matt. 12: 1–8; Luke 14:5). Jesus certainly challenged Jewish legal authority and, as for Roman order, it was to be replaced by the Kingdom of Heaven. So the die had been cast well in advance. While Jesus died a righteous man by the standards of the Kingdom of Heaven, he did not go to his cross innocent of breaking the law as it was represented by the mores of the local populace. Nor was he innocent of disturbing the peace as it was preserved in and through imperial order. He was crucified in the end by the Romans as a political criminal. We can imagine the mixed feelings of anguish and relief on the part of responsible Jewish authorities. Yet we are not in a position to know with any degree of certainty the motives of the principals who were involved in his death.

This outline of essential developments between the death of John and the death of Jesus illustrates how tradition originating with Jesus, which is preserved in the Gospels, can be set within the context of his life situation. The tradition can be seen to come alive against the historical background of the Jews in Palestine when Herod Agrippa was Tetrarch of Galilee and Perea, when John the Baptist had been preaching a baptism of repentance in the Jordan valley, and when Pontius Pilate was procurator of Judea.

In retrospect, on the basis of what can be supported by historical inquiry, is it possible to say something about the character of Jesus and about his public ministry? Jesus' character is the mark he left or "engraved" upon his disciples, including the tax collectors and sinners he admitted into the intimacy of his table fellowship. This fellowship heard Jesus gladly and remembered his words and actions. Members of this fellowship took responsibility for formulating and handing on to the earliest churches such authentic sayings of Jesus as in fact have been preserved in the Gospels.

To the degree that the understanding of life expressed in these authentic sayings was actually represented by Jesus in his own life situation, that is, through his words and actions—to this degree it is possible to speak about the character of Jesus. Confining the inquiry to that nucleus of sayings which beyond a reasonable doubt can be accepted as authentic sayings of Jesus, it is possible to conclude the following:[17] in rebuking self-righteousness and chiding those who resented God's mercy toward sinners, Jesus disclosed something about the kind of person he was. He can be seen as a public figure in relationship to other figures. His contemporaries could understand his human concern for others, and many were moved by it. They saw not only his friendship for tax collectors and sinners, but more. They saw a concern for community.

Pretentiousness and self-righteousness on the part of individuals or groups is one of the most serious corrupting influences affecting the health and integrity of communal existence. Individual and collective self-righteousness on the part of authorities, when unchallenged, is like a hard cement by which outmoded and unjust ecclesiastical, economic, political, and social structures are kept defensible in the face of justified opposition from advocates of social or religious reforms. Privileged individuals or castes are secure only so long as it is possible for society to perceive their positions of privilege as clothed with garments of righteousness. To pull aside these garments and to expose hypocrisy and abuse is a revolutionary act of a most radical nature.

Jesus exposed hypocrisy and abuse. For him to rebuke the prideful selfrighteousness of religious authorities was to strike at an important source of contra-redemptive influence in his own life situation and to encourage the continuation of the individual and covenantal renewal that was taking place in response to his preaching. Those whom Jesus had helped to perceive themselves as sinners dependent upon the unmerited grace of God were glad to know that he not only received sinners, but defended this action when it was criticized. And insofar as it was possible, they were moved to go and do likewise.

There was in this compassionate but disconcerting stance of Jesus a dynamic source of redemptive power which worked against the attempt of the established world of Jewish piety to structure human existence on the exclusivistic ground of the mosaic covenant. Such a source of power provided the basis for a distinctive style of life wherein Jesus and his disciples worked joyfully for a reconciling mode of human existence open to God's grace and to a future conditioned by (1) sin and the expectation of God's imminent destruction of sinners; (2) the unbounded sovereign love of God; and (3) a faith which led them to submit to the judgment of God and to trust themselves utterly to the mercy that was intrinsic to and inherent in God's love. This personal structuring and restructuring of their historical existence, this shaping of the realities of their human environment, and the compassion and joy associated with this creative stance sustained and gave theological depth and direction to their fellowship. Clearly there is more to Jesus than this. But this understanding of his public career and character carries the investigator to the very heart of what can be shown as both essential and enduring in Jesus.

It remains to be seen how in less dramatic ways the character of the community which emerged following Jesus' death and resurrection was theologically preformed by other conflicts that beset Jesus during his earthly ministry.

When his disciples experienced different degrees of success and failure, and when praise and blame based on results led to invidious comparisons and dissension among them, Jesus encouraged them to think of their work in relation to a sower who sows indiscriminately. Those who sow will neither be elated because of good results nor discouraged because of poor ones. People may sow, but the results are not in their hands. The one who does God's work is not responsible for others' response to that work. Disciples of Jesus are responsible only for how faithfully they do their work (Matt. 13:3–9).

No amount of success by Jesus or his disciples could completely overcome the anxiety of some of the faithful as the weeks and months passed, and the full restoration of God's sovereign reign over Israel continued to be delayed. To meet the uncertainty this delay caused, Jesus compared the kingdom of heaven with mustard seed and leaven. In this way he reminded the disciples that great things come from small beginnings (Matt. 13:31–33), the corollary of which is that what is impressive and grand can be deceptive (cf. Matt. 24:1–2). Jesus argued repeatedly from everyday examples that it is reasonable to hope and believe that the inbreaking of God's sovereign love into the lives of the disciples would be followed by the coming of his kingdom. A judge who is bound by oath to render justice, even though dishonest and subject to the influence of important people, will nonetheless hear the cry of a helpless widow who faithfully persists in calling out to him for justice. How much more will our heavenly Father hear the faithful when they cry to him for full vindication. Therefore, do not give up petitioning God. That which God holds for the faithful in promise, he will fulfill; that which he has begun, he will complete (see Luke 18:1–8; 11:5–13; 14:28–33). Pray expectantly and with trust: "Thy kingdom come. Thy will be done, On earth as it is In heaven" (Matt. 6:10).

We are encouraged to imagine, from the way Jesus' parables can be understood within the context of his earthly career, that it was along such lines as these that he was able to reason with his disciples over the delay in the kingdom's coming in full force.

It appears likely that there was an additional factor compounding uncertainty over the delay of the kingdom. Perhaps not all the disciples of Jesus were equally reassured that it was proper for him to eat with tax collectors and sinners. If it occurred to some of the disciples that the scribes and Pharisees may have been right in their claim that Jesus made them vulnerable by his relationships with the unrighteous, then it is not difficult to imagine how uncertainty among the disciples would have been compounded by the disturbing criticism of the pillars of Jewish piety. It is also understandable that some of Jesus' disciples would have expressed concern over the presence of persons of questionable character within their fellowship.

A response to this kind of concern appears in Jesus' parable of the wheat and the tares (Matt. 13:24–30). This parable may be viewed as a Magna Charta for the church. In it Jesus teaches his disciples that in due season God, not humans, will separate the just from the unjust. A similar teaching is given in the parable of the dragnet (Matt. 13:47–52). Here the kingdom of heaven is compared to a net cast out into the sea, including within it fish that are both good and bad. What havoc would be wrought if those who were fishing attempted to sort out the catch while the fishing was still underway. No! That can best be done at the end of the day after the net has been brought ashore. Such self-understanding within Jesus' followers—that is, that they should not judge one another (cf. Matt. 7:2–5)—is an essential mark of the church. It means that the fellowship of the church, if it is faithful to this understanding, will normally include sinners as well as saints.

But this does not mean that there are no ethical norms that will characterize the community of Jesus' followers. Jesus' ethical teachings must have left a deep impression upon his disciples. The memory of the church has preserved an important place in the earliest Jesus tradition for these sayings. Moreover, the evangelists, especially Matthew and Luke, have given these ethical teachings a prominent place in their Gospels. Jesus' teaching on loving one's enemies (Matt. 5:43–48) penetrates to the heart of his message and carries the hearer to the central core of the gospel. At the same time it cuts sharply against the grain of human instinct. It has no ground other than the character of God. Because God loves his enemies, we should love our enemies.

Jesus presumably formulated some of his teaching around elements of the folk wisdom current among his hearers. This suggestion is based not merely upon a priori grounds that such practice is a mark of real teaching, but upon the fact that it is sometimes possible to recover teachings from rabbinic literature that are close in thought and language to some of the authentic teachings of Jesus. This suggests that Jesus himself occasionally selected and developed specific teachings. Therefore, the subsequent selection and development of his teachings by those who honored his memory is not an entirely new or unnatural process. As an example, we may consider the following rabbinic sayings: "Did you ever in your life see an animal or a bird which had a trade? And they support themselves without trouble. And were they not created only to serve me? And, I was created to serve my maker. Does it not follow that I shall be supported without trouble?" (Kiddushin 4:14 R. Shim' on ben Eleazer). "He who has what he will eat today and says, 'What shall I eat tomorrow?' behold, this man lacks faith . . . for it is said, 'The day's lot in its day' " (Mekilta of R. Simon to Ex. 16:4).

Other ethical teachings that have a strong claim as authentic to Jesus include the teachings on being angry with the brother (Matt. 5:21–24); on the appropriateness of ethical surgery (Matt. 5:29–30 and 18:8–9); on retaliation (Matt. 5:38–42); on serving two masters (Matt. 6:24). Additional sayings with serious claims to authenticity are those on doing good works to be seen by men (Matt. 6:2–4, 5–6, 16–18); on laying up of treasures (Matt. 6: 19–21); on the eye being the lamp of the body (Matt. 6:22–23); on not casting pearls before swine (Matt. 7:6); on being wise as serpents and innocent as doves (Matt. 10:16); on not fearing those who can kill the body, but who cannot kill the soul (Matt. 10:28–31); on whoever would be greatest must become the servant of all (Matt. 20:26b–27); on not being presumptuous in matters of honor (Luke 14:8–10); on inviting as guests the poor and disadvantaged, who cannot repay (Luke 14:12b–14a); on identifying with the disadvantaged and taking responsibility for their welfare, even in the absence of ethnic obligation and at the risk of one's own security (Luke 10:30–35).

We have seen how it is possible to reconstruct a reliable account of Jesus' public career and message. We can see that this historical reconstruction is commensurate with the story of Jesus in the Gospels, and we can understand in general how the evangelists combined the religious expectations of the Jews with the actual history of Jesus. But specifically what happened? How did the Jesus tradition develop into the various forms it assumes in the Gospels? How were all of these various traditions united within the Gospels as we know them? To understand these developments it is necessary first to consider briefly the importance of Paul and his relationship to those who had been disciples of Jesus, especially Peter.

PAUL AND THE JESUS TRADITION

We turn to Paul's letters for our most important control in delineating the distinctive features of the early Christian environment in which the Jesus tradition developed prior to its incorporation into the Gospels. In Paul's letters one sees a network of eschatologically-oriented churches constituted and enlivened by belief in the saving consequences of the death and resurrection of Jesus Christ. One can be so enamored by the differences between this environment and that of Jesus that one misses the essential continuity between the two—a continuity which explains the historical fact that the post-Easter Christian community developed out of the pre-Easter fellowship between Jesus and his disciples.[18]

Paul's letters reflect some awareness of the gospel traditions. However, the first and perhaps most striking point to notice in these letters is the absence of any explicit reference to the parables of Jesus. This cannot be because Paul's theology was antithetical to the theology Jesus expressed in his parables. The fact is that Paul's theology was essentially the same.[19] So the absence of references to Jesus' parables must be explained some other way.

The answer seems to be twofold. First, the parable form, which was generally suitable to spoken communication, was less suitable to Paul's function as a letter writer. Second, Jesus' parables were addressed to Palestinian hearers. Therefore, they presuppose customs and social relationships native to that locale and culture and less so to customs and social relationships native to the gentile churches of Asia Minor, Macedonia, and Achaia. Since Paul in Gal. 1:23 calls attention to his reputation as one who "is now preaching the faith he once tried to destory" (which therefore must have been a pre-Pauline faith), since he refers to himself as a man in Christ, and since his theology is essentially the same as the theology of Jesus, it follows that there is a case for historical continuity and a developmental relationship between Jesus and Paul.

If the parables of Jesus express the fundamental, controlling images of Jesus' thinking about God—our relationship to God and our relationship to one another—it is then possible to regard the parables as affording primary access to what Paul calls "the mind of Christ." In addition, it is possible to view much of Paul's deepest theological thought as reflecting influence from Jesus' parables. For example, it is as if the parable of the tax collector and Pharisee had burned itself indelibly into Paul's mind. As he wrote about righteousness and justification, he identified himself existentially with one and then the other of these two men—with the Pharisee when he condemned boasting, with the tax collector when it came to the question of justification by faith or righteousness apart from the law, and with the Pharisee again when Paul described himself as blameless over against the question of righteousness before the law.

Consider the compassionate movement of the Good Samaritan to the side of the man left half dead and the corresponding compassionate movement of the father toward his returning son as expressions of Jesus' conception of God's active concern for people. If one were to hold such conceptions in living relationship with the teaching "Whoever would be great among you must be your servant" (Matt. 20:26) and then ponder the christological hymn of Phil. 2:6–11, he or she could see the latter as a mythopoeic statement profoundly in keeping with the theology of Jesus—"who, though he was in the form of God, did not count equality with God a thing to be grasped, but emptied himself, taking the form of a servant, being born in the likeness of men . . . he humbled himself and became obedient unto death, even death on a cross" (Phil. 2: 6–8). This represents development. The death and resurrection of Jesus provide both form and substance to the developed meaning. But the theology is the same. It is a theology of empowerment, of liberation—a divine movement from the privileged position of strength and power to the side of the weak, the disadvantaged, the dispossessed, the despised. It is a movement of compassion, servanthood, self-giving, and risk-taking for the sake of and out of love for the other, of dying that there might be life. This theology called for a revolutionary reversal in the usual hierarchy of human relationships, where the poor served the rich and the weak and dispossessed were enslaved to the strong and powerful. This was a theology which was to affect irrevocably the course of human affairs and to urge humankind in the direction of becoming a family, with God as heavenly Father.

PETER AND PAUL

Ever since the days of F. C. Baur, students of church history have been particularly conscious of the unresolved question, What was the relationship between Peter and Paul? Baur wanted to prove that the impression of apostolic harmony and cooperation left by the New Testament upon the minds of its readers was unhistorical. To a considerable degree, Baur succeeded. His method was to attack the credibility of Acts as a reliable historical source for the history of the apostolic age, just as his younger associate, Strauss, attacked the credibility of the Gospels as reliable sources for the history of Jesus of Nazareth.

The combined effect of the work of Strauss and Baur was devastating. The reaction to their work was certain and lethal. By common agreement between church and state, no student of Baur was allowed to succeed him, and consequently the short-term fate of the so-called "Tübingen school" was sealed.

However, in spite of the reaction against Baur and his students, much of the critical results of the Tübingen school have stood the test of time. Often without proper acknowledgment, many of Baur's views have been adopted unobtrusively into the mainstream of twentieth-century criticism. Slowly but surely the historical-critical approach so relentlessly pursued by Baur and his associates has won its way. And few today would seriously contend that the way forward is to abandon this method of studying the New Testament literature.

But was Baur right in leaving the impression that instead of apostolic agreement and harmony, the early church was characterized by the exact opposite—by apostolic conflict and strife? Granted, Baur was basically correct in recognizing that the special tendencies of Acts undercut any uncritical attempt to base church history on its account of Christian beginnings. But did Baur do justice to the New Testament evidence as a whole and in depth? I think not. Although I accept his view that Acts is a secondary source written a generation or more after Paul wrote his letters, I will attempt to set forth in terms congenial to Baur's historical method an argument for the view that beneath, behind, and surrounding the party strife in Corinth and the open conflict between Peter and Paul in Antioch was a fundamental theological understanding and agreement shared by these apostles, which made cooperation between them possible in spite of the all-too-human pressures upon them to compete and disagree with one another. In so doing, I propose to accept Paul's letters as our primary source for understanding not only his thought, but also his life.[20]

After three years of preaching the faith he had ravaged, Paul went to Jerusalem to visit Peter. This visit lasted fifteen days, and except for James, the brother of Jesus, Paul did not see any of the other apostles. Fourteen years later Paul went up to Jerusalem for another visit. The purpose of this visit was to lay out for those who were apostles before him the gospel he had been preaching during the intervening years, lest he run or had run in vain. Present on this occasion were Peter, James, and John. The practical result of this meeting was a formal decision to reorganize the evangelistic efforts of the church that Paul once persecuted.

Peter, James, and John were perceived by many to be pillars of that church. Now, however, primarily in the light of the success of Paul's evangelistic efforts among the Gentiles, the need for a new organizational structure was recognized. Following a principle of what we may term "gospel expediency," the evangelistic efforts of the church were to be formally divided. Peter, James, and John were to head the mission to the circumcised; and Paul and Barnabas were to head the mission to the uncircumcised. Thus, within seventeen years, Paul had risen from the status of only one of many to whom Jesus had appeared to a place of coequality with the person to whom Jesus first appeared—a person who had been a disciple of Jesus and one who belonged to the triumvirate of the apostolic council in Jerusalem. This was an astonishing achievement verified not only by Paul's statement, but by the important place he is given in Acts. Above all, it is verified by the extraordinary role of his witness in the New Testament canon. Just as Paul had once risen above many of his own contemporaries in Judaism in his zeal for the traditions of the fathers, so within the church he rose over a period of time to a corresponding place of preeminence among those engaged in the gentile mission. He obtained the recognition he sought for the gospel he preached. The desired understanding was formally sealed, and the Jerusalem apostles gave to Paul and his close associate, Barnabas, the right hand of fellowship.

How was this astonishing achievement accomplished? Was it merely the well-deserved reward for fourteen years of successful evangelistic work in Asia Minor and Greece? Hardly! This work itself had been the cause of the controversy that necessitated Paul's trip to Jerusalem.

Consider for a moment the achievement of arranging the conference in the first place. It may be assumed that in certain quarters there was opposition to any agreement to meet with Paul. A meeting to consider the legitimacy of the gospel Paul preached accorded him, in the eyes of his opponents, a dangerous recognition that he later used to his advantage. We know that people suspicious of the gospel Paul preached were surreptitiously brought into the meeting. This is a clear sign of the tensions that had been created in the church by the decision to meet with Paul on the agenda that had been set.

How, then, was this meeting arranged? There can be little doubt that Peter was the only person Paul could have counted on to persuade James and John to be in Jerusalem at a particular time to take part in discussions of his gospel and to help make certain necessary, far-reaching decisions.

Important conferences, of course, are seldom easily arranged. This is especially true when great distances and great personalities are involved. Each principal has his or her own private schedule and agenda. These must be adjusted and coordinated if the meeting is to take place. Someone must want the meeting and must be able to persuade one or more of the others of its importance.

It could be that James or others in Jerusalem wanted this meeting and that Paul was, so to speak, summoned to headquarters. But Paul explicitly rules out this possibility. The initiative to go to Jerusalem had not come from human sources. The conference, as Paul perceived it, was desired by God. Though he does not say so explicitly, it seems likely that Paul himself requested the meeting and was able to justify the need for it.

Since Paul's purpose in going to Jerusalem was to discuss the gospel he preached with those who were apostles before him, it presumably would have been in relation to this gospel that he requested the meeting and justified its need. This gospel of Jesus Christ or "of God," as Paul sometimes called it, was the gospel which was adapted in various modified forms (for example, in Matthew, Mark, Luke, John, Acts, Ephesians, 1 Peter, and so forth) as the gospel of the Christian church. Competing gospels, especially those requiring circumcision, were eventually discarded or withered away.

How, then, was it possible for Paul's gospel or the gospel Paul preached to win the day in a church which once tolerated opposition to it? We must not forget that persons opposed to Paul's gospel were let into the Jerusalem meeting. Later, when the circumcision party from James arrived in Antioch, Peter, whose recognition of the validity of Paul's gospel (a gospel which justified both Jews and gentiles by faith, not by works of the law) had led him to take up the practice of eating with gentile or uncircumcised Christians, withdrew from their table fellowship *out of fear of the circumcision party*. So it would appear that there was a time when opposition to Paul's gospel or to some of the practical consequences of that gospel was tolerated in the church.

When Peter, other Jewish Christians, and even Barnabas withdrew from table fellowship with the gentile Christians, Paul became deeply conscious of the peril in which he and his gospel proclamation stood. Another gospel was certainly being tolerated—one which might not in his eyes have been a gospel at all, but which was nonetheless some people's understanding of the faith, although contrary to the gospel he preached.

How did Paul's gospel win the day? It certainly did win the day to the extent that Paul's letters (including Galatians and the account of the Antioch incident) were given great prominence in the church's canon.

It is clear from what Paul writes about the incident with Peter at Antioch that the question at issue was not theological per se, but concerned actions that were inconsistent with an agreed-upon theology. In fact, according to Paul's testimony, he won the day because he was able to expose Peter's hypocrisy through an appeal to a fundamental theological agreement that he and Peter shared.

When was this agreement reached, and what was its import? It could not have been reached as late as the conference at Jerusalem when Paul discussed the gospel he preached with those who had been apostles before him. That conference itself presupposed that someone besides Paul and his close associates (that is, Barnabas and Titus) understood and was willing to endorse the fundamental theological position from which Paul worked. Who could that person have been but Peter? Barnabas and others of Paul's associates may have played an intermediary role. But in the final analysis, only effective contact with Peter could have enabled Paul to actualize his realization of the need for the meeting with the Jerusalem triumvirate. Moreover, it is not enough to think that Peter was mildly agreeable to the meeting. Paul would have needed his active support since Paul had no power to open doors at the highest levels of the church in Jerusalem by himself. Someone near or at that level needed to do this for him, and who besides Peter could this have been?

Now we can appreciate as never before the importance of the fifteen-day visit Paul made to Peter in Jerusalem three years after his conversion. Concurrence between Peter and Paul over the fundamental apostolic faith, upon which the Christian church rests today, was probably agreed to in principle during Paul's fifteen-day stay. This apostolic faith is not to be identified with either Peter or Paul per se, but with Peter *and* Paul. It is inclusive of both, but not limited to or absolutely identical with either. Paul acknowledged that he also met with James, who was probably involved to some extent in the discussions that took place. No doubt Paul discussed the matter of the resurrection appearances with James and Peter. No doubt he also fully satisfied himself that Jesus' appearance to him, though to one born out of due time, was of the same order as those to Peter and James. But Paul makes clear that his purpose in going to Jerusalem on that occasion was to visit Peter.

So James presumably came into the picture in some secondary role as far as Paul was concerned. In any case, in view of what happened subsequently, it is doubtful that James ever really understood or fully agreed with Paul. And his acceptance of Paul, such as it was, was probably preceded and made possible by Peter's acceptance of Paul.

It is notable that three years had gone by before Paul went to Jerusalem to visit Peter. That was time enough for him to have formulated the questions he wished to ask. At the time he left for the fifteen-day visit to Peter, Paul was already preaching the faith he once ravished. Whether at this early stage he had fully developed what he later termed his "gospel" may be problematic. Nevertheless, it seems likely that Paul had worked out his gospel in principle before he went to Peter. Certainly he had the theological foundation for that gospel before he met Peter because he explicitly says, with reference to that period of his life, that the churches of Christ in Judea only knew him by reputation. And according to that reputation Paul had been "preaching the faith he once ravished." This clearly implies that the faith he preached was the faith of the pre-Pauline Christian community he formerly persecuted.

To suppose that Paul's faith was something other than a particular form of the apostolic faith, shared in one way or another by Peter and the other apostles who had been disciples of Jesus, only creates unnecessary historical and theological problems. Indeed, once it is recognized that Jesus was opposed by some Pharisees for eating with Jews who were living like gentiles (with "tax collectors and sinners"), it is not difficult to reconstruct the reasons Paul had opposed the church. As a Pharisee he could have been opposed to the church of Jesus Christ, as some Pharisees were to Jesus, only if the members of this postresurrection community continued the table fellowship practices Jesus had initiated. In southern Syria and the regions near Damascus, it was likely that the circle of Jews who were living like gentiles would eventually include gentiles themselves—certainly God-fearing Gentiles who had already drawn near to Jewish circles and who would have been keenly interested in a form of the faith where the nonobservant (specifically, the noncircumcised) were fully accepted.

If we conjecture that Paul's opposition to the church was excited in part by some religiously illicit mixture of gentiles and Jews as well as by the report of righteous Jewish Christians accepting nonobservant Jews into their fellowship, then we have an essential ingredient for a solution to the problem of the development from Jesus to the gospel Paul preached. After his conversion Paul preached the faith which he had formerly ravished; he therefore would have preached a faith which already was actualizing the inclusion of faithful nonobservant gentiles, something implicitly entailed in Jesus' practice of accepting nonobservant Jews into his table fellowship. Such a development is clearly consonant with what Paul writes concerning the difficulties created in Antioch by Peter's withdrawal from table fellowship with nonobservant (that is, uncircumcised) gentile Christians. Indeed, one reason Paul felt constrained to confront his colleague was precisely the fact that he recognized how a compromise on this matter was not a compromise of the *bene esse,* but of the *esse* of the fellowship of Jesus Christ.

If Paul's preaching during the three years before he went to Jerusalem to visit Peter had already opened his eyes to the possibility of and the need for evangelizing the gentiles in a way that actualized his conviction that Christ's death abrogated the necessity to keep the law, then his discussions with Peter would certainly have covered the theological grounds for such a development. We do not know whether he discussed Jesus' attitude toward the law; certainly he discussed Peter's own attitude. Since Peter had been a disciple of Jesus, however, the two questions are virtually inseparable, the one entailing the other. If Paul didn't discuss the resurrection appearances and the question of the continuing authority of the law with Peter during his fifteen-day visit, then what did they discuss?

That Peter and Paul did establish a trusting relationship grounded in a deep faith in God and mutual respect for one another seems to be the simplest explanation for all that followed. It helps to explain how Paul, fourteen years later, could lay claim on Peter's sympathetic concern for his welfare and the welfare of the evangelistic work to which he had given so much of himself. It also helps explain how Paul could, when necessary, speak the truth in love to Peter and rebuke his inconsistent actions.

To what extent these two apostles agreed on their Christology or on the details of their faith is, of course, problematic. Indeed, complete agreement of this kind would have been mutually less beneficial than deep personal trust and fundamental theological agreement. From Paul's own statement, this fundamental theological agreement was rooted in their common trust in God's justifying grace in Jesus Christ and in the corollary of this justifying faith, that is, their recognition that one cannot be justified by works of the law. Nowhere does this understanding come to expression more clearly than in certain recorded words and actions of Jesus preserved in our Gospels.[21] So it is intrinsically probable that the considerably developed and richly diverse apostolic faith of Peter and Paul is rooted in the faith of Jesus, which he shared with his disciples and by which he inspired them.

Once it is understood that Peter and Paul concurred on how this faith was to be interpreted to the Gentiles, all else falls into place. Paul's spectacular fourteen-year mission in Asia Minor and Greece was a vindication of what must have been at first a minority position in Jerusalem, endorsed at most by Peter and James. In any case, it appears that Peter concurred with the gospel Paul preached and that he and Paul mutually supported one another from the day Paul left him in Jerusalem after his fifteen-day visit. Needless to say, Paul's account in Galatians, on which this argument is based, is one-sided and perhaps unfair to Peter at some points. But the point we are trying to make is that Peter and Paul were fundamentally agreed on the meaning of the faith. Confidence in such a conclusion is strengthened because it rests on evidence given by Paul at a time when he was actually constrained to underscore the opposite, that is, his *difference* with Peter. If Paul were arguing for the point we are making, we could not use his statements to support our conclusion with the confidence we do.

This concurrence between Peter and Paul did not and could not guarantee Paul or his churches immunity from the harassment of Judaizers, who may or may not have claimed for their position the authority of the Jerusalem church. Thus, Paul's concern in Gal. 2:2 that he might be running or had run in vain in no way calls into question the possibility of the earlier agreement between him and Peter. In fact, if that earlier agreement was still in place, it helps account for Paul's success in getting a meeting with the Jerusalem triumvirate. It also helps account for the twofold division of the church's mission that was agreed upon during the conference. The fact that Peter and Paul emerged from the conference in positions of mutual preeminence is prima facie evidence in favor of the conjecture that they had a decisive role in organizing the conference and setting its agenda. Nor need this interpretation prejudice the question of whether at any time, either before or subsequent to the incident in Antioch, Peter was in Corinth. Nor need it prejudice the question of whether the "party spirit" in Corinth was at any time or in any way inspired by Peter.

From all this it follows that the story of the formation of the New Testament canon includes the story of how this early and decisive apostolic concurrence and mutuality between Peter and Paul became normative for the leadership of those churches that eventually formed it and abided by its authority.[22]

Seen from this point of view, the essential elements in the New Testament canon were present in principle in the apostolic agreement reached by Peter and Paul (with some possible consultation with James) during the fifteen days Paul visited Peter in Jerusalem just three years after his conversion. Since at that time not a single book of the New Testament had been written, it may at first seem strange to think that the essential elements shaping the canon could have been brought together so early. What would or could these essential elements have been?

First, there would have been the apostolic memory of Jesus. Peter and James were representative custodians of that collective memory. Second, there would have been the resurrection appearances of Jesus. The common bond between Peter, James, and Paul was that Jesus had appeared to each following his death and resurrection.

James had known Jesus as a close relative. Peter had participated in Jesus' public ministry. Paul was a Pharisee who had experienced the saving power of the gospel of Jesus Christ without having had direct contact with him before his death. Whatever diversity there may have been in the way each of these three apostles experienced the postresurrection appearances of Jesus, the tradition upon which Paul built wherever he went was that Jesus had appeared to the Twelve, then to a much larger number, and eventually to all the apostles. The only persons Paul specifically mentions by name besides himself when he passed on this tradition are the two apostles he saw during his fifteen-day stay in Jerusalem, namely Peter and James.

So the postresurrection appearances of Jesus and the concomitant belief in him as the risen Christ who had gained victory over death would have been powerfully present as an essential element in the apostolic concurrence between Peter and Paul. This is a point not easily appreciated by most gentiles who place great weight upon Paul's direct testimony of having seen Jesus. The fact is, however, that Paul himself was reliant upon others who, by virtue of their previous personal acquaintance with Jesus, could recognize him and give credible testimony to his identity. This is an important point, notwithstanding Paul's apparent lack of interest in it.

The apostolic memory of the crucified Jesus is inextricably bound up with the confident belief that he had been resurrected and that he had effectively manifested himself to persons who had never known him before his death. We can even say that without the apostolic memory of Jesus and the appearance of Jesus after his death to some of his disciples, there never would have been a church for Paul to persecute. And without that experience, any appearance of Jesus to Paul would have been something different from the appearance of Jesus to Paul that plays such an important role in the New Testament. Without Paul's conviction that the Son of God whom God had revealed to him was none other than the Jesus who had appeared to Peter, James, and others, his gentile converts could well have separated themselves from everything that rooted the church in Judaism. There can be no doubt that Paul had this conviction. He undoubtedly had it before he went to Jerusalem for his first visit with Peter. It is unlikely that Paul had any reservations about the matter. But any he might have had were resolved, we may assume, by his direct contact with Peter and James. For this visit would have afforded him an opportunity to satisfy himself as to what some of those who had been apostles before him and who had been with Jesus had to say about these matters.

According to more than one source, there was a tradition that after his resurrection Jesus first appeared to James. No trace of this tradition, however, appears in the New Testament. This indicates that for the church which developed out of the apostolic association of Peter and Paul, pride of place as far as resurrection appearances are concerned went to Peter.

Paul himself is quite explicit on this point. He says that Jesus appeared first to Cephas and finally, as to one born out of due time, to him. In this way the appearances of Jesus to Peter and Paul mark the beginning and end of a most decisive period in the history of the New Testament church. For this is the time during which the apostolic faith of the New Testament church was established in principle. Looking back years later, Paul saw and represented himself as consummating this authoritative series of postresurrection appearances. But when was this tradition fixed? In Paul's mind it must have been fixed by the time he left Peter and James at the end of his fifteen-day visit. It presumably was the tradition he passed on to all his churches during his fourteen years of missionary work in Asia Minor and Greece.

In view of the fact that James joined his colleagues (Peter and John) in the Jerusalem triumvirate in extending the right hand of fellowship to Paul and Barnabas under circumstances where the gospel Paul preached among the Gentiles was at issue, we must presume that whatever private reservations James may have harbored personally on this point were not allowed to intrude. Whether the tradition that Jesus had first appeared to James was known to him or whether he contributed to the development of such a tradition, we cannot know. What is clear is that in the New Testament the tradition that Jesus appeared to James is preserved only in one of Paul's letters. The letter of James does not even mention the resurrection, nor does it claim apostolic status for its author. This latter point is in contrast with most of the letters attributed to Paul, including Colossians, Ephesians, all the Deutero-Pauline letters, and 1 and 2 Peter. It is, however, in keeping with the fact that no apostolic status is claimed by the authors of 1, 2, and 3 John, Jude, Hebrews, or Revelation. Indeed, it is a remarkable fact that of all the apostles, only Peter and Paul are represented in the New Testament by letters in which the authors are designated as apostles. This further confirms our impression that the New Testament canon was formed under circumstances where the apostolic witness of Peter and Paul had become normative.

James is mentioned only three times in Acts. When Peter takes leave of those to whom he appeared at the door of the house of Mary, mother of John Mark (Acts 12:17), he is represented as saying: "Tell this [how the Lord had miraculously brought him out of prison] to James and to the brethren." This reference reflects a tradition according to which Peter recognized a special leadership status for James in the Jerusalem church. Later, in Acts 15, James supports Peter's recommendation that the work of Paul and Barnabas be recognized as authentic work of the Holy Spirit.

In Acts 21:18, Paul is represented as talking with James during his last visit to Jerusalem. He was told by James that in the interests of the church he should make it clear that however lenient he was with gentile converts, he himself was fully observant of the law. The paucity of references is hardly commensurate with the important place that James must have held in the Jerusalem triumvirate. There was a "circumcision party" that was identified with James. This party had sufficient power even outside Jerusalem to cause a serious break or disruption in the Christian community as far away as Antioch. For fear of this party, Peter withdrew from table fellowship with gentile Christians into which he had been led by his faith in the grace of God in Jesus Christ. The power and influence of James at that time must have been great indeed. The fact that James is referred to only three times in the Acts of the Apostles should make it clear that this book is a woefully inadequate source for reconstructing his actual role in the history of the church.

Paul gives John a place of special importance in the Jerusalem hierarchy. He is mentioned as the third member of the Jerusalem triumvirate. John's name appears repeatedly along with Peter's in the early chapters of Acts. Apart from accompanying Peter, however, John has no important role to play in the Acts account. The evidence from Acts suggests that the New Testament was shaped by a tradition in which the apostle Peter stands far above his Jerusalem colleagues. The only person with a status of comparable importance is Paul. We are speaking here not of history, but of the canon. The fact that James and John are not featured in Acts tells us something about the church that made Acts the central span in the New Testament bridge from Jesus to the heavenly Jerusalem.[23]

The tradition that Peter and Paul were martyred in Rome, if it can be depended on,[24] affords an important clue to unraveling the mystery of the peculiar prominence given to them in the New Testament canon. But something more is needed. The New Testament leaves unexplained how and why these two apostles (when last seen together they are in a situation of deep confrontation) could emerge in the New Testament canon as irenic pillars of the apostolic faith, standing together in a unified witness to the gospel of Jesus Christ.

It is not enough to show, as we have attempted, that this confrontation took place within the context of a wider, much deeper theological unity that had long held these two apostles together.

For Peter's implied defection was of the most serious nature and witnessed to a potentially dangerous disruption of apostolic mutuality and concurrence.

If this potential cleavage or disagreement was not theological per se, what was it? The New Testament indicates that the disagreement had to do with what was fundamentally a christological problem. Paul indicates as much by pointing out that Peter's withdrawal from table fellowship nullified or made of no avail the death of Christ. It was Paul's contention that Christ's death had brought an end to the law; the law was no longer binding on those who believed in Christ.

We cannot know what Peter might have thought about this point. It is unlikely, however, that he would have wanted to do anything that might diminish the importance of Jesus' death in the eyes of others. He certainly would have been conscience-stricken to think that he had acted hypocritically by withdrawing from table fellowship. So if this confrontation with Paul was a growth experience for Peter in which his vision and understanding of the practical consequences of faith in Jesus Christ were enlarged and deepened, then it would have resulted in a change in Peter's thinking. Of course, Peter could possibly have been unaffected by what happened on this occasion and could have insisted on the appropriateness of his actions at every point. If so, we have no explanation for the picture that finally emerges in the New Testament. For in this picture Peter and Paul are represented as basically agreed concerning the fundamental points at issue—whether and to what extent it was necessary to observe the law and whether it was appropriate to have a common table fellowship between Jewish and gentile Christians.

On these fundamental questions the New Testament may represent a colossal tour de force where historical fact has been twisted beyond recognition. But it is at least equally possible and intrinsically more probable that Peter underwent something of a conversion in his understanding of the full consequences of faith in Jesus Christ. There are a number of passages in the New Testament which can be interpreted to support this view.[25] The omission in Acts of any reference to the problem between Peter and Paul at Antioch and the general picture of apostolic harmony that Acts provides could have been the result of interest in promoting the much deeper, fundamental relationship of concurrence, mutuality, and cooperation that actually had existed between these two apostles.

MODIFICATION AND CREATION OF TRADITION

The modification of the Jesus tradition and the creation of new forms for that tradition were made possible by the Spirit of Jesus, which was manifestly and in manifold manner present and active in the church that came into being in response to Jesus' death and resurrection.

To recognize the basic continuity between the theology of Jesus and Paul as perceived respectively in their parables and letters, including the absence of any apparent need for Paul to reproduce or even refer to the parabolic forms of Jesus' teaching, at once makes clear with what freedom the basic theology embodied in Jesus' teachings was taken over and developed in some early Christian communities. A chief necessity for development in these communities seems to have been prompted by the need to do justice to the theology of Jesus in terms of his death and resurrection. During the time Jesus preached, it was natural for those who heard him and/or worked with him to receive his words in the context of his commitment to God. After his death, however, it was necessary to combine and even coalesce Jesus' words with tradition that clarified his relationship to God. To take Jesus' words by themselves would have abstracted them from the reality that provided the contextual relationships in which they received their meaning and significance. That reality was the committed life of a man obedient to God.

Some efforts to relate Jesus' words to his death (as, for example, changes made in the parable of the wicked tenants) ran counter to a primal intention Jesus had in creating his words, namely to point people to God. And one may judge as too-radical-to-be-normative the freedom sometimes exercised by theologians like Paul who, in an effort to be true to the substance of the faith, often left aside the formal Jesus tradition.[26] Though this freedom permitted theological creativity while leaving Jesus' words undistorted, it did not provide a needed norm by which the proliferation of new tradition could be kept subject to the normative influence of the "remembered" Lord. Eventually the Gospels met this need. Basically they incorporate the words of Jesus within christological frameworks in which his death and resurrection are seen as the culmination of his commitment and dedication to the will of God, to his servanthood, and his sonship. By the time the Gospels were written, however, the Jesus tradition itself had developed significantly through modification of the words of Jesus and the creation of quite new words.

Modification and creation are not two altogether different kinds of development. Both presuppose that the Spirit of Jesus is at work in the developmental process; both allow the Spirit freedom to reveal the mind of Jesus Christ in unexpected ways.

To understand how such development could have occurred, it is necessary to place ourselves among the disciples of Jesus following his death and resurrection. As long as Jesus was alive in the flesh, he could and did inspire and legislate for his disciples. When he was no longer present in the flesh, the disciples were leaderless, except for the tradition Jesus had created (which they cherished as words of the Lord), and the guidance of the Spirit. He had taught them to pray and to have faith in the goodness of the heavenly Father: "Knock, and it will be opened to you" (Matt. 7:7). He had molded them into a community in which they were taught to love and serve one another: "Whoever would be great among you must be your servant" (Matt. 20:26). This entailed listening to one another in a spirit of love and understanding.

Moreover, the disciples had experienced table fellowship with Jesus and with one another. On the night he was betrayed, Jesus had prepared them for his death by providing instructions that would ensure their remembrance of him when they came together for sacred meals. In this way, Jesus was to continue with them through an act of corporate memory. At least this is the way the later followers of Jesus looked back upon their beginnings as a post-Easter community.

This abbreviated account is something of an oversimplification, but it surveys the essential matters required for understanding the development that followed. When the disciples met together, they had power as a group to make decisions on the basis of mutual consent, guided by a sense of what the Spirit was prompting them to do. But on those occasions when important new decisions needed to be made and there was no "word from the Lord" and agreement among them, some provision was needed that would enable the group to work through disagreement to an acceptable solution.

There are indications that certain disciples assumed leadership roles that were more or less permanent and relatively independent of the authority of occasional inspiration. Peter and James, the brother of Jesus, are two names well known in this regard. Paul mentions them together with John as a triumvirate among those who were apostles before him. By alluding to them, even if with irony, as "pillars" (Gal. 2:9), Paul indicated that their leadership was not charismatic. Thus, their leadership was not primarily dependent on the Spirit, which comes and goes and remains unpredictable. Rather, like pillars, their leadership rested on some more permanent basis. With James, leadership apparently rested on blood relationship; with Peter, perhaps on the distinction of having been the first to whom Jesus appeared after his resurrection. Even so, these "stable" leaders did not have the authority to decide on important issues apart from the process of listening to the others, and it is here that a key provision for developmental change was allowed.

Christian Prophets

Some early Christians recognized that Jesus was mystically present in their midst when they were gathered together in his name (Matt. 18:20), that is, when they were properly constituted as a body of his disciples. Their assurance that this provision was divinely ordained constituted the basis for accepting decisions that had been agreed upon in such meetings as binding. On administrative and legislative occasions, the primary though perhaps unexpressed question was and continues to be among many Christians, Who speaks in the Spirit of Jesus? It was the recognizable Spirit of Jesus which could speak through any one of the disciples that guaranteed that any decision they made on earth would be binding in heaven (Matt. 18:18–20).

It is of the greatest importance to realize that at a very early period this provision was extended beyond the circle of the original disciples who had known Jesus in the flesh. This was certainly the provision for discipline among members of the church at Corinth, and it was Paul's confidence that the Corinthian Christians would know from past experience his power to speak in the Spirit of Jesus that enabled him to inspire, condemn, and legislate in absentia for the Corinthian church. If they failed to act as he had directed, then when he arrived at Corinth, there would be the opportunity to see who really spoke in the Spirit of Jesus (2 Cor. 12:19—13:10). This thinly veiled threat reveals the basis for a pre-Pauline type of apostolic power in the church. Although abuses of such ecclesiastical power do occur, this theory and practice still lies at the basis of inspired Christian administrative and legislative processes in the church.

This means that from a very early period, probably going back to the pristine time of the resurrection appearances, there were some in the church who functioned as spokespersons for Jesus. These early Christian prophets gave expression to the Spirit of Jesus. For those who accepted their authority as prophets, their words carried an authority corresponding to words of Jesus.

At a later period this prophetic office was curtailed and placed under episcopal control.[27] But in the archaic period of Christian life, at least as late as the Book of Revelation, any crisis in the life of the Christian community would have provided the occasion for some voice within the church to break forth with a disclosure of the will of God for his people in the form of a prophetic word from Jesus. "I Jesus have sent my angel to you with this testimony for the churches. I am the root and the offspring of David, the bright morning star" (Rev. 22:16). "Behold, I am coming soon, bringing my recompense, to repay everyone for what he has done. I am the Alpha and the Omega, the first and the last, the beginning and the end" (Rev. 22:12–13). "Fear not, I am the first and the last, and the living one; I died, and behold I am alive for evermore, and I have the keys of Death and Hades" (Rev. 1:17b–18). "Those whom I love, I reprove and chasten: so be zealous and repent. Behold, I stand at the door and knock; if any one hears my voice and opens the door, I will come in to him and eat with him, and he with me" (Rev. 3:19–20). We know that these sayings originated with a Christian prophet. Other similar sayings, however, cannot be proven to have originated with early Christian prophets. Still, it is quite possible that they did so originate. As examples we can include such sayings as: "Come to me, all who labor and are heavy laden, and I will give you rest" (Matt. 11:28); "No one knows the Father except the Son and any one to whom the Son chooses to reveal him" (Matt. 11:27b); "I am the way, and the truth, and the life; no one comes to the Father, but by me" (John 14:6).

Christian Scribes

In addition and partially parallel to oral development of the Jesus tradition was development made possible wherever this tradition had assumed written form. Written development, of course, was made possible by scribal activity. Here again it was the practical needs of the Christian community that determined the direction of development.

As with early Christian prophets, Jesus' sayings were modified by the activity of Christian scribes. Sometimes the modification was simply for clarification. For example, the word "debtor," which Jesus and his Jewish Palestinian hearers understood as a synonym for "sinner," was replaced by an unambiguous word for "sinner" for the benefit of gentile readers, many of whom presumably would have found the uninterpreted traditional Palestinian concept "debtor-sinner" confusing (Luke 11:4; 13:2–4). Changes like these were necessitated by changes in environment, where metaphors and other expressions understood by Jesus and his hearers would not be so readily understood by later Christians. This was especially true whenever the original tradition was translated into new languages.

Sometimes, however, traditional sayings were allowed to take on completely new meanings by changes that radically altered their plane of reference. A case in point are the parables about the wicked tenants and the marriage feast. Here Jesus is represented as predicting his rejection by Israel and the destruction of Jerusalem as punishment for this rejection. The alteration that has occurred presupposes certain things: (1) that there were Christian theologians in the period after A.D. 70 who saw the destruction of Jerusalem in such terms; (2) that some Christians at this time believed that Jesus' prophetic powers enabled him to foresee his rejection by Israel and the destruction of Jerusalem in these terms; and (3) that the words of Jesus can be treated as an oracular treasury from which the qualified scribe can bring forth new things out of the old.

A clear example of such scribal work is found in the interpretation of the parable of the sower. Taken as a whole, the parable itself (Matt. 13:3–8) interlocks with a particular situation consistent with the environment of Jesus and his disciples. The clue to the original purpose of the parable as Jesus used it is found in the descending order "one hundred, sixty, and thirty." This has the effect of minimizing or deemphasizing the importance of apparent success in preaching. The situation seems to have been one in which the disciples were experiencing different degrees of succss and failure, with praise and blame based on results leading to invidious comparisons, internal dissension, and demoralization.

To meet this situation and to counteract the negative effects of the unequal success of his disciples, Jesus said: "The Kingdom of Heaven is like a sower going out to sow his field; and as he sowed, some seed fell on rocky ground, some on good. . . ." The point is that the sower sows all parts of the field; some parts are fruitful, some are not. Even the fruitful areas vary in their yield.[28] So it is with God who indiscriminately sends his rain on the just and the unjust (Matt. 5:45). The teaching of this parable is clear. One is neither to be elated over good results nor dismayed over poor results. A person sows, but the results are not in human hands. One is not responsible for the response others make to the word. One who speaks the word is responsible only for how faithfully the good news is proclaimed. We must not discriminate and aim our preaching where we think it will bring the greatest success. We are not to judge who is worthy to hear the word (Matt. 13:24–49; 22:10).

In the explanation of this parable, however, the situation presupposed is quite different. An early Christian scribe, who was interested in the church's ministry of the word, has dropped the sower from view and shifted the emphasis to those "hearing the word." He has then offered an explanation of the hearers' different responses.

CHREIAI

Another way in which tradition concerning Jesus developed was through the creation and use of chreiai. Dibelius' definition of a chreia is oversimplified: "It is a reproduction of a short, pointed saying of general significance, originating in a definite person and arising out of a definite situation." "In the age of the gospels," writes Dibelius, "rhetoricians called such a small literary unit a chreia, as also did the Stoics in the first century B.C."[29]

Many chreiai are indeed very concise as, for example, this one concerning Antisthenes: "One day when he was censured for keeping company with evil men, he replied, 'Physicians attend their patients without getting the fever themselves' " (Diogenes Laertius VI. 6). In other chreiai, however, the sayings are more developed and involve both a question and answer as, for example, those quoted by Zenophon in his *Memorabilia of Socrates* (III. 13). Sometimes the chreiai include action as in the chreia concerning Anaxogoras: "When someone inquired, 'Have you no concern for your fatherland?' he replied, 'I am greatly concerned with my fatherland,' and pointed to heaven" (Diogenes Laertius II. 7).

The chreia form as developed and used by the rhetoricians was admirably well adapted to meet the needs of early Christian preachers. Dibelius was correct in noting the similarity between the Hellenistic chreia and what he called Marcan paradigms. He was also correct in noting that in the synoptic tradition peculiar to Luke there are true chreia forms. He was mistaken, however, in regarding these as the result of the evangelist's literary tendency to cast tradition which came to him in the form of paradigms into the more concise chreia form. It happens that in the Hellenistic literature in which chreiai are found (notably in the lives of various famous men), the pattern is not for the authors to create chreiai, but to incorporate them into their accounts from earlier collections of chreiai. On the basis of a comparative study of the nearest parallels in contemporary literature, it seems likely that the chreiai in the Gospels have been incorporated from earlier written sources.

The chreia, first of all, was designed to be easily committed to memory. It could then be recalled, thus constituting a well-structured text which thereafter could be quoted, paraphrased, illustrated, expounded, etc., at will. This left the speaker (or preacher) free to concentrate upon his or her task without the encumbering handicap of written notes or the embarrassing fear of being "lost for words." The gifted public speaker might find such helps unnecessary, but for the majority they proved to be very useful.

The use of chreiai in the schools of rhetoric was so widespread in the first century and had such a firmly fixed place in the educational system of the empire that Quintilian (ca. A.D. 35–100), though writing in Latin, refers to their composition as a rudimentary activity for pupils who were preparing for the schools of rhetoric.[30] He implies that this discipline was included among the first essentials of general education. Although writing about the situation in Rome, Quintilian describes conditions which also prevailed at the eastern end of the Mediterranean. The point is not that as public orators students would be called upon to create chreiai, but that having written chreiai themselves, they would better understand the principles governing their composition. Thus, they would be better prepared to make the most effective use of extant collections of the chreiai of philosophers and famous men, whose example and words would carry weight in the minds of their hearers. To have invented such chreiai would have defeated the speaker's purpose since it was essential that hearers acknowledge the authenticity of the chreiai used. For all chreiai contain the words or refer to the actions of known historical persons.

It follows, therefore, that just as chreiai concerning Jesus are not to be regarded as having been invented by the evangelists while writing their Gospels, neither are we to think of them as primarily the creation of early Christian preachers. Rather, we should imagine that these early preachers drew upon previously prepared collections of chreiai in which sayings or actions of Jesus had been provided a historical setting and against the background of which the respective sayings or actions were to be understood and interpreted.

Many chreiai are preserved in the Gospels. Matt. 18:21–22 is a chreia consisting of an introduction (v. 21) and a saying of Jesus (v. 22). Immediately following is the parable of the unmerciful servant (vv. 23–35). This parable is intended to illustrate the point in the chreia to which it is joined: that we cannot offer our forgiveness to the brother who sins against us on any calculating basis, but must be prepared to forgive him from the heart, unconditionally, and without the limitation that he not sin again precisely because God has forgiven us a debt of sin infinitely great and humanly impossible to repay.

Luke 12 contains another chreia which is illustrated by a parable (12:13–21). The point in this chreia, that a man must guard himself against all forms of covetousness, is aptly illustrated in the parable of the rich fool.

The use of a parable to illustrate a saying in a chreia was one of the prescribed ways in which the rhetoricians were trained to use chreiai in public speaking.[31]

There are copies of style manuals drawn up by the Greek-speaking rhetoricians, Hermogenes of Tarsus (second century A.D.) and Aphthonius (third century A.D.), in which examples are given of a particular chreia illustrated by an appropriate parable. These manuals were designed to demonstrate to students how they should develop a chreia. Each person using a chreia was free to select whatever parable best illustrated the point made in the chreia. Furthermore, there were other prescribed ways for developing a chreia —for example, by paraphrasing it freely, by bringing out the general principle entailed in it, and where appropriate, by ending with an exhortation to the hearers to act in accordance with this general principle.

It is obvious that all of these prescriptions would have been helpful to early Christian preachers in their use of the chreiai concerning Jesus. In Hellenistic literature outside of these style manuals, chreiai are not developed according to this pattern since by definition this development was designed to enable a speaker to make more effective use of them in oral communication. Therefore, when we find chreiai in the synoptic tradition that are illustrated by parables, we are in direct touch with a particular form of oral tradition. Not that these literary units were first conceived in the mind of some early Christian who, without ever having written them down, passed them on orally to others who repeated the process until they were finally written down in our Gospels. There is scant evidence for that kind of oral tradition. Rather, we are to imagine early Christians creating chreiai which, we may presume, would have been written down and circulated singly or in collections for the use of teachers and preachers in an expanding Christian community.[32]

It is possible that in some cases the same person who formulated a particular chreia might also have been responsible for selecting and attaching a particular parable to it for purposes of illustration. But this point need not be pressed. Perhaps this was due to a later development, reflecting the experience of Christian preachers who found certain parables uniquely well suited to illustrate certain chreiai. In this case, it obviously would be wrong simply to assume that all such parables were necessarily parables of Jesus. On the other hand, one can well imagine that if someone writing down a chreia also knew of a parable of Jesus which aptly illustrated that chreia, that person would be rendering a unique service to those who were to use the chreia by also writing down the parable.

The parables in the synoptic tradition which illustrate chreiai have a distinctively Palestinian cast, and in no case is there any reason to doubt that they are authentic parables of Jesus. This is altogether consonant with these parables having become attached to companion chreiai at an early date. It is noteworthy that these chreiai, including both their sayings and introductions, are also free from signs of later Hellenistic influence. It is equally important that these literary units are singularly free from all traces of the influence of the special needs and interests of the Jewish-Christian community, which was exerting pressure in Palestine and in churches as far away as Antioch in Syria as early as the end of the Christian movement's second decade. All of this points to the close kinship between the tradition preserved in these literary units and the most primitive strata of tradition in the earliest (pre-Pauline) Palestinian Christian communities.

Perhaps one should ask whether at this early date there would have existed in Palestine the need for tradition in this particular form. The answer is yes, almost from the beginning. The earliest Christian communities in Palestine would have found these literary units useful. For even if we were to grant for the sake of argument that orthodox Jewish circles in Palestine may not have been influenced by the educational system of the empire (a historical absurdity), we must allow that the influence of Hellenistic culture upon some Jewish circles in Palestine nevertheless did exist in the first century.[33] One must further allow for the non-Jewish, Greek-speaking population of Palestine and ponder its potential interest in Christian preaching. It is not possible to say precisely when the number of Greek-speaking Christians in Palestine grew to the point where regular preaching was carried on in that language. There is no reason to think that Christian preaching in Palestine was restricted to Aramaic (and/or Hebrew) for very long, if indeed such a restriction ever existed. In circles where the Greek language was spoken, the standards of Hellenistic culture were felt, however imperceptibly, including what the Greeks described at this time as "general education." The chreia was a well-known literary form which, because of its place in Hellenistic rhetoric, probably exerted an influence even beyond the educated classes.[34] We should not necessarily imagine early Christians consciously conforming to rhetorical standards. But if the gospel tradition reflects the influence (conscious or subconscious) of Hellenistic rhetorical practice upon the form of some very early literary units, this should occasion no surprise. All the preconditions for this existed in Palestine some time before the birth of Christian preaching.

Of course one must reckon with the possibility that even among orthodox Jews at this time, sayings of the rabbis were remembered by being formulated in chreia-like constructions. For example, some sayings of Hillel, preserved in Pirke Aboth, are in a form somewhat parallel to the synoptic phenomenon of parables used to illustrate chreiai. One may also compare a similar use of parables in later rabbinic literature.[35]

The original form of the chreia concerning "The Widow's Mite" in Luke 21:1–4 can be reconstructed by the omission of verse 4:

> Looking up, Jesus saw rich people casting their gifts into the Temple treasury. And he saw a needy widow casting in two very small coins. And he said: Truly I say unto you, "This poor widow cast in more than all of them."

Verse 4 is what the rhetoricians termed an *aitia* or "reason." It was one of the standard acceptable additions to attach to a chreia, and its purpose was to explain the general principle incorporated in the chreia. The reason it could be said that the two very small coins of the widow were more than the gifts of all the rich was that "they gave to the treasury out of their abundance; but she out of her want cast in the whole of her substance" (Luke 21:4). This *aitia* opened up the possibility for the rhetorician or preacher to expatiate on the subject of sacrificial giving, to make practical application of the principle under the illumination provided by the picture of the needy widow giving her two tiny coins, and to do this in the power and with the authority of the man to whom the saying in the chreia was attributed.

A developed and expanded version of this chreia is found in the Gospel of Mark. There is a loss of conciseness in this version with the quite unnecessary threefold repetition of the term for "temple treasury" (see Mark 12:41 and 43). The Marcan introduction to the chreia in vv. 41 and 42 is not concise, and the added detail that he "called his disciples to him" in v. 43 is a literary effort at verisimilitude, adding nothing to the chreia. The clearest sign of the secondary character of the Marcan form of this tradition as compared to that of Luke is found in the interpretative gloss added to v. 42, in which it is explained to Mark's readers that the two *lepta* amounted to a *quadrans* in Roman coinage.

LEGENDS AND MYTHS

Legendary Tradition

The origin of legendary tradition concerning Jesus often defies satisfactory explanation. However, it is possible to shed some light upon the forces at work in the case of the birth narratives and other legendary material if they are considered against the background of Jewish-Hellenistic piety.

The expectation of a savior or messiah among pious Jews is bound up with a belief in a correspondence between the messianic future and God's saving activity in and through messianic figures of the past. Thus, in Midrash Koheleth, we read: "As was the first savior (Moses), so also is the last (messiah). . . . And Moses took his wife and his sons, and set them on an ass. So also the last savior—'poor and sitting on an ass' (Zech. 9:9)." This shows that the correspondence can be very loose. When one believes in a pattern of correspondence between the messianic past and messianic future, even the most casual linguistic or conceptual similarity can be made the basis for connecting something the scriptures say has taken place with something that will take place in the time of the messiah.

A corollary of this logic for those who believe that Jesus is the Messiah is to think about the history of Jesus as the Messiah in terms of a corresponding activity of God in the past. This leads to a study of the Scriptures for the purpose of supplying information not only about what is still in the future, but also about what in the earthly life of Jesus must have corresponded to the archaic history of Israel since *he is* the Messiah. The presupposition of this way of thinking is made explicit in Midrash Tanchuma: "What God . . . will do in the future (messianic) time, that he has already done before by the hands of the righteous . . . God will wake the dead, as he did before by Elijah, Elisha, and Ezekiel. He will dry up the sea, as was done by Moses. He will open the eyes of the blind, as he did by Elisha. God will in future time visit the barren, as he did with Abraham and Sarah."

The Gospels are not to be understood as a simple recasting of such messianic expectations into a fictitious narrative about Jesus. There is much valid historical material in the Gospels, and many things expected of the messiah are not projected into the narrative of Jesus in the Gospels as, for example, the drying up of the sea.

Still, it is important to recognize that the story of Jesus' entry into Jerusalem in Matt. 21:1–11 has been told with the prophecy of Zech. 9:9 in view. Moreover, it is clear that the text of the story in Matthew reflects the text of a Greek translation of the Zechariah passage, which is cited in v. 5. In the Hebrew original only one animal is in view ("humble and riding on an ass, (even) on a colt the foal of an ass"), and the point is that the animal is not even a fully developed beast of burden. When Matthew cites Zechariah, however, the ass and the colt are considered two separate animals, and the story is developed accordingly with the disciples' being sent to find the ass and the colt that is with the ass. After finding them, they placed garments upon them, that is, both upon the ass and upon the colt. Under these circumstances, it is clear that texts like Matt. 21:1–11 are largely to be explained in terms of a tradition-forming process that is structured by a belief in divine correspondence between what is read in the Scriptures and what happened to Jesus. This is especially true where the prophets have spoken.

In Matt. 21:1–11 there is no indication of the influence of Scripture at any level other than fulfillment of a prophecy concerning the messiah. However, in the story of Jesus' birth there is, in addition to the prophecy in Isa. 7:14, the influence of the story of the divinely ordained and assisted birth of a son to Abraham and Sarah. Indeed, the correspondence of Matt. 1:18–25 with the story of Abraham and Sarah is so much closer than with the passage in Isaiah that the present text probably represents a modification of a story which originally was only seen in correspondence with the story of God's prototypical visit to Abraham and Sarah.

> And God said to Abraham . . . "your wife . . . shall be called Sarah. And I will bless her, and give you a son of her, and I will bless him [so LXX], and he shall be for a nation, and kings of nations shall be of him. . . . " And God said to Abraham, "Yes, behold Sarah your wife shall bear you a son, and you shall call his name Isaac [cf. Matt. 1:21], and I will establish my covenant with him, for an everlasting covenant, to be a god to him and to his seed after him" (Genesis 17:15–17) . . . And the Lord visited Sarah, as he said, and the Lord did to Sarah, as he spoke. And she conceived and bore to Abraham a son in old age, at the set time according as the Lord spoke to him. And Abraham called the name of his son . . . Isaac (Gen. 21:1–3; cf. Matt. 1:25).

This scriptural passage best explains the structural parallel: "And she will bear a son, and you shall call his name Jesus . . . she (bore) a son; and he (Joseph) called his name Jesus." That the connection of the story of Jesus' birth with Isa. 7:14 was made after this formal structure was developed seems clear from the fact that there is no correspondence between "call his name Immanuel" in Isa. 7:14 and "he called his name Jesus" in Matt. 1:25. In fact, both names are independently explained in the text as it now stands.

The student of the development of early Christian tradition must be alert to the influence of the "correspondence" motif at different levels: (1) at the earliest stage in the development of the tradition, where there may no longer be any explicit reference to the scriptural passage which has had a formative influence on the tradition; and (2) at the later stage represented by the text as it has come to us, where frequently there is an explicit reference to and citation of the scriptural passage that had been in view as the Gospel was being composed.

This second level certainly represents the conscious intention of the evangelist to narrate the story of Jesus in terms of a fulfillment of prophecy motif. But to what extent the evangelist is himself the one who has discovered or created these correspondences between the story of Jesus and matters spoken of by the prophets and to what extent he found such correspondences already made in the materials available to him as he undertook to write his narrative, is very difficult to determine.

The story of Jesus' birth in Matthew in its present form is both romantic and dogmatic. Its dogmatic function is to represent the birth of Jesus as in accordance with the words spoken by the prophet, and therefore thoroughly appropriate for one destined, as God's Messiah, to save his people from their sins. It is romantic insofar as it is an account of how Joseph filled the role of husband to Mary and father to Jesus without begetting. In Hebrew thought, divine intervention in such cases involved opening the womb of a mother which was closed to the seed of the father. Divine intervention did not preempt the full human participation of the father in the begetting of the child any more than it preempted the full participation of the mother in its birth. The substitution of the Holy Spirit as the active agent in the procreation of the child is a Greek concept and represents an interpretation of the Greek text of Isa. 7:14, where the Hebrew word for a "young woman" is rendered by a word meaning "virgin." This allowed the development of a story about the birth of Jesus conforming to that of corresponding figures in history—for example, Alexander, the founder of the civilized world of Hellenic culture, and Romulus, the founder of Rome. This story assists the writer of Matthew to present Jesus Christ, son of David and son of Abraham, as the founder of a kingdom which is sovereign over all earthly kingdoms, even those of Alexander and Caesar. Jesus will save his people because he is "Emmanuel . . . God with us." Similarly, the Gospel stories concerning the appearance of Jesus after his death and his final charge to his disciples correspond to stories about the founder of Rome.

There is strong evidence that the gospel tradition which has been influenced by the "correspondence" motif was formed principally in a Hellenistic, Jewish-Christian environment. This is especially the case in the passion narrative. For example, the narrative detailing Jesus' treatment at the hands of his tormentors and what was said to him as he hung on the cross clearly reflects the influence of what is said concerning the Righteous One in the Hellenistic Jewish work, Wisd. of Sol. 2:1–20. The influence of Isaiah 53 and Psalms 22 and 69 on the formation of the passion narrative scenes also have taken place in a Greek-speaking environment. At least the influence of the Septuagint text of Ps. 69:21 on the formation of the tradition in Matt. 27:34 seems clear.

Mythological Tradition

The origin of mythological tradition is even more difficult to retrace than that of legend. In the Gospels, mythological forms are often used to express God's action in the history of the Christian community through the intervention of the risen Christ. As examples of tradition whose development clearly seems to reflect the crisis which arose over the admission of gentiles into the church, we may take the stories of the transfiguration and Peter walking on the water. These stories belong to a group of stories relating to what might be called "the conversion of Peter." In Luke 22:31–32, Jesus is represented as saying to Peter: "Satan demanded to have you, that he might sift you like wheat, but I have prayed for you that your faith may not fail." Then Jesus adds: "And when you have turned again, strengthen your brethren." This appears to be tradition that originated in a church which benefited from the conversion of Peter. The most explicit of these "conversion" stories appears in Acts 11:1–18. In this passage certain points stand out: (1) following the death and resurrection of Jesus, Peter and the other apostles in Jerusalem, conforming to Jewish custom, did not eat with gentiles; (2) Peter was confronted with the fact that God's grace and Spirit had come through Jesus Christ also to the Gentiles; (3) this led to the conversion of Peter and the practice of eating with gentile Christians; (4) Peter defended this practice before the apostles in Jerusalem; (5) Peter testified that the means of his conversion was a symbolic dream in which God revealed to him that there was now a new ground for salvation—a salvation no longer based on meeting the requirements of the Law of Moses, but one based on grace through faith so that Jew and Gentile alike could now sit together as people of God and share a common table as a family of their heavenly Father.

A less explicit example of a "conversion" story concerning Peter occurs in two forms, one in Luke 5:1–11 and the other in John 21:1–13. In this story (1) the disciples had been fishing all night without success; (2) Jesus gave instructions to make a new effort; (3) Peter, as spokesman for the others, protested and yet followed Jesus' command; (4) the results were amazingly successful; (5) Peter and the others recognized and confessed Jesus as Lord. In John, this is told as a story that took place after the death of Jesus. In Luke, it apparently took place before Jesus' death. As with the story in Acts, however, the history behind the story seems to be that of the early churches' missionary experience and the christological question associated with the problem of evangelizing the Gentiles.

Gentiles were admitted into the church at a very early date. How early is not known. In principle there is no reason to doubt that some of gentile origin were admitted almost from the beginning. These would have included two main types: (1) proselytes, that is, gentiles who had become Jews, and (2) "God fearers," that is, gentiles who were closely drawn to Judaism, but who were not Jews because they had not accepted circumcision or embraced the full yoke of the Law of Moses.

The admission of proselytes into the church would have created no serious problem. The problem would have come with the admission of the "God fearers." It would have accelerated with the full-scale mission to the Gentiles since, at this point, we may presume that large numbers of them whose acquaintance with Judaism was slight or nil presented themselves for membership in the church. The matter came to a crisis over the question of whether the Law of Moses was the supreme authority by which to judge the will and intention of God.

The stories concerning the "conversion" of Peter tell in differing ways the apostle's move from a lower to a higher Christology. Peter began as one who doubted and ended as one who truly believed. What Peter confessed at the end of these stories is summed up in the judgment that Jesus is the Son of God and, as such, a source of authority which transcends the authority of the law and the prophets. This is most clearly expressed in the symbolism of the story of the Transfiguration.

In this story, Jesus took Peter, James, and John up on a mountain. There he was transfigured before their eyes, and they beheld Moses and Elijah with him. Peter's response to this theophany was to rejoice over the divine manifestation of the truth that Jesus had an authority equal to that of Moses and Elijah—a truth symbolized in his offer to build three tabernacles, one for Jesus, one for Moses, and one for Elijah. This represented for the Jew a high Christology. Indeed, those who accorded Jesus a status equal to that of Moses and Elijah were thereby distinguished from all other Jews in a very decisive manner. Moses and Elijah represented the law and the prophets, and to make Jesus equal to the law and the prophets was to accept him as a spokesman authorized to speak for God directly to the people.

Such a christological development tended to separate any Jewish community adhering to such a Christology from a dependence upon the scribes and Pharisees. Having access to Jesus as an authority tended to circumvent the scribes and Pharisees "who sat in Moses' seat."

As high as this Christology was, however, it was not high enough. It did not make clear that God intended to exalt Jesus above all earthly and heavenly authorities and to give him "the name which is above every name, that at the name of Jesus every knee should bow" (Phil. 2:9–10).

This higher and more exalted Christology is symbolized in the story of the transfiguration by a bright cloud that overwhelmed the disciples, and out of which a voice addressed them saying, "This is my beloved Son, with whom I am well pleased; listen to him" (Matt. 17:5; cf. also Mark 9:7; Luke 9:35). The disciples fell on their faces in great fear at this divine disclosure of the awesome status of Jesus. But Jesus came to them in their prostrate position and, after touching them, said, "Rise and have no fear." The story ends with the telling words: "And when they lifted up their eyes, they saw no one but Jesus only." The symbolism of Moses and Elijah disappearing and leaving only Jesus is crystal clear: Jesus is not an authority on par with the law and the prophets, but his authority as the Son of God transcends the law and the prophets. From such an exalted Christology it follows that whenever and wherever the Spirit of God, which is in Jesus Christ, leads Christians into practices that are contrary to the Law of Moses, the authority of Moses is abrogated by the authority of Jesus as the Son of God and Lord of the church. For Peter to accept this higher Christology was for him to be converted from a relatively speaking "lower" Christology. As is indicated in Acts, this conversion took place in the early church in connection with the problem of the admission of gentiles.

The story of Peter walking on the water is of no less interest in this regard. In this story Jesus separated himself from the disciples, sending them on ahead while he went up on a mountain to pray. While the disciples were at sea in a storm-tossed boat, Jesus appeared to them walking on the water. Their response to this apparition was at first fear. But Jesus assured them of his identity with the words, "Take heart, it is I; have no fear." Once again Peter acted as spokesman for the rest and, requesting divine confirmation, said, "Lord, if it is you, bid me come to you on the water." Jesus replied, "Come." Peter then got out on the water and began to walk toward Jesus. But he became afraid and began to sink. Then he cried out, "Lord, save me." And immediately as Peter was sinking Jesus reached out and grasped him by the hand saying, "O man of little faith, why did you doubt?" The story ends with those in the boat confessing to Jesus, "Truly you are the Son of God."

There is little reason to doubt that when this story was first told, it was well understood that the Jesus who reached down to save Peter was the risen Christ. Once removed from its present location in the narrative framework of the Gospel of Matthew, it is correspondingly clear that the Peter who began well, supported by faith in the power of Jesus as Lord, and then faltered because of lack of faith only to be rescued by the risen Christ, was not so much Peter before the death and resurrection of Jesus as the historical Peter of the early church.

Read in this way the symbolism is once again clear and corresponds closely to Peter's personal history as reflected in Paul's first-hand account of an early and very important chapter in church history (Gal. 1:18—2:21). Paul relates that after coming to Antioch, Peter ate with the Gentiles. When a party from James arrived, however, Peter withdrew from table fellowship with the Gentiles, "fearing the circumcision party." The rest of the Jews then followed Peter's example. But Paul, perceiving that Peter and those who were dissimulating with him "were not straightforward about the truth of the gospel," confronted Peter before everyone. The effect of this confrontation for Paul was to set the record straight that he through the law had died to the law that he might live to God. In his argument he appealed to Peter's knowledge that "a man is not justified by works of the law but through faith in Jesus Christ."

Presumably Paul could make this appeal with confidence because at an earlier time, during the fifteen days he had spent in Jerusalem, his visits with Peter had satisfied him concerning Peter's position on this cardinal point. This helps explain how Paul could confront Peter on this formal occasion. Peter was not acting in a manner consistent with his own previously acknowledged understanding of the revolutionary consequences of belief in Jesus Christ. Jesus himself had made clear to his disciples that people are not justified by works of the law, but by faith (Luke 18:9–14). Paul understood the main significance of Jesus' death to lie in this: through the death of Jesus, God has revealed his love for humankind so that it is forever clear that righteousness and justification is no longer through the law, but "by faith in the Son of God, who loved me and gave himself up for me." Paul concluded his argument: "I do not nullify the grace of God; for if justification were through the law, then Christ died to no purpose."

Viewed in this way, what seems to have been at issue in all of these materials concerning Peter is the question of the true status of the risen Christ in the life of the early church. There seems to have been a powerful "circumcision party" that apparently favored a policy according to which, during the interim period until the return of Christ in power, the Law of Moses remained in full effect. This was tantamount to saying that the messianic power of Jesus was still to become really effective as far as the replacing of the law was concerned. Paul, on the other hand, clearly held to a Son of God Christology. Jesus was not viewed simply as the Messiah in the sense that when the messiah comes in the future it will be Jesus, so that the Christian simply awaits the day of judgment in confidence of the outcome. Rather, Jesus' messiahship was already effective, and this was especially and particularly true as far as the continuing authority of the Law of Moses was concerned. Jesus as the Son of God was already empowered through the Spirit to enable the believer to know the will of God and to relate himself or herself to God apart from the law.

The more moderate faction of the "circumcision party" seems to have vacillated. It appears that Peter understood what the gospel required, and he usually could be counted on to walk in a manner consistent with the gospel. For example, when he first arrived in Antioch, he ate with Christians of gentile origin. In removing himself from table fellowship with the Gentiles in Antioch, Peter probably did not consciously repudiate his faith, but simply acted in a manner that could be interpreted as inconsistent with that faith. In the story about walking on water, Peter's faltering steps are represented as due to doubt or a lack of faith. In the story of the transfiguration, however, his willingness to place Jesus on a level with Moses and Elijah is represented as not fully enlightened. Peter did not realize the true status of Jesus as the Son of God, whose authority transcended even that of the law and the prophets.

The origin of these stories concerning Peter is not known. In the story in Acts, the role of imagination expresses itself in the mode of dreaming. It is not impossible that all these stories originated in a similar way and that the ancient belief in the power of dreams to reveal stimulated the imaging process that lies behind their symbolism. For the purpose of understanding the development of tradition, what is especially interesting and important in these stories is their relationship to history. All of these stories are historical, but not in the conventional sense of that term. They are historical in the sense that they all relate to a known historical person and to an important event in the life of that person, an event that has profoundly affected history. But that event did not have its historical focus simply in the earthly ministry of Jesus nor afterwards in the early church. The climax of the event, that is, the effective conversion, seems to have taken place during those christological controversies of the early church that were caused by opposition to the admission of gentiles. The converting forces at play upon Peter, however, were rooted in earlier experiences—in the death of Jesus, and behind that in the historical preaching ministry that preceded that death. The author of Luke-Acts, who had the scope of a two-volume work in which to present his account, had the possibility both of including an explicit story of Peter's conversion in the second volume and foreshadowing this conversion with stories pointing to it that were set within the temporal framework of Jesus' ministry.

With the author of Matthew, however, who chose to present all that he had to say about Jesus Christ and the church within the framework of the life of Jesus, any important event in Peter's life which took place after the resurrection must have been telescoped back into the temporal span of the life of Jesus. This is true not only in the case of such symbolic postresurrection stories as the transfiguration and Peter's walking on water, but also for the theological orientation of the overall framework of Matthew and for much of the content of that Gospel. Matthew is not simply a historical account of the earthly ministry of the flesh and blood Jesus of Nazareth. It is a Gospel of Jesus as the Son of God whose disciples, if they truly understand the will of their Lord, are to commit themselves fully to the mission to the Gentiles—with the assurance that Jesus as the Son of God will abide within them "always, to the close of the age" (Matt. 28:20).

The "historical conversion" of Peter to the higher Son of God Christology which, in the Caesarea Philippi story, is historicized and telescoped back into the earthly ministry of Jesus, is a rock upon which the church of the second and third centuries is founded. As this story makes clear, it is not "flesh and blood" that reveals that Jesus is "the Christ, the Son of the living God." This formulation was used by Paul, as is clear from his words concerning his own conversion. "When he who had set me apart before I was born . . . was pleased to reveal his Son to me . . . I did not confer with flesh and blood." Paul adds: "Nor did I go up to Jerusalem to those who were apostles before me." His famous fifteen-day visit to Peter in Jerusalem came at least three years later. During the three intervening years, Paul had been preaching the faith that *formerly he had tried to destroy* (Gal. 1:23). This faith was grounded in and sustained by the revelation of Jesus as Son of God. Consequently, Paul went to Peter with a "pre-Pauline" faith, which he had at first persecuted and then preached for at least three years. We are not to imagine that Paul invented the faith that he preached or the Son of God Christology which structured it. Neither did Paul receive this gospel of the grace and love of God in Jesus Christ through human beings, nor was it taught to him, but it came to him through revelation (Gal. 1:12). The rock upon which the church rests, therefore, according to this gospel tradition, is faith grounded in divine revelation and not faith transmitted to the apostles by flesh and blood. This understanding of the apostolic faith represents a victory for Paul, not over against Peter who was never clearly antithetical to Paul, but over against those who questioned Paul's apostolic credentials.

The keys of the Kingdom of Heaven that are given to Peter, so that whatever he "bind[s] on earth shall be bound in heaven" (Matt. 16:19), are conditional upon his confession and Jesus' assertion that such faith comes from God. This accords with the tradition in which Jesus extends the divine prerogative to "bind and loose" to all of his disciples (Matt. 18:18). According to this tradition, the keys to the kingdom that once were in the hands of the scribes and the Pharisees who sat on Moses' seat (Matt. 23:2,13) have now been placed in the hands of those who confess Jesus as the Christ, Son of the living God.

Among all of the apostles, Peter and Paul are distinguished as respective heads of the two closely related but administratively separable missions. Paul's words concerning the response of the Jerusalem apostles to the gospel he preached are of the greatest importance:

> When they saw that I had been entrusted with the gospel of the uncircumcision, even as Peter with the gospel of the circumcision (for he who energized Peter for the apostleship of the circumcised energized me also for the Gentiles); and when they perceived the grace that was given unto me, James and Cephas and John, they that were reputed to be pillars, gave to me and Barnabas the right hand of fellowship, that we should go unto the Gentiles, and they unto the circumcision" (Gal. 2:7–9).

Paul made this statement in retrospect after a breakdown of apostolic authority had taken place among the churches he had founded in Galatia. The statement refers to an understanding that was reached at a Jerusalem conference held after Paul had engaged in at least eleven and probably fourteen years of missionary activity, following his fifteen-day visit with Peter. Such an agreement was only possible where there had been some common ground on which both sides could stand. That ground presumably was their common faith in Jesus Christ. We are not to imagine, therefore, that what was lacking was agreement on principle as much as agreement on what in practice was to follow from their common faith.

After the death of Peter and Paul and following the war of A.D. 66–70, the mission to the Jews was virtually eclipsed by the mission to the Gentiles. While fragmentary traditions supporting the mission to the circumcised are preserved in Matthew (some of them even sharply warning against any work among the Gentiles), the Gospel as a whole (revealed in its beginning, end, and climax) calls for a total commitment to the mission to the Gentiles. The earlier division of labor mentioned by Paul seems almost wholly lost from view in Matthew and even more so in Mark, Luke, and John.

Earlier, however, during and following the period of apostolic conflict revealed in Paul's account of what happened at Antioch, there presumably were sectarian developments that resulted in some communities taking different sides in the dispute. Presumably, anti-Petrine tradition would have flourished in communities favoring Paul's general position in the controversy. The words of Jesus to Peter, "Get behind me, Satan! you are a hindrance to me; for you are not on the side of God, but of men" (Matt. 16:23), most likely originated in such a community.

On the other hand pro-Petrine tradition, like that singling him out from among the other disciples as the recipient of the keys of the kingdom, seems to reflect the viewpoint of a community that is prepared to think of Peter in quite positive terms.

The Caesarea Philippi story, where we find the "keys" tradition preserved, seems to reflect a situation in which some effort has been made to accommodate strongly pro-Petrine tradition to tradition which, taken as a whole, is quite Pauline. It is important to realize that the Gospels preserve traditions which reflect developments relating to both a sectarian period, contemporary with the conflict between Peter and Paul, and to a subsequent catholicizing period, when there was a tendency to reconcile earlier sectarian differences. This catholicizing tendency preceded the Gospels and called for their creation. The Acts of the Apostles clearly belongs to a period when differences which had once been acute in the earlier life of the churches were either overlooked or harmonized. As Peter and the Jerusalem apostles are featured in the first half of Acts, so Paul and his associates balance out action in the second. Not the slightest hint of the traumatic confrontation at Antioch between Peter and Paul can be found in Acts. This major omission is a clear sign of the ecumenical forces at work upon the development of the tradition prior to and during the period when the Gospels were being written. Basically what all the Gospels accomplish, each in its own way, is to show that the post-Easter faith, which nourished the mission to the Gentiles, belongs with the beginning of that faith in Jesus of Nazareth. By the time the Gospels were written, however, the tradition concerning Jesus had developed through the period of conflict over the admission of gentiles. Therefore, no evangelist had access to unaltered or undeveloped tradition concerning Jesus. Each wrote in situations deeply influenced not only by the impact that Jesus of Nazareth had made upon his own society, but also by subsequent developments in the post-Easter communities for which they wrote. Of these developments none was more important or far-reaching than the emergence of a conscious and concrete mission to the Gentiles (with official sanction from the apostles in Jerusalem) and the subsequent triumph of that mission over its older sister mission to the circumcised.

THE WAR OF A.D. 66–70 AND THE DEVELOPMENT OF THE GOSPEL TRADITION

We do not know exactly when the mission to the Gentiles became the dominant mission. We know that by the time of the Jerusalem conference where Peter, James, and John extended to Paul and Barnabas the right hand of fellowship, the mission to the Gentiles was in the hands of assertive and inspired leadership. But the mission to the Jews also had strong leadership. In fact, at the time of the incident between Peter and Paul at Antioch, the influence of the "circumcision party" in the practical affairs of the churches seems to have retained preeminence over the interests of the mission to the Gentiles.

We have reason to believe that the war of A.D. 66–70 changed that. The effect of the Jewish defeat was catastrophic not only for

Jews who had rejected the messiahship of Jesus of Nazareth, but also for Jewish Christians who had continued to worship in the national sanctuary and who had pinned their hopes on the success of the mission to Israel. After the destruction of Jerusalem, the handwriting was on the wall for all Jewish Christians. Until A.D. 70, Christians generally found their security within the structures of imperial society enhanced by such claims as they could make to the privileges accorded Jews by the Roman authorities.

Since the time of the Maccabees, when the Jews had been allies with Rome against the Seleucids, the Romans had been deeply conscious of the zealous and dedicated nature of Jewish resistance to any interference with their religious customs or institutions. To be sure, the Romans in the time of Pompey (63 B.C.) had established the point that they had both the power and audacity to possess Jerusalem and the national sanctuary at will. But having made that point, the Romans tended to follow a policy of seeking out and working with amenable religious forces within the Jewish community. Every foolhardy attempt to ride roughshod over Jewish religious sensitivities, whether by client princes like the Herods, or Roman officials like Pilate, or even emperors like Caligula, was overcome by the patient, collective wisdom of the Roman administrative bureaucracy. The bureaucracy recognized that the Jewish nation was not altogether like other nations and would not be completely subjugated except at great cost. In practice this meant that throughout the empire, Jews were usually able to obtain a reasonable hearing from Roman officials for any legitimate grievance.

Christian communities at first had no independent legal status in the eyes of Roman officials. They were recognized either as belonging within the sphere of Jewish authority and dealt with through the recognized leaders of the local Jewish community, or they were recognized as separated from the Jewish community and treated as a new religion without special prerogatives. In the latter case they were subject to the considerable perils and insecurities that intermittently faced new cults in the empire.

It seems clear from Paul's letters that in Asia Minor, Macedonia, and Achaia, churches which were primarily the fruit of the gentile mission very early found their worldly security enhanced through a system of mutual interdependence. Each local congregation recognized its unity with other Christian churches and gave this unity practical importance by acknowledging the authority and leadership of representatives, who exercised a supervisory power over other nearby and sometimes far-distant Christian communities.

There is no corresponding firsthand evidence concerning the situation among churches in Palestine and Syria in the period before the war of A.D. 66–70. We may assume that in areas where the mission to the Jews predominated, there was a similar recognition of apostolic authority among different congregations, but with major differences. In Palestine and Syria and in cities like Damascus and Antioch or, for that matter, any large cosmopolitan center of the empire where large and flourishing Jewish communities existed, the first forms of Christian social existence would have sprung to life within circles that were generally recognized as Jewish. The acceptance of the Jewish scriptures and the following of Jewish customs by these Christians would have made this identification natural and inevitable. This meant two things. First, local authorities would have recognized synagogue leaders as responsible for the social conduct of Christian families or churches. Any complaint against resident Christians would have been handled first through the local Jewish courts. At least, that would have been regarded as due process by the nearest representative of Roman authority. Second, legitimate social grievances or needs of Christian congregations that required action by local authorities would have been brought by Christian leaders first of all to the attention of some person or persons of influence within one of the local synagogues. In other words, such worldly security as was enjoyed by early Jewish Christian communities in Palestine and Syria was achieved partly through maintaining a viable relationship with at least one nearby synagogue.

Wherever such viable associations between local Jewish-Christian congregations and Jewish synagogues could be maintained, the mutual advantages to both groups were probably considerable. Christians could enjoy at least some of the political and social privileges that were accorded Judaism as a legal religion. There probably were corresponding commercial and political advantages that could be furthered wherever a local Jewish community had a reasonably harmonious liaison with local Christians. If the local synagogue authorities were to be held legally responsible for the social and political behavior of local Christians, they would naturally benefit from peaceful and effective relationships with Christian leaders.

The effect of this mutually beneficial arrangement, however, was to encourage a sense of dependence of the daughter upon its mother, the church upon the synagogue, and generally to retard any practical social or political expression of the spiritual unity that all Christians felt through their common faith in Jesus as the Christ. It is notable that both in Paul's letters and in Acts, such large scale cooperative social efforts undertaken by early Christians, such as collections for the poor and relief for victims of famine, were undertaken by the leaders of the gentile mission. There is no evidence that churches which were strictly the fruit of the mission of the circumcised could launch and effectively carry through projects of this kind for the primary benefit of Christians. Such social and political power as the Jewish Christian churches possessed was presumably hampered or limited by and administered through synagogue channels.

In Palestine and Syria such unity as was achieved in theory from time to time in conferences like the one Paul describes (Gal. 2:1–10) was difficult to maintain in practice. This is made clear by what Paul says happened in Antioch (Gal. 2:11–21).

The careful scrutiny to which Jesus and his disciples had been subjected by the scribes and the Pharisees in Galilee and Judea was continued by Pharisees like Paul who, at least in some cases, exercised disciplinary control over Christian communities in Syria. The pre-Christian Paul, a Pharisee, relates that he persecuted the church beyond measure and made havoc of it (Gal. 1:13,23; cf. Acts 8:3; 9:1–21; 22:4,19; 26:10 ff.; 1 Cor. 15:9; Phil. 3:6).

The first phase of this conflict between the early Christians and Jewish authorities was characterized by bitter strife. This phase did not abate with Paul's conversion, but continued to poison and acerbate relationships, as is made clear in Paul's letters and in the later accounts in Acts. The effect this pressure from the Pharisees and other synagogue authorities who functioned as guardians of the law had upon the development of the Jesus tradition was divergent.

On the one hand, defiance of the Jewish religious authorities fostered further development of sayings which Jesus had himself addressed to the Pharisees. For example, to Jesus' woe against scribes and Pharisees for building memorials to the prophets (Matt. 23: 29–31) has been added the bitter words, "You serpents, you brood of vipers, how are you to escape being sentenced to hell?" (Matt. 23:33). Actual persecution of Christians is probably reflected in the additional words: "Therefore I send you prophets and wise men and scribes, some of whom you will kill and crucify, and some you will scourge in your synagogues and persecute from town to town" (Matt. 23:34).

On the other hand, acquiescence to pressure from Jewish authorities in some Christian circles led to a conservative tendency to select and develop such sayings of Jesus as could support a mission strictly for Jews. For example, Jesus' prophetic programmatic utterance, "Think not that I have come to abolish the law and the prophets; I have come not to abolish them but to fulfil them" (Matt. 5:17), which he had used to counter misrepresentations of his intentions with regard to the law, was later interpreted in a manner that definitely served the interests of a quite conservative Jewish-Christian community. Thus the scribal addition: "For truly, I say to you, till heaven and earth pass away, not an iota, not a dot will pass from the law" (Matt. 5:18). Such an attitude may have had some justification in Jesus' natural desire to be a loyal son of Israel and the corollary, that is, his general tendency to remain an observant Jew. But the effect of these words in the early church clearly ran counter to those developments of the Jesus tradition which we see working themselves out in the Pauline churches. In fact, the even later words which come next in the developed form of the tradition show an anti-Pauline tendency at work: "Whoever then relaxes one of the least of these commandments and teaches men so, shall be called least in the kingdom of heaven" (Matt. 5:19).

The eventual practical outcome of these bifurcating tendencies was the development of a dual apostolic missionary effort: Peter, James, and John to the circumcised; Paul and Barnabas to the Gentiles.

The controversial charge of Jesus to the twelve disciples, "Go nowhere among the Gentiles, and enter no town of the Samaritans, but go rather to the lost sheep of the house of Israel" (Matt. 10:5–6), may have originated with some early Jewish-Christian prophet in support of the mission to the circumcised. But it no less clearly supports the practical solution worked out by Paul and the Jerusalem apostles. For it gives Jesus' sanction to a division of labor that strictly limits the mission of the Twelve to the lost children of Israel. It does not preclude Paul's conviction that he had been called as an apostle and that God had revealed his Son to him that he "might preach him among the Gentiles" (Gal. 1:16). It leaves that door open, and Paul would have been more than content to walk through it.

The sociological advantage of the twofold division of the Christian mission was that it allowed the Jewish-Christian churches to develop a pattern of peaceful coexistence with the wider Jewish community. At the same time, it extended the greatest degree of freedom to Paul and his co-workers in their missionary activity among the Gentiles. It was inevitable, however, that difficulties should arise in places like Antioch, where a strict division of the two missions would have been hard to maintain. We do not know how this division worked out following the death of those who were parties to the agreement. In any case, the destruction of Jerusalem in A.D. 70 radically changed the whole complexion of things and erased from the effective memory of the post-war churches any regard for the earlier twofold division of the Christian mission. There is not the slightest trace of this pre-war, twofold division of the mission in Luke-Acts, Mark, John, or any other later New Testament writings.

In order to grasp how this radical change took place and to appreciate its importance for understanding the occasion and need for the Gospels, it will be helpful to imagine what it would have been like to live in a Christian family in Antioch during and following the terrible Jewish-Roman war.

We may conjecture that the effect of the war upon a particular Christian family in Antioch would depend upon how closely that family was identified with the Jews. In large scale and long, drawn out military operations, the Romans sometimes supplemented their regular legions with auxiliary forces. In the case of the war with the Jews, these auxiliary forces were recruited in large part from Syria, which afforded ease of access to Palestine by land and sea. The organized resistance of the Jews was formidable and called for the enlistment of large numbers of Syrian troops. The carnage and bloodshed of the war, which became more and more intense and costly as it reached its climax, marked this protracted war as a particularly senseless conflict in the eyes of the Syrian public. It was inevitable that the perennial anti-Jewish feelings that had long been latent in Mediterranean society should come to the surface in those cities which were losing sons in what Syrian and Roman authorities would have represented as a needless uprising by fanatic and unreasonable people. Antioch was perhaps the most important of all the major cities most affected by the war. As the casualty lists lengthened, the intensity of anti-Jewish feeling in a city like

Antioch would have heightened accordingly. This situation, then, would have presented difficulties in Antioch not only for Jews, but for all Christians who were regarded as Jews.

The Jewish community in Antioch, as in all great cities, was pluralistic in character. The commercial and political destiny of the city determined the character of its social fabric and in turn influenced the political and commercial orientation of the various Jewish synagogues. Antioch was the most important meeting place of east and west in the Roman Empire. Presumably there were Jewish families in the city which maintained contact in both directions. It seems probable, however, that most Jewish families and therefore most synagogues in Antioch were culturally and commercially oriented toward either the east or the west. This ambidexterous capability of the Jewish people was rooted in the realities of their homeland, which was open by sea to the west and by land to the east.

Christianity reached Antioch basically from two different directions: from Judea through Caesarea and Joppa by sea, and from Galilee through Damascus and Heliopolis by land. Therefore, it may be presumed that from the beginning the larger Christian community in Antioch, like the larger Jewish community, was oriented both toward the east and the west, with different churches and synagogues reflecting this basic "bridge" structure of Antiochian society in different ways.

PART II

From the Gospel Tradition to the Gospel Genre

THE SEQUENCE OF THE GOSPELS

Introduction

In order to understand how the gospel tradition developed into the form which we now find in the four canonical Gospels, it is essential that we understand the literary relationships among these documents and, in particular, the temporal sequence in which they were composed. It is especially important to know which Gospel was written first. All of the canonical Gospels bear a striking resemblance to one another. Matthew, Mark, and Luke are remarkably similar, but John also is clearly more closely related to these three than to any other comparable literary composition.

Taken together, these four Gospels plus the so-called apocryphal gospels constitute a distinct literary genre. The problem of explaining or understanding the origin of this genre is chiefly a problem of explaining how the multiform gospel tradition was edited and given biographical shape for the first time. After this is understood, it is a relatively simple matter to explain the other gospels as literary modifications of this Christian adaptation of Hellenistic popular biography.[36] It must be emphasized that there is nothing about the gospel tradition itself that necessitated its taking the overall literary form of popular biography. This was the result of conscious literary creation.

The author of the first gospel was the gospel genre pioneer. Once the gospel form was created, it was capable of infinite modification. Even if the first gospel was oral, it would still be true to say that the author of that oral gospel was the gospel genre pioneer and that his oral composition established the original gospel form on which all subsequent gospels are patterned. The notion that the gospel tradition naturally assumed the form of a gospel by virtue of some unconscious process of oral transmission is groundless. It has no support from the church fathers, who have passed on the earliest traditions about the gospels, and it has no support from modern literary studies. It is clear that much of the gospel tradition found in our Gospels once circulated in the form of oral tradition. But this does not mean that oral tradition assumed the form of a gospel by some unconscious group process. That happened only as the result of thoughtful and creative work designed to give this multiform tradition a new and more effective overall form. Each successive evangelist was free to exercise his creative genius in composing his gospel. Each also had the advantage of access to the work of his predecessor or predecessors, and the literary evidence supports the judgment of Augustine that no one of the evangelists did his work in ignorance of what his predecessor or predecessors had done.

Augustine *traduced* that the Gospels were written in the sequence Matthew, Mark, Luke, and John. This order is familiar to us as the canonical order. It has been more or less uniformly followed in most New Testament arrangements since Athanasius.

However, this canonical order was never meant to represent the historical sequence in which the Gospels were written. The order—Matthew, Mark, Luke, John—serves a canonical purpose, which we will need to consider. At this point, we want to discover the historical sequence in order to understand the development of the gospel genre. The position of any document in a series of closely related documents may be a matter of indifference *in some circumstances*. But for historians who want to know the purpose of these documents and to understand their importance in relation to the historical process of which their composition was a part, it is a matter of primary concern to know their temporal relationship, that is, the historical sequence in which they were composed.

This is such an elementary point that it may be regarded as a truism. The confusion over the "synoptic problem" that has characterized modern thinking about Christian origins, however, is so all-pervasive that it is necessary to review this matter in an elementary manner. Perhaps, as a result, a way out of our present historical and theological impasse may then be found.

The best way to proceed in thinking clearly about this matter is to make a distinction between "external" and "internal" evidence. Internal evidence comes from the documents themselves; external evidence comes from outside these documents. Both kinds of evidence are important. Thus, what one can learn from studying the

Gospels themselves is important, and what one can learn from evidence outside the Gospels is also important.[37] The discussion of the external evidence as it bears on the question of the sequence in which the Gospels were written generally begins with a consideration of the words of Papias, Bishop of Hierapolis, who lived during the first half of the second century.

External Evidence—Church Fathers

Papias

Papias produced an exegetical work on the Gospels consisting of five books. This work has not been preserved, but it was known and cited by Eusebius, Bishop of Caesarea, in his famous and indispensable *Ecclesiastical History*.[38]

Eusebius cites Papias's work three times. The first is of value in clarifying the exact place of Papias in the history of the transmission of the gospel tradition. Eusebius is concerned that Irenaeus has written that Papias was a "hearer of John." He wants it understood that this cannot mean that Papias knew John the apostle. Therefore, to make clear that Papias in no way had been a hearer and eyewitness of any of the apostles, Eusebius quotes at length from the preface of Papias's work:

> And I shall not hesitate to set down for your benefit, along with the interpretations, all that I ever carefully learnt and remember from the elders, for of their truth I am confident. For, unlike most, I did not take delight in those who have much to say, but rather in those who teach what is true; nor in those who recount the commandments of others, but rather in those who recall the commandments given to the faith by the Lord and derived from the truth itself. And if ever anyone chanced to come who had actually been a follower of the elders, I would inquire as to the discourses of the elders, what [the elders reported that] Andrew or Peter had said, or what Philip, or what Thomas or James, or what John or Matthew or any other of the Lord's disciples had said, and what [the elders reported that] Ariston and John the Elder, disciples of the Lord were saying. For, I did not suppose that information out of books would be nearly so helpful to me as the words of an abiding and living voice.[39]

It is clear from Papias's arrangement of names that he distinguishes the apostles (Andrew, Peter, Philip, Thomas, James, John, and Matthew), whom the elders had heard, from Ariston and John the Elder who, at the time Papias was in contact with the elders, were still active. Since Ariston and John the Elder were not of the Twelve, they would have presumably belonged to a wider circle of transmitters of tradition and would have (at least in the eyes of Papias) stood in some authoritative relationship to the living oral tradition going back to Jesus and his original followers. Eusebius reports that Papias included in his work accounts of the words of the Lord from Ariston and traditions from John the Elder.

Thus it is easy to understand that what Eusebius (later in the same book) cites from Papias about the Gospels has been studied with the greatest interest. Eusebius's second citation from Papias is as follows:

> And the Elder used to say this: "Mark, indeed, having been the interpreter of Peter wrote down accurately all that he could recall of what [Peter had said] was either said or done by the Lord—although not in the correct order. For he [himself, that is, Mark] had not heard the Lord, nor had he followed Him, but later on, as I said, he followed Peter who used to adapt his teaching to the needs [of his hearers], but not with a view to putting together the Lord's oracles in orderly fashion: so that Mark was not off target in thus writing down things as he recalled them (that is, from his memory of what he had heard Peter say). For he kept a single aim in view, namely, to omit nothing of what he had heard (Peter say), and to include no false statements in his account.[40]

This is a remarkable passage in several respects. First, Papias is referring to a matter on which the Elder apparently commented repeatedly. This is clear from the use of the imperfect tense in Greek, when Papias reports that the Elder "*used* to say." He "used" to say it in the sense that he did not say it on one particular occasion, but whenever the matter came up.

The matter that repeatedly came up clearly had to do with Mark's arrangement of topics. The Elder admits this was faulty, presumably by comparison to some unmentioned standard. If one understands the purpose of Mark, it will be clear that this fault was not fatal. For Mark's purpose was simply to put down in writing everything he could recall of what he had heard Peter say, and to be careful to state these matters truthfully. Since Peter himself adapted what he had to say to the varying needs of his hearers and not to any need for these reports to be arranged in a continuous written narrative, Mark did not have from Peter a set arrangement for the topics in his Gospel. Mark's work, then, can best be judged in terms of his own purpose, and it is wrong to fault him for something he could not have been expected to do correctly. Mark himself had not been a follower of Jesus, so he was not in a good position to arrange his material in the proper order. He was dependent on Peter, who never wrote a gospel and who, therefore, never undertook the task of giving his reports an order that would fit them into a continuous narrative. Taking this into consideration, Mark has done quite well and can best be appreciated when it is known that he has preserved the witness of Peter fully and truthfully. This is how John the Elder reasoned whenever he heard Mark's Gospel criticized—according to Papias, as recorded by Eusebius.

Eusebius continues:

> Such then is Papias's account of Mark, and about Matthew this was said, "Matthew collected *ta logia* in the Hebrew language, but each interpreted them as he was able."[41]

These words of Papias have never been satisfactorily explained. They have been variously understood to mean that Matthew wrote his Gospel in Hebrew; that he compiled the words of Jesus in Hebrew; that he wrote his Gospel in Greek, though in Jewish style, and so forth.

Although the words "each interpreted . . . as he was able" indicate some dependence of the interpreter concerned upon the work of Matthew, nothing can be concluded from this concerning the relationship between the Gospel of Matthew and the other Gospels. Nor can one conclude from the fact that Eusebius cites what Papias wrote about Mark before he cites what Papias wrote about Matthew, that Papias regarded Mark as earlier than Matthew. What Papias wrote has its importance for understanding reaction to Mark in the early second century. And Papias's words exerted an influence upon later writers. However, from the words of Papias cited by Eusebius, one can safely conclude little, if anything, about the sequence in which the Gospels were composed. It is quite otherwise when we come to the next piece of external evidence.

Clement of Alexandria

Clement of Alexandria lived in the second half of the second century and was in personal contact with a number of elders from different parts of the Mediterranean world. To appreciate the widespread network of informational sources open to Clement, it is useful to cite his own words, which are quoted by Eusebius in Book 5 of his *Ecclesiastical History*.

> Now this work is not a writing composed for show; but notes stored up for my old age, a remedy against forgetfulness, an artless image, and a sketch of those clear and vital words which I was privileged to hear from blessed and truly notable men. Of these, one, the Ionian, I met in Greece, another in south Italy, a third in Coele-Syria, another was from Egypt, and there were others in the east, one of them an Assyrian, another in Palestine of Hebrew origin. But when I met the last, and in power he was, indeed, the first, I hunted him out from his concealment in Egypt and found rest.[42]

The last Elder mentioned undoubtedly refers to Clement's famous teacher, Pantaenus, whom he met in Alexandria in the early eighties of the second century. This means that most of the contacts that Clement established with the various teachers he met were made during the previous decade. Thus the testimony which these elders passed on to Clement carries us in a reliable way well back into the first half of the second century.

In Book 6 of his *Ecclesiastical History,* Eusebius writes as follows:

> And, again in the same books [Hypotyposeis], Clement has inserted a tradition of the primitive elders with regard to the order of the gospels as follows. He used to say that those gospels were written first which include the genealogies, and that the gospel according to Mark came into being in this manner: When Peter had publicly preached the word at Rome, and by the Spirit had proclaimed the gospel, that those present, who were many, exhorted Mark (as one who had followed him [that is, Peter] for a long time, and remembered what had been spoken), to make a record of what was said; and that he did this, and distributed [copies of] the gospel among those that asked him. And that when the matter came to Peter's knowledge, he neither strongly forbade it nor urged it forward. But that John, last of all, conscious that the outward facts had been set forth in the gospels [that is, those with genealogies and Mark], was urged on by his disciples [as Mark had been urged on by the Christians in Rome], and, divinely moved by the Spirit, composed a spiritual gospel. This is Clement's account.[43]

It is difficult to know to what extent Eusebius is closely citing Clement and to what extent he may be paraphrasing him. Is the whole or only the first part of this account which Eusebius has taken from Clement to be regarded as tradition Clement received from the primitive elders? If it is the whole, then we would reason as follows: since the gospels with genealogies are clearly Matthew and Luke, they were written first.[44] Nothing is said about which was actually first and which was second. Mark and John were both clearly written after Matthew and Luke. Between Mark and John, it was John that was written last of the four.

This presumably represents what Clement believed was authentic tradition. A comparison of what is said here about the circumstances under which Mark wrote his Gospel with what Papias said on the same topic leaves grounds for reasonable doubt concerning the historical reliability of that part of Clement's account. The tradition Clement said he received from the primitive elders that bears on the question of whether Matthew and Luke were written before Mark and John, or whether John was written last of all, is not subject to this kind of doubt. Nothing in what Papias reports conflicts with or causes any difficulty for accepting this tradition. It appears to be quite unmotivated and, as far as is known, it constitutes the earliest reliable existing external evidence that bears on the question of the sequence of the Gospels.[45]

The reference to the plural "elders" should be noted. Because of the plural, it may be concluded that Clement did not know this as a tradition passed on by a single elder, but that it was a tradition known and received in different places in the second century church.

Another possibility is that the account as a whole is composite and that Clement drew together all he could recall from what various elders had said. In this case one item would have concerned the temporal relationship of Matthew and Luke, which had genealogies while the others did not. "Those with genealogies were written first." Another item would have concerned John. "John was written after the others and intended to complement them in a 'spiritual' manner." The item about Mark could have been a developed form of the tradition known to Papias. It need not have included any reference to a sequential relationship to the other Gospels. It appears to deal mainly with the question of Mark's relationship to Peter and Peter's attitude about Mark's work. If Clement knew from the other traditions that Matthew and Luke were written first and that John came last, it would have been a simple deduction for him to place Mark after Matthew and Luke and before John. This would fully explain what Clement says about the order of the Gospels. Here again, however, there is no apparent motive for the item about Matthew and Luke. So the very least that can be said is that Clement's tradition supports the view that Mark and John were written after Matthew and Luke.

Unless there is some reason to doubt the tradition concerning

John, we can conclude that Clement's account supports the view that John was written last. If so, it follows that the account also supports the view that Mark was written third. It would appear that this deduction is unaffected by any doubt that might be cast upon the reliability of the details Clement relates concerning the circumstances under which Mark was written. In other words, the reliability of Clement's tradition concerning the circumstances under which Mark was written can be considered independently of the question concerning Mark's position in the sequence in which the Gospels were written. Mark's place as third can be logically deduced solely from the tradition Clement records concerning the other three.

All this is said without prejudice to the ultimate outcome of a critical evaluation of Clement's tradition about Mark and Peter. Since there is room for doubt concerning that part of Clement's account, it has been necessary to isolate that question and to proceed as we have in order to clarify the importance of Clement's statement for understanding the far less complicated matter of the sequence of the Gospels.

Irenaeus

Irenaeus of Lyons, an older contemporary of Clement of Alexandria, was also a widely traveled man. He was especially well acquainted with the churches of Asia Minor and the Rhone valley in southern France, and with the church in Rome. About the time Clement ended his extensive travels and settled in Alexandria, Irenaeus, who had become the bishop of Lyons, wrote his famous work *Against Heresies*.

In the third book of that work, Irenaeus adduced proof from the Scriptures to combat the heresies of his day. The first chapter of this book contains a passage that refers to the Gospels. Eusebius, in Book 5 of his *Ecclesiastical History,* has preserved the original Greek text of this important passage.

> Matthew published a written gospel among the Hebrews composed in their own language [or dialect, or style], while Peter and Paul were preaching the gospel in Rome and founding the church there. After their decease, Mark, the disciple and interpreter of Peter, did also hand down to us in writing the things that used to be preached by Peter. And Luke, as well, the companion of Paul, set down in a book the gospel which Paul used to preach. Afterwards, John, the disciple of the Lord, the one who had leaned upon his breast, also set forth [in writing] the gospel, while residing at Ephesus in Asia.[46]

This statement by Irenaeus, though including information bearing on the question of sequence, does not purport to treat the four Gospels in the strict order of their composition. What Irenaeus writes that affects our understanding of this question is limited to what can be deduced from his words. First, he writes that Matthew wrote his Gospel while Peter and Paul were active in Rome. If this refers to a gospel written in Hebrew, it says nothing about the compositional sequence of our canonical Matthew, which was written in Greek. Next, Irenaeus writes that Mark was written after the death (or departure) of Peter and Paul. This places Mark after a Hebrew Matthew, but says nothing about the sequential relationship between canonical Matthew and Mark. When Irenaeus writes "Luke, the companion of Paul . . . " we are probably meant to recognize the parallel with the preceding "Mark, the disciple and interpreter of Peter. . . . " That is to say, Irenaeus treats Mark and Luke together because each of them was closely associated with the apostles Peter and Paul respectively.

It seems most natural to understand Irenaeus as implying that Luke, as Mark, composed his Gospel after the death of Peter and Paul. However, there is no indication of any sequential relationship between Mark and Luke. Matthew was written while Peter and Paul were active in Rome; that is one period of time. Mark and Luke were written after the deaths of Peter and Paul, which marked the end of one and the beginning of another period of time. Concerning John, however, Irenaeus clearly includes a sequential reference. He says that John wrote "afterwards," that is, after Mark and Luke had written their Gospels.

Hans von Campenhausen notes that the order of the Gospels followed by Irenaeus is generally Matthew, Luke, Mark, and John, and he observes that this order would seem to be "the order most familiar to Irenaeus himself."[47] The evidence for this view is drawn from the same work of Irenaeus, *Against Heresies,* and relates to the order in which Irenaeus cites the Gospels as he builds his case against heresy. Thus, in Book 3, in defense of his thesis that the Creator God is one and the same as the God declared by the gospel, he first takes up proof from Matthew (3.9.1–3), second from Luke (3.10.1–5), third from Mark (3.10.6), and fourth from John (3.11.1–6). Also, in discussing the Gospels in relation to different heretical groups, he treats them in the same order—associating Matthew with Ebionites, Luke with Marcionites, Mark with Docetists, and John with Valentinians (3.11.7).

In Book 4 of *Against Heresies,* in refuting the view that God was not the Father of Christ, Irenaeus refers to the Gospels in the order Matthew, Luke, Mark, and John (4.6.1).

The order of the Gospels followed by Irenaeus in these parts of his work corresponds to the order that is supported by the witness of Clement. However, in discussing the symbols of the four evangelists, Irenaeus follows the unique order John, Luke, Matthew, Mark (3.11.8). His reasons for doing this are not clear, but von Campenhausen thinks they are theological.[48]

So it would appear that Irenaeus is free to discuss the Gospels in any order that best fits his purposes. In the case of the passage with which we began our discussion, Irenaeus's purpose is quite clear. This passage comes at the very beginning of his refutation from Scripture of the views of the heretics. It is necessary to unite the gospel preached by the apostles of the Lord with the Scriptures now in the hands of an embattled church, beseiged on all sides by damnable heretics. This Irenaeus accomplishes by appealing to his doctrine of the Spirit. After the resurrection of the Lord, the apostles were empowered from on high by the Holy Spirit. They thereupon departed to the ends of the earth, preaching the gospel. At this point, Irenaeus takes up the contribution of Matthew, which was to put the gospel that the apostles were preaching into a written form. This Matthew did among the Hebrews, in their own language, and at a time when Peter and Paul were preaching the same apostolic gospel in Rome. His purpose was to establish that these two apostles were also to be credited with written gospels through their close associates, Mark and Luke. For this reason he next speaks in succession of Mark and Luke, connecting their Gospels with the "preaching of Peter" and "the gospel Paul preached" respectively. As a possible sign that he does not mean the order Mark-Luke to be understood sequentially, Irenaeus includes no separate time reference for Luke. We cannot be sure that he was greatly concerned about the question of compositional sequence. In fact, it is clear that his overriding consideration is theological, that is, to connect written gospels with the preaching of specific apostolic figures. It cannot be said, however, that Irenaeus is oblivious to temporal considerations. Otherwise there would have been no purpose for him to have noted that one Gospel was written when Peter and Paul were in Rome and the other three after Peter and Paul had died.

The reason Irenaeus mentions Peter before Paul is presumably a reflection of historical fact, namely that Peter was an apostle before Paul. That in fact is the order in which their careers are treated in the Acts of the Apostles. But that is certainly not the church's judgment of the relative importance of these two apostles. When early Christian writers refer to "*The* Apostle" (absolutely), it is generally a reference to the Apostle to the Gentiles, that is, to Paul.

There is every reason to think, therefore, that Clement's sequence "Peter-Paul" reflects a well-recognized historical sequence. Peter came before Paul in the history of the church or, to apply Irenaeus's categories, "in the plan of salvation."

It should be obvious, however, that this historical priority of Peter to Paul says nothing about the compositional relationship between the Gospels of Mark and Luke. Irenaeus, in the passage under consideration, has just referred to Peter and Paul. He is about to write something about the Gospels which by tradition are linked to these two apostles. It is natural and perfectly reasonable that he discuss them in the order set by that tradition. There is no reason at all to think that Irenaeus intended his readers to conclude that Mark was written before Luke. Yet it appears possible that Origen did just that.

Origen

Origen almost certainly knew the work of Irenaeus, and Clement was his teacher. It is with no little interest, therefore, that we turn to Origen's statement on this matter. He takes up this topic in his *Commentary on Matthew*. Origen's statement has been preserved by Eusebius in Book 6 of his *Ecclesiastical History*:

> In the first of his [commentaries] on the gospel according to Matthew, defending the canon of the church, he gives his testimony that he recognizes only four gospels, writing somewhat as follows, " . . . having learnt by tradition concerning the four gospels (which alone are unchallenged in the Church of God under heaven), the first [gospel] written was that according to Matthew, who was once a tax collector, but afterwards an apostle of Jesus Christ, who published it for those who, from Judaism, came to believe, composed as it was in the Hebrew language. And second, was that according to Mark who wrote it in accordance with Peter's instructions, whom also Peter acknowledged as his son in the catholic epistle, speaking in these terms: *She that is in Babylon, elect together with you, saluteth you; and so doth Mark my son* [1 Pet. 5:13]. And third,

that according to Luke, who wrote the gospel that was praised by Paul, for those who from the gentiles [came to believe] after them all, that according to John."[49]

This is a remarkable statement. Origen may have once been a pupil of Clement. But much had happened since Clement first penned his statement about the Gospels. Each of the four Gospels is but a separate written expression of the *one* apostolic gospel that was being preached everywhere, long before any written gospel was composed. The unexpressed subject of the ascriptions "according to Luke" and "according to John" is the one glorious gospel of Jesus Christ. Such a theologically comprehensive concept combined with such uniform linguistic usage in the ascriptions to each Gospel bespeaks a conscious and deliberate ecclesiastical act. None of the statements about the Gospels prior to that of Origen reflect any consequence of this act of ecclesiastical publication. The order of the Gospels Origen follows is the order given in the statement Irenaeus makes about the Gospels' origin. But this order is neither the one Irenaeus follows when he discusses the reasons that there are four and only four Gospels, nor is it the order he follows when he draws proof from the Gospels.

It appears most likely that by the time of Origen, the fourfold Gospel canon was formed on some common ground of ecclesiastical authority located between the church in the Rhone Valley and Alexandria in Egypt. From that center, this canon was promulgated by teachers like Origen as if it had always been so.

There is no reason to think that Origen had evidence to support the order, Matthew, Mark, Luke, and John, an order he does not mention. In fact, it is possible that when he systematically moves from first to second to third and to the last of all, he does not himself think of this order as the historical sequence in which these Gospels were composed.

Eusebius includes Origen's statement because of its bearing on the *number,* not the *order,* of Gospels in the church's canon. He probably accepted Origen's order as the canonical order. On the other hand, Eusebius includes Clement's statement because of its bearing on the *order* of the Gospels. In his own statement about the Gospels, Eusebius is very judicious. He adds nothing to our knowledge about their order. What he writes about order corresponds to what he knew from Origen and Irenaeus. He does not say, however, that Mark and Luke were published in that order. That is left ambiguous, as well it might be, since Eusebius knew the tradition on order from Clement, which places Mark after Luke.

Summary Statement

Eusebius neither contradicts nor confirms the order Luke-Mark or the order Mark-Luke. His statements are compatible with either and/or both as well as with anything that is said about order by Clement, Irenaeus, or Origen. All, including Eusebius, agree that John is fourth. No one disagrees that Matthew was the first to write a gospel, though Clement alone implies that Matthew was before Mark and John, not that he was first. Papias, Irenaeus, Origen, and Eusebius all appear to speak of a Hebrew Matthew. The order Luke-Mark is supported by Clement and, in balance, by Irenaeus when his overall witness is carefully examined. Origen has either misunderstood Irenaeus or, more likely, followed the order already fixed in the fourfold Gospel canon. The relationship between the witness of Irenaeus and that of the fourfold Gospel canon remains unclear.

If the order of the fourfold Gospel canon was known to Irenaeus, why does he not follow it except for *one* known occasion? On the other hand, if the fourfold Gospel canon was fixed and published in Rome under the influence of Irenaeus's "history of salvation" theme, then both the comprehensive theological conceptualization and the canonical order would be explained. "First to the Jews and then to the Gentiles" places the more Jewish Matthew before the other three. Mark comes next because it represents the apostle Peter who, though he had close ties to Jewish Christianity, favored admitting gentiles into the church and was martyred for that faith in Rome. Then comes Luke, which represents Paul the apostle to the Gentiles. Finally comes the work of John, who was regarded as author of both the fourth Gospel and the Book of Revelation. The same church which places John at the end of the fourfold Gospel canon will in the end prevail in retaining the Revelation of John as a fitting close for its canon of Scripture, all in accordance with the plan of salvation envisioned by Irenaeus.

The canonical order of the Gospels and the order of Origen are the same, and that order is readily susceptible to a theological explanation. The order Matthew, Luke, Mark, and John, supported in part by the witness of Clement, in part by the witness of Irenaeus, and clearly contradicted by no one (unless it is Origen) is not readily susceptible to any such theological explanation. It is an enigma, unless it is what it is purported to be—a historical order supported by the earliest and most explicit, external evidence available.[50]

Additional External Evidence[51]

The "Anti-Marcionite" Prologue of Luke

This prologue, which has an anti-Marcion tendency, was probably written between A.D. 160 and 180. In it we are informed that Luke wrote his Gospel in Achaia after Matthew had been written in Judea, and after Mark had been written in Italy.[52]

The "Monarchian" Prologue of Luke

This prologue, presumed to be later than the anti-Marcionite prologue of Luke, gives the same information: that Luke was written in Achaia after Matthew had been written in Judea, and after Mark had been written in Italy.[53] The wording of this prologue is so close to the wording of the anti-Marcionite prologue that it indicates this agreement may be explained by literary dependence. Therefore, the tradition of these two prologues, which places Matthew and Mark before Luke, is actually the same tradition.

The "Monarchian" Prologue of Mark

This prologue, which is generally dated in the time of Jerome, is one of four prologues arranged in the order Matthew, John, Luke, Mark. This is an arrangement that seems to reflect (1) an order of dignity: the apostles Matthew and John first, followed by the disciples of apostles, Luke and Mark; and (2) the chronological order attested by Clement of Alexandria, where Mark comes after Matthew and Luke. In any case, this prologue shares the view that Mark wrote after Matthew and Luke: "Lastly [Mark], at the outset of his book of the gospel . . . did not [as some think] demur from referring to [Christ's] human birth, since he had already seen it in both the preceding [gospels]. Rather, his first object was to devote himself to the evidence how Jesus was cast into the desert. . . ."[54]

Comments upon this prologue made by the ninth-century Irish monk, Sedulius Scottus, indicate that this prologue was traditionally understood to presuppose the testimony of Clement: " . . . Matthew and Luke, who, according to some, as the Ecclesiastical History relates, wrote their gospels before Mark. . . ."[55] The reference to "the Ecclesiastical History" clearly refers to Eusebius E. H. 6.14.5.

A little further on, Sedulius Scottus explains that Mark omitted the birth narratives because he knew that they had already been recorded "in the first two evangelists, namely in Matthew and Luke." Since Sedulius Scottus makes these comments while explaining the passage from the "Monarchian" prologue of Mark cited above, there would seem to be no grounds for doubting that the tradition that Mark wrote after Matthew and Luke can be traced from the second century through the fourth and into the ninth century. In addition, there would seem to be no grounds for doubting that the chief authority for this tradition, at least in the ninth century, was found in the testimony of the elders cited by Clement.

Early Latin Manuscripts

In early Latin manuscripts of the Gospels, prior to the revision by Jerome, one generally finds the arrangement Matthew, John, Luke, Mark. This is the same sequence followed in the arrangement of the "Monarchian" prologue of Mark.[56]

Questionum ex Novo Testamento Pars Secunda

This work, wrongly attributed to Augustine, provides a doctrinal justification for a chronological order of Matthew, Luke, Mark, John. "Since it is definite that the books written . . . are four in number . . . it is necessary to know what their order is . . . Matthew is to stand first . . . after him comes Luke . . . Mark is third . . . lastly comes John. . . ."[57] It is assumed that the author wrote at a time when the received canonical order of Matthew, Mark, Luke, John was well known. In that case, he must have written in a place where a different tradition, which placed Mark after Luke and Matthew, was known and respected.

Jerome's *De Viris Illustribus*

The so-called "Greek" order of the Gospels adopted by Jerome for the revision of the Latin Vulgate translation subsequently spread far and wide in Christianity the chronological order of Matthew, Mark, Luke, and John. However, Jerome himself gives indirect testimony to a tradition that places Mark after Luke. In his *De Viris Illustribus,* Jerome treats these persons in the following order: Peter, James, Matthew, Judas, Paul, Barnabas, Luke, Mark, and John. It is also interesting that Jerome, in writing about Luke, does not say that Luke wrote his Gospel after Matthew and Mark, even though he must have known such a tradition and even though he followed the order Matthew, Mark, Luke, and John in his Vulgate translation.

Jerome's *Epistula ad Damasum*

In this letter, Jerome is conscious of introducing an arrangement of the Gospels that was not the one usually followed at that time in the Latin church. To justify the change, he writes: "Therefore, this short preface introduces only the four gospels, whose order is the following: Matthew, Mark, Luke, and John; they [the Latin manuscripts of the gospels] will be brought into agreement with the Greek manuscripts."[58]

The Eusebian Canons

Eusebius of Caesarea based his famous gospel canons on Ammonius of Alexandria's harmony of the Gospels. In their present form these canons appear to reflect the sequence Matthew, Mark, Luke, and John. But there are traces in some of the ten canons of the influence of the order Matthew, Luke, Mark, and John. In the first canon, where Eusebius treats all passages which are found in all four Gospels, the arrangement is Matthew, Mark, Luke, and John. In the second canon, where John is omitted, the sequence is Matthew, Mark, and Luke. In the third canon, where we would expect the arrangement to be Matthew, Mark, and John, it is in fact Matthew, Luke, and John. The arrangement Matthew, Mark, and John comes fourth. The fifth canon presents passages that occur in Matthew and Luke, where we would expect Matthew and Mark. The sixth canon presents passages found in Matthew and Mark. The eighth canon presents passages found only in Luke and Mark in that order, rather than Mark and Luke. Finally, the tenth and last canon, which includes passages that are unique to each Gospel, presents them in the same sequence as the first canon.

This is a remarkable set of facts. It is most simply explained if the original arrangement of these canons observed the sequence Matthew, Luke, Mark, John. Then, at a later stage, the first, second, and tenth canons were rearranged to conform to the "canonical" order of Matthew, Mark, Luke, and John. Other canons were left to reflect the earlier sequence of Matthew, Luke, Mark, and John. The reverse seems less likely since the revision would begin at the most obvious points, beginning and end, and would leave unrevised, if anything, the less prominent parts of the harmony.

Summary

The arrangement of the canonical Gospels in the early church generally followed one of three sequences: (1) Matthew, John, Luke, Mark; (2) Matthew, Mark, Luke, John; (3) Matthew, Luke, Mark, John. The first arrangement is partially explained by the order of dignity which places the Gospels associated with the names of apostles Matthew and John before those by disciples of apostles, Luke and Mark. That Matthew preceeds John is universally attested in the church. That Luke preceeds Mark is supported by the testimony from Clement. This first arrangement, then, is explained by appeal to the order of dignity combined with tradition concerning chronological order. The second arrangement is attested as early as Origen and is found in the "anti-Marcion" and "Monarchian" prologues of Luke. It was taken over by Jerome from its "Greek" origins and made normative for his Vulgate translation. In the third arrangement (as in the second), Matthew as first and John as last is universally attested in the early church. That Mark follows rather than preceeds Luke is attested by Clement. There is, therefore, no difficulty explaining the first and third arrangements. The situation is different with the second arrangement. That Matthew was first and John was last is easily explained. But how do we explain Mark being placed before Luke, especially since it contradicts the testimony of Clement? One possibility is that this was the true historical sequence, that is, that Luke was written after Matthew and Mark, as is stated in the ancient prologue of Luke. Still, this would create an inexplicable historical contradiction between this tradition and that which Clement received from the Elders.

The best explanation that can be offered is no more than a conjecture. Is it possible that the canonical order of Matthew, Mark, Luke, John was the order of the original fourfold Gospel canon? If so, the following reasons can be given for this arrangement. First, there is the fact that Matthew, Mark, and Luke are closely related to one another and form a natural group separable from the later and more spiritual John. Mark (connected with Peter) and Luke (connected with Paul) help explain the order, Mark and Luke, which corresponds to the historical order of Peter and Paul. Finally, there is the possibility that the fourfold Gospel canon was arranged in the sequence Matthew, Mark, Luke, John because it was believed that this was the best order in which to read the Gospels. Matthew,

Mark, and Luke before John, and Mark after Matthew but before Luke. When the theology and purpose of Mark are taken up, the canonical benefits of this order will become clear. Mark constitutes a bridge between Matthew and Luke and unifies the first two Gospels.

The Secondary Character of Luke to Matthew

The prologue of the Gospel of Luke makes clear that other evangelists had previously taken in hand the task of narrating an account of the fulfillment of the things which had happened among the Christians. The three surviving narratives that could qualify as having preceded Luke are Matthew, Mark, and John. Of these three, Matthew is the only Gospel which was universally regarded in the early church as having been written before Luke. Matthew certainly has the character of a narrative that gives an account of the "fulfillment" of the things which had happened in the church. For these reasons alone, the historian would expect Luke to exhibit some secondary characteristics. In particular, the historian would look for evidence that the author of the Gospel of Luke had used or had been influenced by the Gospel of Matthew.

The first indication that Luke not only knew but also made use of Matthew is the fact that the overall shape of his work is strikingly similar to Matthew. Most of the topics covered by Matthew are also covered by Luke. The independent manner in which Luke covers these helps to explain why he regarded his work as necessary. The extraordinary agreement between the topics Luke includes and those in Matthew indicates that he has taken his topics from Matthew or from a narrative source, either preceding or following Matthew, that stood in a very close compositional relationship to Matthew. Based on the topics they cover, neither Mark nor John, either singly or together, could have served as a model for Luke as well as Matthew could. The earlier existence of some hypothetical gospel like Matthew is always a possibility. But such a hypothetical source is quite unnecessary unless there are reasons to think that Luke did not know Matthew.

A reason that is sometimes given in support of the view that Luke did not know Matthew is that Luke put much of the same material found in Matthew into a very different order. However, this was a prerogative Luke had as an author, and he amply explains this in his prologue. Another reason given in support of the view that Luke and Matthew are independent of each other and dependent on some hypothetical source is that Matthew is the one who sometimes preserves tradition in its more original form, while at other times Luke does this. Luke's prologue also explains this very well. Luke has taken pains to examine all sources available to him and to consider anew the entire matter. Therefore, Matthew would have been only one of his sources. It is to be expected that in some instances Luke would have incorporated material from his other sources, which could have preserved certain traditions in more original forms than those same traditions had in the Gospel of Matthew. The parable of the lost sheep appears to be a case in point.

In many cases, however, and especially where the verbatim agreement between Matthew and Luke is high, the Matthean form of the tradition is more original, and the Lucan form is better adapted for the use of gentile readers.[59]

The Secondary Character of Mark in General

E. P. Sander's Appendix

Since most readers will have been taught the priority of Mark, the best place to begin considering the matter of Mark's secondary character is with E. P. Sander's compilation of those passages in Mark which have been adjudged to be secondary to Matthew and/or Luke by competent authorities who accept the theory of Marcan priority. These scholars are, in this instance, to be regarded as "disinterested" if not "hostile" witnesses, and their judgment that Mark is secondary cannot be discounted on the basis of any predisposition to favor Matthean or Lucan priority.

The number of passages in Mark regarded as secondary by a particular individual was never sufficient to cause any one of these scholars to reject Marcan priority. However, when considered together, these secondary passages turn out to be so all-pervasive in Mark as to constitute a serious case in favor of regarding the whole Gospel as secondary. The scholars Sanders cites are representative: J. Weiss, R. Bultmann, V. Taylor, Matthew Black, Karl Kundsin, B. H. Streeter, and V. H. Stanton. The passages in Mark regarded as secondary to Matthew and/or Luke are: Mark 1:1,11,14,15,29, 33,35; 2:3; 4:31–32; 6:3,8–9,13; 7:24–31; 8:27–33; 9:14; 9:30f.; 9:35–37, 43–47; 10:11,37,43–45; 11:17,25; 12:25,28–34,36; 13:

1–2,9,11,13b; 14:17–21,22–25,30,58,62,72; 15:5,25,44–45. According to this compilation there are only two chapters in Mark where there are not one or more passages which have been judged secondary in some degree to the parallel passage(s) in Matthew or Luke or both.[60]

It should be emphasized that this list, drawn from Sander's compilation, represents only a small part of the evidence indicating the secondary character of Mark, that is, only passages that a representative group of scholars *holding to Marcan priority* perceive as secondary.

F. P. Badham

Once we turn to authors who do not think that the evidence warrants belief in Marcan priority, the list of passages that indicate the secondary character of Mark is much more extensive.

For example, F. P. Badham lists as evidence for the secondary character of Mark its "un-Judaic" character.

Un-Judaic Character of Mark

Referring to the theory that Mark has been Judaized by Matthew, Badham writes: "Though it is conceivable that a gospel prepared for gentiles [Mark] should afterwards have received some Judaic coloring [Matthew], it is almost impossible to imagine a colorist so attentive to minutiae as the present case would require."[61]

> In reporting the incident of the corn plucking and the cure of the withered hand, our second evangelist omits all mention of "the law," and of the priestly exemption for purposes of ritual; and in place of the rabbinical rule about sheep falling into pits, he gives us the general principle as to saving life or killing. He again omits all mention of "the law" in reporting the lawyer's question.[62]

In comparing parallel traditions in Mark and in Matthew, where we read: "Some . . . say Elijah," Mark omits "and others Jeremiah" (Mark 8:28; Matt. 16:14); "pray that your flight may not be in the winter," Mark omits "or on a sabbath" (Mark 13:18; Matt. 24:20); "the desolating sacrilege," Mark omits "spoken of by the prophet Daniel" (Mark 13:14; Matt. 24:15); "no sign shall be given," Mark omits "except the sign of Jonah" (Mark 8:12; Matt. 16:4). Badham continues:

> He [Mark] omits the name of the high priest who condemned Christ, presumably because of little interest to his readers (Mark

14:1,53); and for those ignorant of the topography of Jerusalem, he explains that the Mount of Olives overlooked the Temple (Mark 13:3). Aramaic words are used, not causally, as in Matthew 5:22; 27:6, but at calculated points, and with the manifest object of impressing an audience unfamiliar with Aramaic (see Mark 5:41; 7:11; 7:34); and though "Eli, Eli," in Matthew 27:46 may seem analogous, it is not really so, being requisite to explain the jibe about Elias.[63]

In his story of the rich ruler, Mark (10:17–31; cf. also Matt. 19:16–30) omits the promise that those who have followed Jesus "will also sit on twelve thrones, judging the twelve tribes of Israel."[64] In his treatment of the story of the Syro-Phoenician woman (7:24–30), Mark omits the first repulse and Christ's declaration of being sent only to "the lost sheep of . . . Israel" (Matt. 15:24).[65]

Badham continues:

> Before quitting the subject of the un-Judaism of our second evangelist, attention is due to his constant explanation of Jewish customs and softening down of Jewish terminology. The *Preparation* is explained as "the day before the Sabbath," and the first day of unleavened bread as that "on which the Passover must be slain." We are informed that "common" is synonymous with "unclean"; that John's disciples and the Pharisees were in the habit of fasting; that amongst Jews it was of traditional obligation to wash the hands before eating and after marketing; . . . "Greek" takes the place of "Canaanite"; "healed" is twice explained by "taught"; "long robes" replace the large fringes and broad phylacteries of Matthew 23:5; and for the oriental metaphor of bearing the shoes is substituted "unloose the latchet."[66]

Badham concludes that the "un-Judaism" of Mark is "consistent" and "systematic."[67]

Glosses and Inflation

In a chapter on "Glosses and Inflation" Badham says that "Mark develops his material, softens asperities, explains ambiguities, heightens effects and generally strains after emphasis and intensity."[68] Badham lists over 150 examples of these "glosses and inflations." He admits that in many cases, *considered separately,* this data could be explained as instances where Matthew has "pruned" or "toned down" the tradition. Yet, he claims that considering them together enables one to see that they argue for the secondary character of Mark.

The following fourteen examples from Badham's lists are clearly worthy of notice:

1. "And going a little farther he fell on his face and prayed, 'My Father, if it be possible, let this cup pass from me' " (Matt. 26:39). "And going a little farther, he fell on the ground and prayed that, if it were possible, the hour might pass from him. And he said, 'Abba, Father, all things are possible to thee; remove this cup from me.' " (Mark 14:35–36). Badham notes that the additional assertion "all things are possible to thee" is made by Mark "lest the divine power should seem to be limited."[69]
2. "And they had then a notorious prisoner, called Barabbas" (Matt. 27:16). "And among the rebels in prison, who had committed murder in the insurrection, there was a man called Barabbas" (Mark 15:7). Badham notes that the Greek word translated "notorious," but sometimes rendered "renowned," is actually ambiguous. He suggests that Mark has explained the ambiguity.
3. "He went to Pilate and asked for the body of Jesus. Then Pilate ordered it to be given to him." (Matt. 27:58). "Joseph of Arimathea . . . took courage and went to Pilate, and asked for the body of Jesus. And Pilate wondered if he were already dead; and summoning the centurion, he asked him whether he was already dead. And when he learned from the centurion that he was dead, he granted the body to Joseph" (Mark 15: 43b-45). Badham notes that Mark's additional words preclude "any cavil that Christ merely revived from a swoon."[70]
4. "When the disciples saw it, they were indignant, saying, 'Why this waste?' " (Matt. 26:8). "But there were some who said to themselves indignantly, 'Why was the ointment thus wasted?' " (Mark 14:4). Badham regards Mark's "some" as a softening of Matthew's "disciples."[71] This goes against the view put forward by Marcan priorists that it is Matthew who has a tendency to soften Mark.
5. "Whoever divorces his wife" (Matt. 19:9). "And if she divorces her husband" (Mark 10:12). Badham notes that these words in Mark provide for "a contingency impossible under Jewish law, but common enough in Greece and Rome."[72]
6. "From that time Jesus began to preach, saying, 'Repent, for

the kingdom of heaven is at hand' " (Matt. 4:17). "Jesus came into Galilee, preaching the gospel of God, and saying, 'The time is fulfilled, and the kingdom of God is at hand; repent, and believe in the gospel' " (Mark 1:14–15). Badham notes that Matthew's "began to preach" reads in Mark "preaching the gospel of God," and that Matthew's "repent" reads in Mark "repent, and believe in the gospel." Then he connects this with Mark's "whoever loses his life for my sake *and the gospel's* will save it" (Mark 8:35b), where Matthew simply has "whoever loses his life for my sake will find it" (Matt. 16:25b).[73]

This emphasis upon the absolute use of "the gospel" or the use of the expression "the gospel of God" is very Pauline; it appears to be a Paulinism that has been taken over by the author of Mark. Since the whole church eventually came to adopt this Pauline usage, there is no reason to think that Matthew or Luke would have omitted this feature of the developing tradition. It follows that the use of this expression in Mark and its absence in Matthew and Luke, indicates that Mark is secondary to Matthew and Luke, and that Mark was written in a church which had a great regard for Paul and his gospel.

7. "And his garments became white as light" (Matt. 17:2c). "And his garments became glistening, intensely white, as no fuller on earth could bleach them" (Mark 9:3).[74] This illustrates Badham's observation of Mark's heightening of effect as well as his straining after "emphasis and intensity."
8. "And as Jesus was going up to Jerusalem" (Matt. 20:17). "And they were on the road, going up to Jerusalem, and Jesus was walking ahead of them" (Mark 10:32a).[75] This is certainly a heightening of effect. One can actually visualize Jesus out ahead of his disciples, leading them up to the holy city.
9. "Rise, take up your bed and go home. And he rose and went home" (Matt. 9:6–7). "Rise, take up your pallet and go home. And he rose, and immediately took up the pallet and went out before them all" (Mark 2:11–12).[76] Here again Mark heightens the effect by picturing the paralytic walking out before everyone, and he strains after emphasis and intensity by having him do this actually carrying his pallet with him.
10. "The daughter of Herodias . . . pleased Herod" (Matt. 14:6). "Herodias' daughter . . . pleased Herod and his guests" (Mark

6:22).[77] Mark's more developed account heightens the effect of Herodias's daughter's dancing by enlarging the audience that she pleased.

11. "Prompted by her mother, she said, 'Give me the head of John the Baptist here on a platter' " (Matt. 14:8). "And she went out, and said to her mother, 'What shall I ask?' And she said, 'The head of John the baptizer.' And she came in immediately with haste to the king, and asked, saying, 'I want you to give me at once the head of John the Baptist on a platter' " (Mark 6:24–25).[78] Beginning with Matthew's text, all can be explained. The homiletical nature of Mark's developed text is clear. The mother is not inside the room with the men. Therefore the daughter must go outside to consult her. After receiving the daughter's request for advice, the mother gives it. The daughter hurriedly returns to the king and repeats the request, word for word, climaxing it with the phrase that closes Matthew's text—"on a platter."

    The text of Matthew is less developed. To reverse the process and have Matthew create out of Mark's text his concise but dramatic statement is more difficult to explain. Such writing as is found in Matthew in this instance is crafted by the imagination working from the essentials of the story rather than from some developed text. This is not a question simply of a shorter or longer text. Matthew's text tells a story. Mark's text tells the same story, but with great elaboration. This elaboration serves to heighten the effect of the request for John's head *on a platter*! In the process, however, it *strains* after emphasis and intensity and, to that extent, loses some dramatic power. As literature, the phrase "on a platter" is anticlimatic after Herodias's daughter departed and returned in haste. But homiletically it can be effective. The story in Mark's hands comes alive with the addition of the vivid details of Herodias' movements.

12. "He sent and had John beheaded in the prison" (Matt. 14:10). "And immediately the king sent a soldier of the guard and gave orders to bring his head. He went and beheaded him in the prison" (Mark 6:27).[79] To bring out the fact that the king sent someone with orders to do the deed, as Mark does, strains after emphasis.

13. "Every one who has left houses or brothers or sisters or father

or mother or children or lands, for my name's sake, will receive a hundredfold, and inherit eternal life" (Matt. 19:29). "There is no one who has left house or brothers or sisters or mother or father or children or lands, for my sake and for the gospel, who will not receive a hundredfold now in this time, houses and brothers and sisters and mothers and children and lands, with persecutions, and in the age to come eternal life." (Mark 10:29–30).[80] Matthew's reference to a "hundredfold" reward is ambiguous; it leaves unclear when this reward will come and what form it will take. Mark's text removes this ambiguity by (1) indicating that the "hundredfold" reward will come "now in this time" as distinguished from "the age to come"; (2) clarifying that the extended family of the church will replace previous family relationships; and (3) indicating that the reward will paradoxically include "persecution."

14. " 'Why this waste? For this ointment might have been sold for a large sum, and given to the poor' " (Matt. 26:8b–9). " 'Why was the ointment thus wasted? For this ointment might have been sold for more than three hundred denarii, and given to the poor.' And they reproached her" (Mark 14:4b–5).[81] The enormous alleged expense of the ointment and the reproach of the woman by her accusers strain after emphasis and intensity.

Further Selection from Badham's Data

Badham's point—that these cases be considered together—can be made most effectively by listing without comment some of the remaining examples he presents. As Badham says, the data speaks for itself.[82]

MATTHEW	MARK
"Who gave thee this authority" (21:23).	"Who gave thee this authority to do these things" (11:28).
"Offer" (8:4).	"Offer for thy cleansing" (1:44).
"This man" (9:3).	"Why does this man speak thus" (2:7).
"Save in his own country" (13:57).	"Save in his own country and among his own kin" (6:4).
"Cried out" (8:29).	"Crying with a loud voice" (5:7).

MATTHEW	MARK
"This wisdom" (13:54).	"The wisdom that is given to him" (6:2).
"From the beginning" (19:4).	"From the beginning of creation" (10:6).
"The care of the world, and the deceitfulness of riches" (13:22).	"The cares of the world, and the deceitfulness of riches, and the lusts of other things entering in" (4:19).
"Less than all seeds" (13:32).	"Less than all seeds that are upon the earth" (4:31).
"Yielded fruit" (13:8).	"Yielded fruit, springing up and increasing and brought forth" (4:8).
"Must suffer many things from the elders" (16:21).	"Must suffer many things, and be rejected by the elders" (8:31).
"Afterwards he sent unto them his son" (21:37).	"He had yet one, a beloved son: he sent him last unto them" (12:6).
"Thou son of God" (8:29).	"Jesus, thou son of the Most High God" (5:7).
"Brought all who were sick" (14:35).	"Began to carry about on beds those that were sick" (6:55).
"Told it in the city" (8:33).	"Told it in the city and in the country" (5:14).
"And followed him" (20:34).	"And followed him in the way" (10:52).

EMPHATIC POINTING

MATTHEW	MARK
"Taketh from it" (9:16).	"Taketh from it, the new from the old" (2:21).
"Destroy this temple and build in three days" (26:61).	"Destroy this temple that is made with hands and in three days build another made without hands" (14:58).
"Be not anxious" (10:19).	"Be not anxious beforehand" (13:11).

MATTHEW	MARK
EMPHATIC POINTING (continued)	
"Sleep on now" (26:45).	"Sleep on now: it is enough" (14:41).
"Why trouble her" (26:10)?	"Let her alone: why trouble her? She hath done what she could" (14:6).
"Behold, I have told you beforehand" (24:25).	"Take ye heed; [behold] I have told you all things beforehand" (13:23).
"This night" (26:34).	"Today, even this night" (14:30).
"From heaven or from men" 21:25).	"From heaven or from men? Answer me" (11:30).
"Saw no one save Jesus only" (17:8).	"Saw no one anymore save Jesus only with themselves" (9:8).
"But with God all things are possible" (19:26).	"But not impossible with God; for with God all things are possible" (10:27).
"I have observed" (19:20).	"I have observed from my youth" (10:20).
EXCESSIVENESS	
"Peter saith" (26:35).	"Peter saith exceeding vehemently" (14:31).
"They wondered" (15:31).	"They were beyond measure astonished" (7:37).
"Cried out the more" (20:31).	"Cried out the more a great deal" (10:48).
"Marvelled" (8:27).	"Feared exceedingly" (4:41).
"He heard the word" (19:22).	"His countenance fell at the word" (10:22).
"When he heard the word, he went away sorrowful" (19:22).	"With a fallen countenance at the word, he went away sorrowful" (10:22).
"Saying" (9:18).	"Besought him much, saying" (5:23).

MATTHEW	MARK
EXCESSIVENESS (continued)	
"They marvelled" (22:22).	"They marvelled greatly" (12:17).
"Behold the heavens were opened" (3:16).	"He saw the heavens rent asunder" (1:10).
"There came one to him" (19:16).	"There ran one to him and kneeled to him" (10:17).
"They followed him on foot from the cities" (14:13).	"They ran there together on foot from all the cities and outstripped them" (6:33).
REDUPLICATION AND REDUNDANCY	
"When they deliver you up" (10:19).	"When they lead you to judgment, and deliver you up" (13:11).
"Take him" (26:48).	"Take him and lead him away safely" (14:44).
"I know not" (26:70).	"I neither know nor understand" (14:68).
"Was silent" (26:63).	"Was silent and answered nothing" (14:61).
"Do ye not yet perceive" (16:9).	"Do ye not yet perceive neither understand" (8:17).
"Said" (21:13).	"Taught and said" (11:17).
"Saying" (8:2).	"Beseeching him . . . and saying" (1:40).
"Was hungry" (12:3).	"Had need and was hungry" (2:25).
"In the resurrection" (22:28).	"In the resurrection when they rise" (12:23).
"For the elect's sake" (24:22).	"For the elect's sake, whom he chose" (13:20).
"Your tradition" (15:6).	"Your tradition which ye have delivered" (7:12).
"From the beginning of the world" (24:21).	"From the beginning of the creation which God created" (13:19).
"Casting lots" (27:35).	"Casting lots upon them what each should take" (15:24).

MATTHEW	MARK
REDUPLICATION AND REDUNDANCY (continued)	
"They beat" (21:35).	"They beat and sent away empty" (12:3).
"She arose" (9:25).	"She arose and walked" (5:42).
"Who followed" (27:55).	"Who followed . . . and came up with him to Jerusalem" (15:41).
"The boat was covered with waves" (8:24).	"And the waves beat into the boat, insomuch that the boat was now filling" (4:37).
"His leprosy was cleansed" (8:3).	"His leprosy departed from him, and he was made clean" (1:42).
"And the woman was made whole from that hour" (9:22).	"Straightway the fountain of her blood was dried up, and she felt in her body that she was healed of her plague" (5:29).
"Is it lawful to give" (22:17).	"Is it lawful to give? Shall we give, or shall we not give" (12:14–15).
"[Herod] promised with an oath to give her whatsoever she should ask" (14:7).	"(Herod) saith, ask of me whatsoever thou wilt and I will give it to thee. And he swore, whatsoever thou shalt ask of me, I will give it thee, even to the half of my kingdom" (6:22b–23).
AFTERTHOUGHTS	
"The poor ye have always with you" (26:11).	"The poor ye have always with you, and whensoever ye will ye can do them good" (14:7).
"Will faint by the way" (15:32).	"Will faint by the way, for some of them come from afar" (8:3).
"Herod heard" (14:1).	"Herod heard, for his name had become known" (6:14).
"For the sake of Herodias" (14:3).	"For the sake of Herodias, for he had married her" (6:17).
"This man blasphemeth" (9:3).	"He blasphemeth. Who can forgive sins but God" (2:7).

MATTHEW	MARK
AFTERTHOUGHTS (continued)	
"False witnesses came" (26:60).	"False witnesses came, and their witness agreed not together" (14:56).
POSTSCRIPTS	
"Not of the dead, but of the living" (22:32).	"Not of the dead, but of the living. Ye do greatly err" (12:27).
"Choked them" (13:7).	"Choked it, and it yielded no fruit" (4:7).
"But the blasphemy against the Spirit shall not be forgiven" (12:31).	"Whosoever blasphemes against the Holy Spirit never has forgiveness, but is guilty of an eternal sin: for they had said, 'He hath an unclean spirit' " (3:29–30).
"Making void the word of God" (15:6).	"Making void the word of God: . . . and many such like things ye do" (7:13).

Summary

This kind of evidence does not in any single instance prove the secondary character of Mark. At most, it is tacit evidence in support of that view. Taken together, however, it constitutes an impressive body of data that is fully consonant with the view that Mark is secondary. When taken together with evidence adduced by other scholars, it strongly suggests that Mark is secondary to Matthew.

Pierson Parker

In 1953, the University of Chicago published *The Gospel Before Mark* by Pierson Parker. Parker argued that Mark could not have been Matthew's main source because the material in Matthew that was paralleled in Mark was organically united to the material in Matthew which was *unique* to that Gospel. Considered together, these materials suggested to Parker that there was an earlier gospel which was closer to the Jewish Christian origins of the Christian community than Mark. Both Mark and Matthew had made direct use of this earlier gospel, which Parker designated K. Mark was secondary to K in general and to Matthew in passages where Matthew had preserved the original text of K more exactly than Mark.

Since Parker did not dispense with Q and continued to think of Mark as a source for Luke, his hypothesis retained some of the major features of the two-source hypothesis. In 1979, at the request of colleagues in the Society of Biblical Literature, Parker prepared a paper entitled "A Second Look at *The Gospel Before Mark*." In this paper, which was printed with the official seminar papers for the 1979 meetings of the Society of Biblical Literature, Parker wrote:

> The book's central thesis still seems, to me, inescapable. *Our* Matthew did not derive from *our* Mark. Instead, both canonical gospels were taken from a common *Grundschrift* which had first appeared, probably, in Aramaic, and which, for convenience, I labeled "K" (*koinos*).[83]

After taking into account developments in the intervening quarter century—specifically the revival of the hypothesis that Luke used Matthew, and Mark combined his Gospel out of Matthew and Luke, together with the statistical studies of A. M. Honore, Charles E. Carlston, and Dennis Noelin—Parker suggested a way of disposing with "the anomolous Q," and, at the same time, bringing "Griesbach and the K hypothesis and some others closer together."

According to Parker's suggestion, which he is careful to say is put forth "*very* tentatively," there were in the beginning two primary sources—not Mark and Q, but Proto-Matthew (K) and Proto-Luke. Matthew was, of course, primarily dependent upon Proto-Matthew, but he also made use of Proto-Luke. Luke depended upon Mark and Proto-Luke. This is a more serious modification of the two-source hypothesis since it dispenses with Q. Nevertheless, it retains Marcan priority as far as Luke is concerned and denies that Mark is directly dependent on Matthew. Both Matthew and Mark have direct access to Proto-Matthew.

In a section entitled "Some Items of Literary Criticism," Parker acknowledges that Mark is usually more prolix or verbose than Matthew. He claims that it is the tendency of a later writer to condense. For Parker, since Matthew is less prolix and Mark is more prolix, Mark is "usually" the more primitive, though Matthew is "often" the more primitive.

Parker's premise is to be denied. There is no canon or criteria of literary criticism which correlates style with chronology. Each case must be considered on its own merits. Because Matthew or Mark has in a given instance used more words than the other evangelist in the parallel passage says nothing about which is the secondary text. Everything hinges on the *nature* of the difference. In all the passages cited from Badham's list, the extra words in Mark's text were explicable on the assumption that they were glosses on or expansions of the tradition.

Parker reports that he found fifty-four instances where Mark is more succinct than Matthew. His premise is that in these instances Mark's text, *because it is more succinct,* is secondary to Matthew. Nevertheless, he remains open to the possibility that in all instances the words in Matthew that are not in Mark could prove to be examples of either secondary glosses or expansions of the tradition. It would still be the case, however, that these fifty-four instances would equal only one-third the number of instances where Badham noted *Mark's* extra words as signs of *Mark's* secondary character.

On the other hand, were Parker to be proved correct in his view that there is a tendency for a secondary author to be more succinct, and were we to wipe out everything we have learned from Badham about "glosses" and "expansions" as evidence for the secondary character of Mark, we would still have the un-Judaic character of Mark. Parker and Badham agree that this feature of Mark's text is an important argument for its secondary character.

In a section entitled "The Second Gospel is Secondary," Parker sets forth under four main headings over 100 reasons for regarding Mark as a secondary gospel. I have taken what seems to me the most important of these and, for the most part, present them very much word for word as Parker has formulated them.

The Second Gospel (Mark) Is Late

Parker argues that whatever the calendar date of Mark, its viewpoint is "often strangely subsequent to those of Matthew, Luke, and even John." As examples, Parker notes that "Mark is the only gospel which, like the Apostles' and Nicene Creeds, never alludes even remotely to Mary's husband. And it is the only New Testament book that calls Jesus 'son of Mary' (6:3)." Also, Mark "is the only gospel that uses an unqualified *to euangelion* to designate the Christian enterprise (1:14; 8:35; 10:29; 13:10; 14:9)."

Parker observes that in numerous other places Mark "looks definitely less original" than Matthew. For example, in Matt. 3:13, Jesus came to the Jordan River expressly *to be baptized* by John—an idea, writes Parker, "quite alien to the rest of the New Testament." In Matthew, moreover, the teaching of Jesus is at times almost word for word like that of John the Baptist: compare Matt. 3:2 with 4:17; 3:7f. with 12:37f., 23:33; 3:10 with 7:19; 3:12 with 13:20. Parker concludes: "No Christian would have welcomed these subordinations of Jesus to John, still less have invented them. Almost certainly, therefore, they came to Matthew out of the earliest tradition."

In Matt. 15:4 we read: "*God* said, honor thy father. . . ." This agrees with Jewish and Jewish-Christian concepts of scriptural inspiration, Parker notes, whereas in Mark 7:10 this tradition becomes "*Moses* said. . . . " Since this would be "clearer to gentiles and accord better with their attitudes toward the Torah," it is a sign that Mark, in comparison to Matthew, is a later gospel.

Errors in the Second Gospel (Mark)

Parker notes that "the mistakes in Mark are so various *and so numerous* that it seems futile to try to explain them away." He concludes: "This evangelist just *cannot* have been familiar with Palestine, its people, or its religion."

MISTAKES ABOUT JUDAISM

1. Mark 5:22: "One of the rulers of the synagogue." Diaspora synagogues may sometimes have had more than one ruler, as at Pisidian Antioch (Acts 13:15), but Palestinian synagogues normally had only one.
2. Mark 7:11: The explanation of *corban* is "very inadequate."
3. Mark 14:12: "On the *first* day of unleavened bread *when they sacrificed the Passover,*" confuses Nisan 15 with Nisan 14.
4. Mark 14:13 (also Luke 22:10) says that the disciples were to be met by a man carrying a pitcher of water. "Since adult male Jews never did that, it would have aroused jeers, and excited the very attention that Jesus sought to avoid."
5. Mark 14:55 and 15:1 taken together suppose that *the entire Sanhedrin* met *twice* for Jesus' hearing. "This is most improbable."
6. Mark 15:42, "When *evening was already come,* because it was Friday (*paraskeue*) that is, the day before the sabbath . . . "

This means "either *that* Friday began with *that* sunset, and Jesus had died on Thursday; or else the evangelist forgot [or did not know] that the Jewish day began at evening."

7. Mark 15:46 says that *that same evening* Joseph of Arimathea "*bought* a linen cloth." Again, "either it was now Friday, and Jesus had died on Thursday, or else somebody has quietly got around the Jewish sabbath laws."

8. Mark 7:3,4 is a "caricature" of Judaism and could not have been written by a Jew or by "anyone familiar with Judaism." This "caricature" is made worse by the gratuitous remark at v. 13, "and many such like things you do."

MISTAKES ABOUT SCRIPTURE

1. Mark 1:2 wrongly "ascribes Mark 3:1 to Isaiah."

2. Mark 1:11 "misquotes Isaiah 42:1. So does Luke 3:22, but not Matt. 3:17."

3. Mark 2:26, " 'Abiathar' should be 'Ahimelech.' "

4. Mark 10:19 "misquotes the Decalogue" and inserts an extra commandment: "Do not defraud."

5. Mark 15:34 has Jesus quoting Psalm 22:1 in Aramaic (*Eloi*). Had Jesus done this, "bystanders could hardly have supposed he was calling for Elijah. Jesus must have used Hebrew *Eli,* as at Matt. 27:46."

MISTAKES ABOUT GEOGRAPHY

1. Mark 6:21 says that Antipas' birthday was for "the chief men *of Galilee*." Yet, in Mark 6:27, Antipas had the baptist beheaded in prison and his head brought to the party. Therefore the festivities were still in progress, and the guests must have been in Machaerus, Herod's southern palace, where John was imprisoned, according to Josephus. This was a good 100 miles from Antipas's Galilean headquarters. "Did 'the chief men of Galilee' walk all that way to a birthday party?" Or did the author of Mark "simply have no idea how far it was from Tiberias to John's prison?"

2. Mark 7:31 says that Jesus and his disciples journeyed "out from the borders of Tyre . . . through Sidon, to the sea of Galilee, through the midst of the borders of Decapolis." This is geographically nonsensical. "How many have been the headaches of commentators, trying to make sense out of that!"

3. Mark 8:10 refers to "the district of Dalmanutha." As far as is known, there was no such place in Galilee. (The difficulty was

recognized early because there are many textual variants in the manuscripts.)

4. Mark 8:27 refers to *"villages of* Caesarea Philippi." Matt. 16:13 correctly refers to *"the district of* Caesarea Philippi."

Parker concludes: "Those are too many geographical absurdities. Our author cannot have been told much about Palestine, still less ever have seen the country."

MISTAKES ABOUT CURRENT HISTORY

1. Mark 6:14–27 repeatedly refers to Herod Antipas as a "king." Matthew commits this error only once (14:9). "The correct title 'tetrarch' appears in Matt. 14:1, Luke 3:19; 9:7; Acts 13:1; but *never* in the second gospel [Mark]."

2. Mark 6:17 says that Antipas married the wife of his brother *Philip.* According to Josephus, Ant. XV. v. 4, she was actually the wife of a different brother.

Doubtful Statements about Jesus

1. According to Mark, Jesus occupies at least six different houses: in Capernaum (2:1; 9:33), on a mountain (3:13,19), somewhere in Galilee (7:17), in "the borders" of Tyre and Sidon (7:24), at the foot of the Mount of Transfiguration (9:28), in Perea (10:10). "Moreover, each of these has room also for Jesus' disciples plus other folk! How did Jesus come by all this real estate?"

2. According to Mark, Jesus had a strong desire for secrecy, which he sometimes "carried to irrational lengths." At Mark 5:43, Jesus "wants it *kept secret* that Jairus's little girl has been brought back from death!" At Mark 7:36, a deaf-mute, after being healed, hears and speaks—yet "Jesus again demands that he not let anyone know about it!"

At Mark 7:24, Jesus asks that his whereabouts be kept secret. "No other gospel reports a desire for secrecy that early."

Parker concludes: "We seem to be dealing here . . . with a literary idiosyncrasy of the second evangelist."

The Second Evangelist (Mark) Was a Gentile

JESUS' MISSION TO GENTILES

1. "At Mark 3:8, Jesus has followers from Idumea. No other gospel says that."

2. "At Mark 5:18–20, a gentile, an erstwhile demoniac, goes at

Jesus' bidding on an extended mission to the Decapolis." In Luke 8:37b–39 the mission is more restricted and is not mentioned at all in Matthew.

3. "At Mark 7:31 and 8:1, Jesus himself conducts a mission to the Decapolis." At most, Matt. 15:39 may be understood to mean that the second feeding (4,000) "had occurred *somewhere* on the eastern shore."

4. "At Mark 13:27, the elect are to be gathered 'from the uttermost parts of the earth,' a phrase absent from Matthew and Luke."

5. "At Mark 14:9, '*The* gospel shall be preached *throughout* the whole world.' Matt. 26:13 is more limited: '*This* gospel [referring to what the woman had done] shall be preached *in* the whole world.' "

6. "At Mark 11:17 we read 'My house shall be called a house of prayer *for all the gentiles* . . . ' " Neither Matthew (21:13) nor Luke (19:46) have "for all the gentiles."

ABSENCE OF JEWISH DETAILS

1. "Mark 1:14f. lacks . . . an elaborately Jewish description of Capernaum (Matt. 4:13)."

2. "Mark 7:37 lacks the phrase, 'they glorified the God of Israel' (Matt. 15:31)."

3. "Mark 13:5ff., the Marcan apocalypse, lacks from Matt. 24:9ff., the following: v. 9, 'You will be hated by all gentiles for my names sake'; v. 11, 'false prophets will arise and lead many astray'; v. 12, 'because of violations of the law, the love of many will grow cold.' "

4. "Mark 13:17–19 fails to urge Jesus' followers to pray that they not have to flee on the sabbath (Matt. 24:20)."

5. "Mark 6:7–13 lacks Matt. 10:5, 'go nowhere among the gentiles, and enter no town of the Samaritans, but go rather to the lost sheep of the house of Israel.' " This passage "would have been both unclear and probably offensive to early gentile Christians."

6. "Jewish Christians, in propagandizing fellow Jews, made heavy use of *testimonia* [collections of messianic quotations from Jewish scriptures]. Such apologetic would carry far less weight with gentiles." Parker notes that this explains why the first half of Acts has fourteen appeals to *testimonia,* whereas the second half has only three, *two of which are addressed* to Jesus. Thus, only one out

of seventeen *testimonia* in Acts is addressed to gentiles! "Mark lacks nearly every *testimonium* of Matthew (Matt. 4:15f.; 8:17; 12:18–21; 13:14f.,35; 17:5; 21:4,5,15,16); and it has none to take their place. In fact, Mark's only *testimonia* are four that it shares with Matthew *and Luke*." [Similarly the parables of Jesus are characteristically Jewish and Palestinian. Excluding the parable of the seed growing secretly, Mark's only parables are four that it shares with Matthew *and Luke*].

MOSAIC LAW ABROGATED

1. "Mark 2:23–28 [where Jesus' disciples are criticized for plucking ears of grain on the sabbath], lacks the appeal to the law found in Matt. 12:6."

2. "Mark 7:19b, a comment by the evangelist, asserts that Jesus 'declared all foods clean.' "

3. "Mark 9:4 names Elijah before Moses. To subordinate the lawgiver in that way would have struck Jews as bizarre. Matt. 17:3 and Luke 9:30 name Moses first."

4. "Mark 12:31,33,34 subordinate the Torah to love, and to the kingdom, in contrast to Matt. 22:36–40."

JEWISH FEATURES EXPLAINED

Parker notes that Mark "does not explain matters of gentile knowledge, such as who Pilate was." However, Mark does "explain *Jewish* customs and traditions, as though these were unfamiliar to his readers."

1. "Not only is Mark 7:2ff. a caricature. No Jew would have needed any explanation here, however accurate."

2. "Only Mark (12:42) explains that a *lepton*, a coin used in Palestine, was worth half a *quadrans*."

MARK ADAPTS HIS GOSPEL TO GENTILE INTERESTS

1. Sometimes, instead of explaining, Mark "just uses phrasing that was more readily understood by non-Jews. Where Matthew's 'heaven' *means* God, Mark always *reads* 'God,' as does Luke. Where Matt. 12:50 has 'my father in heaven,' again Mark 3:35 (and Luke 8:20) reads simply 'God.' Matt. 24:15 reads, 'standing in *the Holy Place,*' but Mark 13:14 has, 'standing where he ought not.' "

2. "Mark 15:25 sets the crucifixion at 'the third hour.' By Jewish ways of counting time that would mean 9 a.m., which is much too early; but by Roman it meant noon, and that agrees with John 19:14, and also, apparently, with Matt. 27:45 and Luke 23:44."

3. "Mark 4:28 contains the word *automatos*." This concept is "most un-Jewish, whereas it appears repeatedly in Greek literature." Parker cites O. Weinreich, *Tübinger Beitrage zur Altertumswissenshaft* (1929), 330ff.

4. Mark 10:12 forbids women to divorce their husbands and remarry. "But Jewish law already forbade that! The teaching would have seemed outlandish to a Jew of Palestine, but was an appropriate expansion for those of pagan background."

ARAMIC IS, TO THE SECOND EVANGELIST [MARK], A FOREIGN AND EXOTIC TONGUE

Mark uses Aramaic at 7:34 (*Ephphatha*) and 8:41 (*Talitha cumi*) "as if these were incantations for healing, which he then explains." At 3:17 and 10:46 "he similarly explains the meanings of Aramaic surnames."

MARK IS DEROGATORY OF THE APOSTLES

Mark "displays almost unremitting impatience with the Jerusalem apostles—which is understandable if they opposed admission of the uncircumcised to the church."

1. "Mark 6:52 and 9:32 picture the twelve as 'uncomprehending.' "

2. "Mark 4:13; 8:17e; 9:19 represent Jesus as upbraiding the disciples 'severely.' "

3. "Mark 14:20 underscores the fact that *one of the twelve* betrayed Jesus."

4. "Mark 9:14–29 fails to include Jesus' word to his disciples, 'nothing shall be impossible to you' (Matt. 17:20)."

5. Mark 3:21 is derogatory of Jesus' "friends."

6. Mark 6:4 is derogatory of "his own kin." [All of these features of Mark serve gentile interests where it is important to discount the claims of special status based upon kinship to Jesus, being of Jewish origin, or of having a special relationship to those who were closely or remotely connected with the Twelve or the Jerusalem apostles.]

MARK'S ATTITUDE TOWARD PETER

1. "Mark *never acknowledges Peter's authority*. Contrast Matt. 16:17–20; Luke 22:28–32; John 21:15–17."

2. "Mark never calls him [Peter] 'Simon Peter.' Contrast Matt. 16:16; Luke 5:8; and 16 times in John."

3. "Mark says nothing about his [that is, Peter's] walking on water. Contrast Matt. 14:28–31."

4. "Mark 7:17 only has 'his disciples' ask Jesus to explain a parable, whereas at Matt. 15:15 it is Peter who asks."

5. "Mark 14:31 says Peter declared his faithfulness 'exceeding vehemently.' "

6. "Mark 14:54 has the bitter note about Peter 'sitting and warming himself' at the officer's fire."

7. Note that "only Matthew (26:70–74) puts Peter's denials in proper Jewish form, (a) a simple denial, (b) denial with an oath, (c) denial with a curse."

8. "Mark contains very little that reads like personal reminiscence, and *nothing at all* that need have come from Peter. Peter ignored, Peter denigrated—are these the ways that John Mark would write of his friend?"

CONCLUSIONS

Parker concludes as follows:

> To sum up, the second gospel [that is, Mark] favors gentiles. It proclaims a marked universalism. It ignores matters of interest to Jews. It plays down their Torah. It runs down the Jerusalem Christian leaders. It reinterprets the Christian message along gentile lines. And it displays vast ignorance of Judaism, of Palestinian geography and history, and of the Hebrew scriptures. Often it seems misinformed about Jesus himself.

Under the heading *Anomalies in the Theory of Marcan Priority,* Parker notes that "to maintain the priority of Mark, in the face of all this evidence [we have given only a part of what Parker has presented], one must have recourse to a large set of assumptions." Parker puts these assumptions very boldly:

1. "Impatience with Jerusalem church leadership was early; cordiality toward it was late."

2. "Neglecting or erring about the Hebrew bible was early; adherence to it was late."

3. "Explaining Judaism to readers was early; assuming they were familiar with Judaism was late."

4. "Ignorance of Palestine and of Jerusalem was early; acquaintance with these was late."

5. "When Mark is more wordy than Matthew, Matthew has shortened; when Mark is less wordy than Matthew, Matthew has added."

6. "Patristic tradition need not be explained. If it disagrees with the hypothesis, it may be disregarded. If the fathers erred, it is not necessary to inquire what led them astray."

Taken separately, no one of these assumptions so succinctly formulated by Parker, can by itself be said to be devastating to Marcan priority. But taken together as a set, they constitute a web of logical considerations which argues convincingly for the secondary character of Mark, comprehensively entraps Marcan priority and, along with the many other considerations adduced by Stoldt and others, bundles it up for critical oblivion. Advocates for Marcan priority may find a way out of the logical predicament in which they are bound. But this will not be achieved without great effort, if it can be achieved at all.

Summary Statement

We began this section on "The Secondary Character of Mark in General" with a consideration of the compilation made by E. P. Sanders. From that compilation we learned that even adherents of Marcan priority recognize the secondary character of Mark in some instances and that, when the passages they judge to be secondary are considered together, there are only two chapters in Mark that do not contain one or more secondary passages.

Next, we considered the compilation of passages in Mark that Badham regarded as evidence for Mark's indebtedness to Matthew. Finally, we considered the evidence compiled by Pierson Parker.

Taken together, the evidence from these three compilations is impressive. It is important to emphasize that there are no corresponding compilations made by defenders of Marcan priority to show the secondary character of Matthew and/or Luke to Mark.[84]

To the compilations made by E. P. Sanders, F. P. Badham, and Pierson Parker may be added the compilation of nine notes included in Chapter 7 of *The Synoptic Problem*: (1) "The Synoptic Tradition Concerning Uncleanness (pp. 243–244)"; (2) "The Synoptic Tradition on the Sign of Jonah (pp. 244–245)"; (3) "The Synoptic Tradition Concerning the Parable of the Wicked Tenants (pp. 248–250)"; (4) "The Synoptic Tradition on Divorce (pp. 255–257)"; (5) "The Synoptic Tradition on Cleansing the Temple (pp. 258–262)"; (6) "The Synoptic Tradition on Tribute to Caesar (pp. 262–264)"; (7) "The Synoptic Tradition on the Woes to Scribes and Pharisees (pp. 265–266)"; (8) "The Synoptic Tradition on the Widow's Mite (pp. 266–270)"; (9) "The Apocalyptic Discourse (pp. 271–278)."

These nine notes illustrate how, by the use of form and redaction criticism, one can best explain the relationships among the Gospels, assuming the hypothesis that Luke made use of Matthew and Mark made use of Matthew and Luke. These notes add further weight to the case that can be made from the evidence compiled by Sanders, Badham, and Parker that Mark is a secondary gospel.

Further evidence that Mark is probably secondary to Luke as well as to Matthew, can be shown best when the origin and purpose of Mark is discussed.

Meanwhile, our reappraisal of evidence bearing on the question of the sequence of the Gospels has shown the plausibility of the view that both Luke and Mark are probably secondary to Matthew. This means that the ground has been cleared for a fresh approach to Matthew. Before undertaking this task, it may be helpful to recapitulate the argument that is structuring our discussion.

This argument may be summarized as follows: Jesus and his disciples were Jews living in Palestine. In due time the community that began in Palestine spread out into the Mediterranean world. As this extra-Palestinian expansion took place, more and more Gentiles sought membership until, finally, it developed into a community that was predominantly gentile.

Matthew is clearly the most Jewish Gospel. It is also the Gospel that best reflects the Palestinian origins of the Christian church, including the bitter persecution of Christians in Palestine by the same authorities who persecuted Jesus and his original disciples. Luke is also very Jewish. But there are many passages in Luke where, in comparison with Matthew, Luke is better adapted for use by Gentiles outside of Palestine. There are no examples where Matthew is better suited for use by gentiles than Luke or Mark.

While unmistakably retaining traditions of Jewish and Palestinian origin, Mark is, of the three, the best adapted for gentile readers wno are not acquainted with Palestinian culture. Tnus, in terms of historical development, it is a methodologically sound procedure to begin with Matthew and then go on to Luke and/or Mark.

RENEWAL AND POSTWAR SYRIAN CHURCHES

Matthew, a Postwar Gospel

The date of Matthew is difficult to determine. Scholars generally regard Matthew as having been written after the Jewish-Roman War of A.D. 66–70.

If Matthew were dependent upon Mark, then Matthew would be dated after Mark. But if, as appears to be the case, Matthew were written before Mark, it cannot be dated later than the date given Mark. Since the date of Mark remains uncertain, we are free to attempt to date Matthew on its own terms.

We have seen that there is no decisive external evidence for dating our Greek Matthew. So we turn to internal evidence. Here conventional argumentation, which is based on references in Matthew that appear to reflect the events of A.D. 70, falls short of being convincing. The Jewish scriptures provide language and imagery that describe earlier destructions of Jerusalem. These descriptions could have influenced the wording of Matthew. Thus, it is not necessary to think that Matthew's wording presupposes the events of A.D. 66–70, though some of it certainly fits those events.

The question of dating the Gospels needs careful reappraisal, which can hardly be carried through successfully if pursued on the basis of mistaken or confused views of the fundamental question of sequence. Since the question of sequence is less difficult than the question of dating, the sequence question should be settled first on the grounds of sound methodology.

This book has been written from the viewpoint that the most probable sequence of the Gospels, that is, the one that the balance of external and internal evidence best supports, is Matthew, Luke, Mark, and John. This viewpoint takes the middle ground on the question of dating, claiming neither that the Gospels are early (that is, pre-A.D. 70) nor late (second century). All four could easily have been written between A.D. 70 and 90.

If Matthew were written in the early seventies, Luke-Acts could have been written not long after, certainly by the late seventies. Mark could have been written in the early eighties, and John in the late eighties. To attempt to be more precise than this would only mislead readers. There is, after all, little basis for precision in dating the Gospels. What is needed, however, is a serious attempt to reconstruct the history of the development of the gospel tradition from Jesus through the latest Gospel. The following is the beginning of an attempt to do this. To the extent that this attempt makes sense, it lends support to but does not prove the dating assumed.[85]

The Syrian Setting of Matthew

The Gospel of Matthew, though postwar and universal in its final outlook, preserves a great deal of tradition which had developed earlier to meet the needs of eastern-oriented Jewish Christian communities in northern Palestine (Galilee) and southern Syria (Damascus).[86] Luke-Acts, on the other hand, appears to be a work composed to meet the needs of western-oriented postwar churches which earlier had enjoyed close ties to Christian communities in Judea (Jerusalem, Caesarea), and whose outlook is strongly influenced by the needs of the mission to gentiles. Such considerations have suggested a provenance for Matthew as far east as Edessa and a provenance for Luke-Acts as far west as Rome. In fact, however, all requisite conditions for explaining the provenance of both may be found in one and the same great metropolitan center—Antioch on the Orontes in Syria.

Regardless of where Luke and Matthew were written, the basic difference in their respective orientations remains. Antiochian society was a convenient and valid microcosm of the "bridge" society of the eastern Mediterranean world, where the church was born and first flourished. We must look to this eastern Mediterranean world to understand the historical background of Matthew and Luke and the forces that were at work in the development of the traditions incorporated in each.

The effect of the war upon Jewish Christians in Antioch and elsewhere in the eastern Mediterranean world would have been polarizing. These Christians could either identify with their compatriots in Palestine in the national defense of the sanctuary, or they could reject the Jewish cause and reconcile themselves to national defeat and the destruction of Jerusalem. For Antiochian Christians, this later course did not lead automatically to a rejection of Judaism. It is likely that there were Jews in Antioch who saw the war as ill-advised and therefore lent their support to the side of the Romans. However, for any Christian to recognize that the Temple in Jerusalem was not essential to the accomplishment of God's purpose was to step back to some degree from an identification with Jews and to take a significant step in the direction of gentile Christianity.

More important would have been the pressures of the war on Christian families in Antioch which had close ties with gentile society. The war would have placed such families under pressure to explain in words and even prove by deeds that Christianity was not to be confused with Judaism. Suddenly all that was distinctive about the church vis-à-vis the synagogues would have been seen by Christians in a different light. Previously these differences would have been minimized to preserve the advantage of claiming the legal privileges of Judaism as an accepted religion in the empire. Now these differences were to be maximized in the interest of disassociating Christians from the terrible and mad killing that took place before and within the walls of Jerusalem. Some Antiochians attributed this mad killing to the fanaticism of the Jews.

The overall effect of the war upon Christians in Antioch was a shift in the balance of power within the total Christian community into the hands of those who saw the future of the church primarily in terms of a mission to the Gentiles. No doubt some Jewish Christian churches went in other directions. These cases represented a parting of the ways. Henceforth the Christian church, as it developed into its classical form in the second and third centuries, was fully committed to the mission to the Gentiles. This shift did not take place overnight, and it probably called for untold hours of unrecorded and unheralded conferences between Christian leaders. At every such conference there was one quite important point upon which formerly estranged churches could agree.

It now seemed obvious that an ecclesiology involving dependence upon the synagogue had become counterproductive. Following the war, great pressure was brought by Antiochians upon Roman officials to withdraw all special privileges from Jews. This pressure was resisted by the Romans, who recognized their need for Jewish support—support which, on the whole, they had been able to count on since the time of the Maccabees. So strong were anti-Jewish feelings in Antioch, however, that Christian leaders could argue that the time had come to cut all apron strings holding the church to the synagogue. Such worldly security as Christians in Syria had previously enjoyed through their "Jewish" contacts with local synagogues was henceforth to rest upon their mutual recognition of their "Christian" obligation to assist one another. In addition, there was a related advantage for Christians as a whole if they arranged their collective interests to be represented by a leadership completely untainted by what had happened in Jerusalem.

This would have called for new leadership in the churches that was forward-looking and capable of achieving spiritual renewal through reaffirmation of the verities of the faith. Churches that had separated earlier during the traumatic period of sectarian rivalry revealed in the letters of Paul (some of Appollos, some of Cephas, and some of Paul, and so on), could now be reminded of the fact that what they held in common was more important than what formerly divided them. What they held in common and united them in one body was their faith in Jesus Christ. Each church was enlivened and disciplined by its own ineluctable and indestructible memory of Jesus. Each had preserved traditions, oral and written, concerning his words and deeds. Some cherished legendary stories of his birth, others stories of what marvelous things happened at the time of and following his death. It remained for someone to recognize the need to bring all of these diverse churches already united by their faith in Christ into a more perfect unity of common resolve.

The Gospel of Matthew is a literary expression of this postwar unifying ferment. The evangelist himself may not have been the one who, with pen in hand, composed the gospel. The work of composition could have been accomplished in a school.[87] Generally, however, there is a dominant, moving spirit in most schools. In this case, the Gospel of Matthew would represent the moving spirit or *modus operandi* of a particular theological school. This would have been a very important school in which Pauline and anti-Pauline traditions, among other conflicting traditions, were being reconciled in a particular way. In Matthew, Paul's position is placed on the lips of Jesus, addressed to Peter (Matt. 16:17), and combined with a strong pro-Petrine tradition (Matt. 16:18–19). These verses are omitted in Luke-Acts. There Paul's position is placed on the lips of Peter and addressed to the circumcision party before the apostles in Jerusalem (Acts 11:1–18). Thus, both Matthew and Luke-Acts, though in different ways, unify Peter and Paul. Without the benefit of Paul's personal firsthand account of his relationship to Peter and the circumcision party in Galatians, 1—2, it would be virtually impossible to perceive the way in which this earlier conflict is reconciled in Matthew and Luke-Acts.

LITERARY METHOD OF MATTHEW (Matt. 4:12–25)

The summary of the beginning of Jesus' ministry in Galilee in Matt. 4:12–25 may be analyzed as follows: In 4:12–16, the evangelist introduces a fulfillment of prophecy quotation with his stylized formula (v. 14). Verses 12–13 are clearly from his hand. It is important to grasp the line of reasoning that led the evangelist to select this passage from Isaiah (9:1–2). The prophet was speaking about the day of salvation. The evangelist understood the prophet to have intended to speak about Jesus as the instrumental agent of God's saving activity. Through Jesus the people who sat in darkness have seen a great light. The evangelist knew that this was true, and he knew that this light had come to the Gentiles as well. Therefore this passage, in which the prophet spoke of salvation coming to "Galilee of the Gentiles," was taken over by the evangelist as the structural backbone or organizing principle governing the theological and geographical framework of Jesus' prepassion ministry.

Jesus had a ministry in Galilee. There is no question (cf. Matt. 11:20–24) about that. In the Gospel of Matthew, however, there is a theologically motivated focus to this Galilean ministry. Here Jesus goes about "*all* Galilee" (4:23). Stories about his work around the Sea of Galilee, in the regions of Caesarea Philippi and of Tyre and Sidon, underscore the extent to which Jesus' ministry reached out to and beyond the land of Zebulun and of Naphtali. Without a doubt, Jesus worked in Capernaum, (cf. Matt. 11:23). This Gospel clearly implies that he left Nazareth to go and dwell in Capernaum *in order to fulfill* the word of the prophet Isaiah. The evangelist wants the reader to understand that Capernaum, which is by the Sea of Galilee, fulfilled the word of the prophet—that the people sitting in darkness in the land of Zebulun and Naphtali by *the way of the sea* have seen a great light. This requires that one understand "by the way of the sea" to refer to the shores of the Sea of Galilee and not, as Isaiah meant, to the shores of the Mediterranean.

The evangelist clearly intends this identification with the Sea of

Galilee. Furthermore, after completing the ministry in Galilee proper and before this prophecy could be completely fulfilled, people sitting in darkness "across the Jordan," that is, in the land east of the Jordan River (Perea), had to see the light of salvation. Therefore, in this Gospel it was necessary for Jesus to go into the region *across the Jordan* (19:1) and for people there also to be healed in great numbers, before he proceeded to Jerusalem for the climax of his work. That the geographical framework of this section of Matthew's Gospel (that is, 19:1—20:16) is motivated primarily if not solely by the literary-theological considerations suggested by this analysis, is confirmed by the absence of any reference to location in the tradition it uses.

This means that the major geographical movements outlined in the redactional framework of this Gospel (as given in 4:18,23; 13:1; 15:29; and 19:1) are motivated primarily by theological rather than historical considerations. For this reason it should not be surprising that attempts to base historical reconstructions of the life and message of Jesus upon the historical reliability of this framework and chronology have ended in failure. The Gospel of Mark presupposes this same geographical outline without giving the fulfillment passage from Isaiah, which provides the basis. To reverse the relationship, making Matthew dependent upon Mark, requires one to believe in a redactional procedure without precedent. According to this view, Matthew has perceived that Mark's geographical outline originated in a unique interpretation of Isa. 9:1–2. Matthew has decided to supply the passage and to elaborate upon it in 4:12–14 by offering, through an equally unique exegesis, a theological motivation for Jesus' leaving Nazareth and dwelling in Capernaum.

Because these redactional passages clarify the way in which the evangelist conceives the ministry of Jesus and reveal his skill in organizing his material, it will be helpful if we bring together these particular passages and view them in sequence and as a whole.

"As he walked by the sea of Galilee . . . " (4:18).

"And he went about all Galilee, teaching in their synagogues and preaching the gospel of the kingdom, and healing . . . " (4:23).

"That same day Jesus went out of the house and sat beside the sea. And great crowds gathered about him, so that he got into a boat and sat there; and the whole crowd stood on the beach. And he told them many things in parables . . . " (13:1–3a).

"And Jesus went on from there and passed along the sea of Galilee. And he went up into the hills and sat down there. And great crowds came to him, bringing with them the lame, the maimed, the blind, the dumb, and many others, and they put them at his feet, and he healed them. . . . " (15:29–30).

"As they were gathering in Galilee, Jesus said to them, 'The Son of man is to be delivered into the hands of men, and they will kill him, and he will be raised on the third day.' And they were greatly distressed" (17:22–23).

"Now when Jesus had finished these sayings, he went away from Galilee and entered the region of Judea beyond the Jordan; and large crowds followed him, and he healed them. . . . " (19:1–2).

It is important to realize that all of these passages are redactional and that the evangelist is their author. They represent an idealized conception of Jesus' ministry.

What the evangelist knows about the actual Jesus, that is, Jesus of Nazareth, is what has come to him in the developed tradition handed down in the churches. This is a rich tradition of great variety, including historical, mythological, and legendary materials. The one major ingredient that is lacking is a conceptional outline for his narrative, an overall framework by which the diverse materials at his disposal can be unified into an intelligible whole. This is what the evangelist has provided. In making this contribution, he has drawn upon not only his classical Jewish literary heritage, but also upon contemporary Hellenistic literary models.

HELLENISTIC RHETORIC

Hellenistic rhetoric provided the evangelist with the topics he was to treat in his Gospel, if he were to succeed in evoking praise and emulation of Jesus. The reading public of the ancient world was educated in the schools of Hellenistic society. At the time the evangelist did his work, these schools were spread throughout the Roman Empire. The education received was constitutive of and sustained Hellenistic culture. Education available to Christians was influenced by the education received in these schools. This was called *egkuklios paideia,* that is, general education; the Romans translated this *artes liberales*. In the secondary schools the two most important branches of the curriculum were philosophy and rhetoric. Of these, rhetoric was the more influential.

Historical research provides a clear idea of what was involved in teaching this esteemed subject. After a student completed his studies in primary school, he would leave the grammarian who had taught him and become an apprentice of a specialist in eloquence, a rhetor (Latin for "orator"). Rhetors were everywhere. One reason for the prestige of rhetoric was the practical value it had during Athen's golden age. Isocrates, the great contemporary and rival of Plato, was the founder of rhetoric. Under him it became the study of the art of effective oral communication in public.

This practical importance, combined with the great influence of Athens, led to the inclusion of rhetoric in the education of an increasing number of the future citizens of Greek city-states. However, the rise of Macedonian rule over the Greek city-states and the subsequent loss of political liberty deprived eloquence of its original significance. Nevertheless, the institutionalization of eloquence in the educational system guaranteed rhetoric a place in the curriculum long after it had lost its original political value. In fact, once it lost that reason for being, rhetoric was free from the restraints of practicality and could flower and develop in a very complex manner and sometimes in quite artificial ways.

Of the three "kinds of speech" which had been recognized in theory since the time of Aristotle—the deliberative, the judicial, and the epideictic—the former two did not completely disappear, but were relegated to the background as a result of the decline of the city system. The only kind of speech that survived and flourished was epideictic—eloquence or the eloquence of the set speech, the art of the lecturer.

> This had not merely survived, it had developed, and it was now in a thriving condition, seeping into all the neighboring subjects and invading everything. . . . *Reading was done aloud, so that there was no borderline between the written and the spoken word; the result was that the categories of eloquence were imposed on every form of mental activity—on poetry, history and even philosophy.* Hellenistic culture was, above all things, a rhetorical culture, and its typical literary form was the public lecture.
>
> By a curious reversal of fate, the orator's artistic prestige was ultimately to invest him with a certain political importance. In Roman times, whenever a city produced one of these artist-in-words, and he turned out to be a successful professional lecturer, it was glad to have him as its spokesman—not merely at public ceremonies like the festivals and the games—that was only a matter

of set speeches and comparatively unimportant—but in far more weighty matters. If the city got into trouble with the king, or the province, it would naturally choose him as its ambassador—not only because he was the best person to plead its cause, the most persuasive arguer, but also because his personal authority as an orator, *an authority deriving from the universal prestige accorded his art, ensured, a priori, that he would be received with attention, goodwill and respect. . . .*

But we must be careful not to stand this matter on its head and mistake the effect for the cause; rhetoric did not lie at the root of Hellenistic culture as a primary, paradoxical fact and so burst forth naturally into flower in the field of education. On the contrary, it was secondary and derivative. The primary fact is that ever since the time of Isocrates and the Sophists, and in spite of all the political and social revolutions that had taken place, eloquence had been the main cultural objective, the crown and completion of any liberal education worthy of the name.

There are gaps in our knowledge, and it is not easy to reconstruct the history of the old schools of rhetoric, but we know enough to be able to say that the tradition was never broken. From the time of Isocrates, rhetoric was always, in practice, accepted as the normal means to the highest flights of education.

Why? You may say, routine, for teaching is not exactly a happy hunting ground for innovators—things are inclined to go on long after their original raison d'etre has disappeared into the mists of oblivion. But the exceptional popularity of rhetoric in the schools of old needs something more direct to explain it, and I believe that this exists in Isocrates' remarkable *teaching about the Word.* Learning to speak properly meant learning to think properly, and even *to live properly.* In the eyes of the ancients, eloquence had a truly human value transcending any practical application that might develop as a result of historical circumstances; *it was the one means for handing on everything* that made man man, the whole *cultural heritage that distinguished civilized men from barbarians.* This idea underlies all Greek thought, from Diodorus Siculus to Libanius. Is it surprising, therefore, that rhetoric should have remained at the heart of all their education and all their culture?[88]

This remarkable section of Professor Marrou's epoch-making study of education in antiquity has been cited *in extenso* because it contains so much that is important for the student of Matthew and because until recently little attention has been given to ancient rhetoric for understanding this Gospel. The passages italicized in this citation of Marrou's work may be commented on as follows.

1. Marrou's statement that the great pioneer of rhetoric, Isocrates, first became the educator of Greece *and then of the whole ancient world* prompts the question, Does that include the Jews?

We know that certain Jewish communities were influenced by Hellenistic culture. Philo of Alexandria is the classic example of a Hellenistic Jew. Elias Bickerman has argued convincingly that the Jewish synagogues came into being in response to the challenge of the Hellenistic schools. But David Daube has gone even further and has proven the influence of Hellenistic rhetorical practices on orthodox rabbinic exegeses.[89]

2. If reading were done aloud in the ancient world so that there was *no distinction between the written and spoken word,* is it possible that the composition of the Gospel of Matthew (which, though written, is so well suited for being read aloud) could have been completely free of the all-pervasive influence of Hellenistic rhetoric?

If the categories of rhetoric were imposed on every form of mental activity, would that include mental activity involved in conceiving the purpose and creating the form of Matthew? Would it include the mental activity involved in the selection and arrangement of materials to be included? If rhetorical categories were imposed on *poetry, history, and philosophy,* what would that mean for the "gospel" as a literary genre?

3. If there were a *universal prestige* accorded the art of rhetoric, which ensured that a person practiced in the art *would* be received with *attention, goodwill, and respect,* would any person living in the Hellenistic world and breaking new ground in writing the first gospel of its kind have neglected the consideration of that art in composing his work? The answer is emphatically no. Such neglect would have been extremely counterproductive.

4. Does Isocrates' *teaching about the Word* have any importance for explaining the popularity of the Gospels among Hellenistic Christians? If rhetoric meant not only learning to speak and think properly, but also learning *to live properly,* is it possible that the ethical words of Jesus, which after all were very Jewish, were received with respect and good will outside Jewish circles in part because they were incorporated within a framework which can be shown to be a creative example of the effectiveness of Hellenistic rhetoric?

5. If rhetoric in the ancient world was the *means for handing on the cultural heritage* of Hellenistic civilization, then the Gospel of Matthew can be viewed as an innovative and successful manifesta-

tion of a determined effort by leaders of certain Syrian churches to hand on the cultural heritage of a new civilization. This was a civilization based not upon the revolutionary achievements of Alexander the Great and the classical scriptures of ancient Hellenes, but on the rival achievements of Jesus of Nazareth and the scriptures of ancient Israel.

It may seem paradoxical that the Syrian church should adopt Hellenistic rhetoric to advance the cause of an essentially competing civilization. Prof. Marrou, however, has shown that such was the normative posture of Christianity toward Hellenistic education as a whole. Moreover, the history of revolutionary movements in general offers many examples of how a new civilization borrows from the one it eventually replaces.

The purpose of this lengthy digression is to call into question any tendency to discount the probability that Matthew was profoundly influenced by Hellenistic rhetoric.

A study of the literature and art of churches in the Mediterranean world, which coexisted with Hellenistic civilization after the advent of Christianity, makes it clear that the Gospels exercised profound influence in forming the mind and character of Mediterranean Christianity. In other words, the Gospels were used in educating those Christians who otherwise were dependent upon education offered in the schools of the Greco-Roman world. On a priori grounds, therefore, it is to be expected that the first Gospel written would have been shaped so that it might be received by the mind of the ancient Mediterranean world. That means that it would have been shaped by Hellenistic rhetoric.

At this point we are not concerned with the full importance of Hellenistic rhetoric for understanding Matthew, but simply with how such rhetoric can help explain the shape of this Gospel, that is, how Matthew begins and ends, and the topics he treats. Rhetorical training was specialized in different categories. There was a category called "comparison," which included such exercises as comparing Achilles and Hector. The "thesis" category required discussion on a topic of general interest. A frequent exercise was treating the question, Should one marry? Still another category was legal tenet, which involved defending or questioning a particular law like, Is it forbidden to kill an adulterer caught in the act?[90]

The most important category for our purpose was "encomium." Here one was trained in the most efficient way to eulogize.

> Topics for encomia of a man are his race, as Greek; his city, as Athens; his family, as Alcomaeonidae. You will say what marvelous things befell at his birth, as dreams or signs or the like. Next his nurture, as, in the case of Achilles, that he was trained and educated. Not only so, but the nature of the soul and body will be set forth, and of each under these heads: for the body—beauty, stature, agility, might; for the soul—justice, self control, wisdom, manliness. Next, his pursuits; what sort of life he led—that of a philosopher, orator, or soldier and most properly his deeds, for deeds come under the head of pursuits. For example, if he chose the life of a soldier, what did he achieve in this? Then external resources, such as kin, friends, possessions, household, fortune, etc. Then time; how long he lived, much or little, for either gives rise to encomia. A long-lived man you will praise on this score; a short-lived, on the score of his not sharing those diseases which come from age. Then, too, from the manner of his end, as that he died fighting for his fatherland, and, if there were anything extraordinary under that head, as in the case of Callimachus, that even in death he stood. You will draw praise also from the one who slew him, as that Achilles died at the hands of the god Apollo. You will describe also what was done after his end, whether funeral games were ordained in his honor, as in the case of Patrodus; whether there was an oracle concerning his bones, as in the case of Orestes; whether his children were famous, as Neoptolemis. But the greatest opportunity in encomia is through comparisons, which you will draw as the occasion may suggest.[91]

Clark suggests that Plutarch, in writing his *Lives of Famous Men,* was influenced by the rules of the encomium.[92] Philip Shuler has analyzed Plutarch's *Lives* to ascertain what evidential basis exists to support Clark's suggestion.[93] There is ample evidence in *Lives of Famous Men* to indicate that Plutarch followed these rules. In some of his biographies he followed the rules more closely than in others. Moreover, the kind of evidence in Plutarch's biographies, supporting the judgment that they have been influenced by the rules of the encomium, also exists in the four Gospels.

We return to the question of how the evangelist solved the problem of providing a conceptional outline for his Gospel—"an overall framework in which the diverse materials at his disposal could be organized into an intelligible whole." We now see that there were literary resources in his culture upon which he could draw.

Were there people in the Hellenistic world who could read and write Greek, but who knew nothing about rhetoric? Such people would certainly have been educational anomalies. There is no reason to regard the author of Matthew as an educational misfit in the culture in which he lived and communicated effectively and successfully. On the contrary, it is patent that he was a gifted writer who was able to function with extraordinary competence. He did not operate from rote memory, but freely and creatively as a person who understood his environment and knew exactly how best to produce his desired effect.

The evangelist did not follow the rules of the encomium mechanically, like a school boy. Even if no tradition had come to him on the topic of the physical appearance of Jesus, he could have composed such material. Therefore, the absence of this topic in Matthew is probably deliberate. Certainly other considerations were obviously in the evangelist's mind as he composed his Gospel. These other considerations had to do with the influence that Jewish scriptures, and above all the Book of Isaiah, had in forming his thinking. The very idea of writing his Gospel may have come to the evangelist from reading Isaiah. It is clear that he believed that what was written in the Scriptures had been fulfilled in what had happened to and through Jesus. He found in Isaiah a passage that clarified the significance of Jesus' ministry in Galilee. Jesus went to Galilee to fulfill the words of Isaiah. Jesus went about all Galilee preaching, teaching, and healing so that the people sitting in darkness in Galilee of the Gentiles might see a great light. Jesus left his home town of Nazareth to dwell in Capernaum because that city was by the sea, which he believed to be the meaning of Isaiah's prophecy. Finally, Jesus crossed the Jordan on his way to Jerusalem to fulfill the words of Isaiah that people "across the Jordan" would also see the great light. In sum, when Isaiah and the rules of encomia are taken together, they explain the topical outline of Matthew.

ISAIAH AND THE HEALING MOTIF IN MATTHEW

The redactional passages of the evangelist may be grouped into several categories. One of the most important of these categories is "healing summaries." Matt. 4:23–25 is the first of these summaries. That it is redactional is suggested by its summary character and confirmed by its literary kinship with other "healing summaries" in 8:16–17, 9:35, 14:35, and 15:29–31.

This summary statement anticipates and foreshadows accounts of Jesus' teaching and healing yet to be presented. The evangelist already has at hand a passage from Isa. 53:4, which he will incorporate with his characteristic fulfillment formula in 8:16–17. This fulfillment passage identifies Jesus with the servant of the Lord in Isaiah, who "took our infirmities and carried our diseases." Jesus fulfilled this work of the prophet by casting out demons and by healing diseases.

The relationship between 4:23–25 and 8:16–17 makes clear that the diseases and torments specified in 4:24—demon possession, epilepsy, and palsy—are representative of the "infirmities and diseases" with which Jesus coped successfully in fulfilling the word of the prophet (Isa. 53:4). Therefore, the stories where Jesus casts out demons (8:28–34; 12:22; 15:22–28) and heals epilepsy (17:14–18) and palsy (8:5–13; 9:2–7) are simply particular examples of exorcisms and healings which he performed in all Galilee (4:23). As is made clear in 8:16–17, this was done to fulfill prophecy—indicating that the general geographical outlines of Jesus' ministry before going to Jerusalem, and the decision about what content to include are theologically rather than historically motivated. This does not prove that Jesus was not an exorcist or a healer. But it does mean that one cannot appeal to these stories of exorcisms and healings without taking into account both the way in which the fulfillment of prophecy motif and the correspondence motif (cf. above) influenced the development of legendary and mythological traditions concerning Jesus. Moreover, the way in which these motifs have influenced the geographical outline of Jesus' ministry and the selection of much of the material in the Gospel must also be kept in mind.

In Matt. 15:29–32, which is another redactional passage belonging to the category of healing summaries, Jesus is represented as healing the "the lame, the maimed, the blind, the dumb, and many others." A study of Matt. 11:5, however, shows that this list is also ultimately derived from passages in Isaiah that contain eschatological promises (for example, 29:18ff.; 35:5ff.; 42:7,16–18; 61:1).

It is clear, therefore, that the evangelist is working in a context in which traditions concerning Jesus had been developing according to a theory that Jesus, during his earthly ministry, fulfilled promises made by the prophets. This theory was then further applied by the evangelist in developing the narrative framework of his Gospel. The historian, then, who is interested in the origin of the stories concerning Jesus' miracles, should carefully investigate the language and imagery of the prophets and of Jesus to see whether there was an experiential basis they had in common.

Historical study reveals that when Isaiah spoke of the blind seeing, the dumb speaking, and the lame walking, he was using metaphorical language to express the healing power of God over against people who were blind to truth, deaf to the Word of God, and crippled by sin. Jesus used similar metaphorical language in his parables when he referred to the dead being made alive (Luke 15: 24,32). With the prophets and Jesus, the forgiving, redeeming love of God for the repentant sinner is the basis for salvation. It is the reality, however conceived, that lies behind all biblical imagery concerning the blind receiving their sight, the lame walking, the lepers being cleansed, the dumb speaking, the dead being raised, and the poor having good news preached to them (Matt. 11:5).

Jesus makes this quite clear in the parallel construction:

> This my son was dead, and is alive again; he was lost, and is found (Luke 15:24).

To be dead is to be lost and to be alive is to be received and forgiven by God. To be lost is to be effectively separated from the love of the heavenly Father. To be found is to discover one's true home within the covenant of God. It was the lost sheep of Israel whom Jesus called to repentance. They were the sinners he came to save. In receiving repenting sinners into the intimacy of his table fellowship, he was expressing and confirming in realistic terms the forgiving love of God who, though he cannot abide sin, does not will the death of a single sinner. Therefore, there is more joy in heaven over the repentance of one sinner than over the righteousness of ninety-nine (Luke 15:7,10).

Paul thought in similar terms, though he recast them christologically. People who were "dead in trespasses" could be made "alive in Christ" through the love of God shed abroad in their hearts (Romans 4—8). Jesus spoke for a God who moved lost sinners from death to life. For Paul, the God of Abraham is the God "who gives life to the dead" (Rom. 4:17).

THE WISDOM MOTIF

Of basic importance to the community of faith for which the evangelist Matthew wrote was access to the secret wisdom of God, which was afforded through the words of Jesus as the living Lord of its cultic life.[94] Some of these words had been preserved in the written traditions of the various and particular Christian communities in Syria, which were of primary concern to the evangelist. These communities received these words as direct and immediate oracles from the living God. That this God was traditionally understood in these communities in Jewish terms was "formally" very important.

Therefore, the evangelist made a conscious effort to maintain and develop formal ties with certain cherished writings in the community, such as the book of the prophet Isaiah. But speaking "substantially," the church of Matthew transcended its particular Jewish past by the evangelist's determination to view Jesus christologically as the unique Son of God, whose authority as a divine spokesman transcended even that of Moses and the prophets. Finally, the evangelist determined to present Jesus as the uncompromising advocate of a mission to the Gentiles.

As a quid pro quo for the acceptance of his work among ecumenically open but tradition-conscious churches, the evangelist's concern was to preserve the detailed "forms" of the past while creating an enlarged "new form" for the present. This led him to incorporate within Matthew large and *virtually unaltered* collections of the words of Jesus as these collections came to him from the major churches for whom he intended his Gospel. In this way, separate and distinctive collections of the words of Jesus in traditional form were, as far as we know, set forth in a *new* overall form for the first time. By this very daring and creative act, the evangelist introduced a development into the traditioning process which later facilitated a de-Judaizing and de-Palestinizing of the "words of Jesus" (as in Luke and Mark), and eventually paved the way for their radical reinterpretation and reformulation (as in John).

It was precisely because of the decisive importance of these words as bearers of the hidden and secret wisdom of God (Matt. 7:28–29; 11:25–30; 13:34–35,54) that the community of faith eventually tolerated and even appreciated their alteration and reformulation in the interest of communicating their full and sometimes new meaning.[95] But this was a later development. At the moment in the church's history when Matthew was created, the freedom to alter the form of these "oracles of God" was hindered by the practical necessity to avoid unnecessary resistance to the evangelist's project as a whole. This best explains why conflicting and antithetical words of Jesus are left unchanged in Matthew. Sometimes these words even seem antithetical to the evangelist's own views (cf. 10:5–6 and 28:19–20). It was for the *first* evangelist to break ground in a quite new way. In carrying out his pioneering responsibilities, he was conservative in handling materials he had received. These different collections of Jesus' sayings represented the vested interests of the churches in which they had been preserved. They constituted the cherished treasures of diverse Christian communities which were being offered up to the great new church that would celebrate, renew, enhance, and enrich its collective faith and life in and through the first Gospel.[96]

Of all these churches, one of the most important is the one which contributed the collection of sayings preserved in Matt. 5:3—7:27. This may be deduced not merely from the great length of this collection and its placement before the collections contributed by other churches, but may be inferred from the intrinsic quality of the traditions represented within the collection. What the evangelist introduces as a sermon on a mount near the beginning of Jesus' ministry in Galilee is a brilliant and precious gem in the jewel-bedecked crown of his achievement. It is a featured portion of his Gospel.

Any church which could have collected, preserved, and edited sayings of Jesus as they are found in Matthew 5—7, assuming that the church would have seriously attempted to live out of the understanding implicit in these sayings, would have been a church of great spiritual power. Even so, this collection does not stand alone. It is harmoniously included in a whole that is greater than its parts. It is thus assured attention from *many* churches—a priceless pearl in a magnificent setting. When the evangelist writes, "Go make disciples of all the Gentiles . . . *teaching them to keep whatsoever I have commanded you,*" the reader is naturally reminded of what proceeded forth from the mouth of Jesus with astonishing authority when he began to teach the crowds at the beginning of the Sermon on the Mount.

These words have had a special power of attraction. In order to begin to appreciate the importance they would have had for the first readers of this Gospel, it will be helpful to review some citations from Apollonius of Tyana. The king of Babylon is reported to have said: "This is Apollonius, whom my brother Megabates says he saw at Antioch, the object of the greatest honor and reverence of all good men there."[97] While it is difficult to be certain of Apollonius's history and dates, what follows is valid as a representation of the refined rhetorical tastes of Hellenistic audiences. It puts us in touch with the realities with which the evangelist contended in his efforts to win for Jesus the good will and respect of Hellenistic hearers.

With reference to Apollonius is written:

> His style of speaking was not lyrical and swollen with poetic expressions; nor was it full of unusual words or affectedly Attic, for he disliked being more than moderately Attic [a good description of Matthew's Greek], nor did he indulge in subtlety or prolixity, and he was never known to equivocate or to walk back and forth before his audience; but when he discoursed, he spoke as if from a tripod, and would say "I know," or "Thus I think," or "Where does that lead you?," or "You must know." His expressions of opinion were concise and clear-cut as a diamond; his words were remarkably well chosen and apt, and what he uttered had the ring of royal edicts.
>
> Being twitted by a quibbler with never asking questions, he said: "While I was young I did ask them, and now it is not my business to ask but to teach what I have learned." And when the other retorted, "How then shall a wise man debate?" he answered: "Like a lawgiver who ought to first convince himself that he is right, and then to tell his people what they must do."
>
> By this method he was eagerly listened to at Antioch, and brought men to his own way of thinking who had been utterly opposed to every sort of study.[98]

The Sermon on the Mount is admirably designed to represent Jesus' teaching in a most attractive manner. In reference to the Beatitudes in general and their introductory character, Martin Luther was moved to remark: "That is, indeed, a fine, sweet, friendly beginning of his teaching and sermon. For, he does not proceed, like Moses, or a teacher of the law, with commands, threats, and terrors, but in a most friendly manner, with pure attractions and allurements, and pleasant promises."[99]

Jesus may not proceed as Moses, but he does function as a lawgiver in this material. He exhorts: 5:16, 23–25, 29–30, 34–37, 39–42, 44–48. At times his admonitions take on the character of negative commands: 6:1–7, 16–18, 19–21, 25–31; 7:1–5,6. He never asks questions except in a rhetorical vein to press home the point of his positive commands: 7:7–11, 15–20. He never equivocates or walks back and forth before his hearers. He sits atop a mountain and intersperses his discourse with "I say to you" or "Amen, I say to you." His expressions are concise and clear-cut as a diamond. His words are remarkably well chosen and apt and have the ring of highest authority.

The evangelist succeeds in bringing Jesus forward in his most winsome stance as a wise man who is ready and willing to tell his people what they must do if they are to enter the kingdom of heaven. The Sermon on the Mount, as it stands in Matthew's Gospel, sets forth conditions for admission into the kingdom of heaven in terms of a righteousness that must exceed the righteousness of the scribes and the Pharisees (5:20), yet cannot tolerate the slightest laxity with regard to the smallest detail of the Law of Moses (5:18–19). Those who hunger and thirst after righteousness are blessed, because they shall be filled (5:6). If this hungering and thirsting leads to persecution, it will only guarantee admission into the kingdom of heaven (5:10). There rewards for being reproached, persecuted, and villified unjustly for loyalty to God will be great (5:11–12). Seeking God's kingdom and his righteousness must come before all else and provides the only assurance of future security (6:33).

Not everyone who honors Jesus, confessing him to be Lord, will enter the kingdom of heaven, but only those who are obedient to the will of God (7:21–23). Neither the gift of prophecy nor the power to exorcise demons or perform miracles will avail admission into the kingdom. If persons endowed with such gifts are not obedient to the will of God, they will only be rejected by Jesus on the day when the kingdom comes in power (6:22–23).

The righteousness that exceeds that of the scribes and Pharisees not only takes the measure of, but goes beyond and sometimes corrects the popularized requirements of the commandments of Moses (5:20–48). Righteousness done to be seen by others is never rewarded by the Father in heaven (6:1–6, 16–18). But this should not lead to keeping good works secret. For when they are known, they light the world and glorify the heavenly Father (5:15–16).

This theological construction, though it goes far in explaining the present form of these materials and is in part faithful to some authentic teachings of Jesus, is neither that of the evangelist nor directly from Jesus. It is largely the work of an earlier redactor who belonged to the community in and for which this collection of sayings was originally gathered and edited.

Through bitter experience, this community had learned how to exist in time. It had been persecuted for its faithfulness to God's will. Yet it persisted in its determination *to do* the will of God and regarded the way of patient obedience as superior to any alternate possibility. Therefore, it eschewed the more alluring forms of Christian existence which featured such exotic gifts as prophecy, casting out demons, and performing miracles in Jesus' name.

This community had accommodated itself to a minority status for an indefinite period. For it the Kingdom of God was no longer imminent, and solace was found in belief in rewards "in heaven" (6:20). This was an "idealized" eschatology. The chief virtues of this community were all those of a relatively powerless minority group that had to survive in a hostile environment: blessed are those who mourn, who are meek, merciful, peacemakers, and who accept persecution, reproaches, and injustices joyfully.

This is a Jewish Christian community standing in direct, unbroken historical continuity with Jesus. The attitude toward gentiles in this community's Jesus tradition clearly reflects the Jewish provenance of this tradition. The solicitousness with which the feelings of gentile Christians had been treated in some communities (for example, Pauline) had not led this community to eliminate or erase even quite pejorative statements (cf. 5:47; 6:32; and especially 6:7).

Jesus undoubtedly recognized the distinction between Israel and the Gentiles that was inherent in Jewish scriptures. In his teaching, he may well have drawn upon received stereotypes to make his points—especially in irony (cf. 5:43–48). At times it is impossible to decide whether a particular reference to gentiles originated with Jesus or came into the Jesus tradition as it developed in the primitive Palestinian-Jewish-Christian communities (cf. 6:7–8 and 6:32).

In this community, the law and the prophets are regarded as fulfilled by the generalized moral dictum: do unto others as you would have others do unto you (7:12). However, strict observance of the Mosaic dietary and ceremonial commandments is also important with regard to the degree of recognition accorded and reward given in the kingdom of heaven. Those who scrupulously observe the law in all its details and who teach others to do the same will be called great in the kingdom of heaven. On the other hand, those who break even one of the least of these commandments and teach others to be similarly negligent shall be called least in the kingdom of heaven (5:18–19).

This is a compromise position. Observance of the law is not required for admission into the kingdom. Therefore, this community is capable of allowing for a certain validity in the claims of Pauline communities that "one does not achieve righteousness by the works of the law" (Gal. 2:16–21). Still, the advantage of those who observe the law in all its details is preserved through a doctrine which allows degrees of greatness in the kingdom. Admission into the kingdom may rest on the righteousness of God, who reckons as righteous even transgressors—for example, "he sends rain on the just and on the unjust" (5:45). Within the kingdom, however, distinctions will be made; those who observe the jot and tittle of the law will be appropriately rewarded. Those who discount the importance of the law, even in its minute detail, have not understood the intention of Jesus (5:17–20). They may be likened to false prophets who would be known by their fruit (cf. 7:15–19). This compromise position seems to have been worked out in reaction to an antinomian position that may have had some relationship to Pauline influence. Paul himself, however, came close to such a compromise in his teaching about rewards (cf. Romans 6—13). The compromise in Matt. 5:3—7:27 finds its ostensible support in teachings of Jesus. However, this is achieved by a particular selection from and expansion of authentic Jesus tradition and by neglecting clear implications of doctrine deeply embedded in the most authentic levels of that very tradition.[100]

THE MOTIF OF MARTYRDOM AND THE PASSION OF JESUS

Preliminary Considerations

Although the Sermon on the Mount is of great importance for understanding the Gospel of Matthew, it is not the single best key for understanding the evangelist's main purpose. The collection of sayings addressed to the Twelve in Matt. 10:5–42 is of equal if not greater importance. A community which could hand on the fiery saying of Jesus—"Do not think that I have come to bring peace on earth; I have not come to bring peace, but a sword" (10:34)—was a community which was prepared to be devisive if necessary (10:35–37).

It would appear that Matthew could no more afford to alter the tradition in this collection than he could afford to alter the tradition preserved in 5:3—7:27. This is suggested by the fact that this collection contains Jesus' charge, "Go nowhere among the Gentiles. . . ." (10:5), whereas the evangelist himself was responsible for representing Jesus as saying, "Go . . . make disciples of all nations [Gentiles]. . . ." (28:19). This is a patent contradiction. It has traditionally been resolved in Christian communities by according normative authority to the closing words of the risen Christ.

Why would an evangelist give a collection containing such a discordant tradition a place in his Gospel? What kind of overriding consideration could explain this otherwise counterproductive compositional decision?

One can assume that the evangelist was convinced that this community's missionary tradition (10:5–15) and eschatological zeal (10:23) were part of the original deposit of faith handed on by the apostles. But beyond this, what compositional considerations can be adduced to illuminate the purpose of including this extraordinary collection of Jesus tradition in a popular religious biography of Jesus?

Matt. 10:5–42 and the Martyrdom of Jesus

While pride of place in Matthew is given to the Sermon on the Mount, the theology of this "sermon" (Matt. 5:3—7:27) was not normative in structuring any other part of the Gospel. To be quite specific, the evangelist has drawn nothing from 5:3—7:27 in composing any other part of his Gospel.

It is quite otherwise with 10:5–42. The remarkable series of "passion prediction" passages in 16:21, 17:22, 20:17–19, and 26:2 have clearly been composed with Jesus' sayings in 10:5–42 in view. The common references to being dragged before the Jewish authorities, being delivered over to the Gentiles, and being flogged indicate as much.

There is further evidence of the compositional nature of these "passion prediction" passages. The basic framework of Matthew's Gospel from chapters 4 through 19 is theological and geographical. The evangelist has used Isaiah to construct this framework. The list of topics treated in Matthew has been significantly influenced by the rules of the encomia: genealogy, birth narrative, public career of Jesus—including his seven great discourses, an account of his end, and stories of remarkable things that happened following his death.

The main compositional question that remains is this: How has the evangelist united into one dramatic whole his powerful and detailed narrative of Jesus' end (called for by the rules of the encomia and including both what precedes and what follows his account of "how Jesus stood in death") with the rest of his Gospel? The answer is clear. He has done this with a series of redactional passages which bear the distinctive literary characteristics of his own hand. These passages foreshadow Jesus' betrayal into the hands of Jerusalem authorities who are to flog and kill him, following which he will be raised from the dead.

Two of these "passion prediction" passages are introduced into Matthew's composition before chapter 19 (at 16:21 and 17:22) and two after (at 20:17–19 and 26:2). Thus, the evangelist skillfully ties together that part of his narrative structured by Isa. 9:1–2 with all that follows. In 19:1—20:16, in a concluding fulfillment of Isa. 9:1–2, Jesus enters the region "across the Jordan," the Gentiles sitting in darkness "see a great light," and Jesus starts "up to Jerusalem." By the time readers reach this section of the Gospel, they are quite prepared to hear Jesus say to his disciples: "Behold, we are going up to Jerusalem; and the Son of man will be delivered to the chief priests and scribes, and they will condemn him to death, and deliver him to the Gentiles to be mocked and scourged and crucified, and he will be raised on the third day" (Matt. 20:18–19).

Matthew's use of this series of "passion prediction" passages serves to underscore the fact that the example Jesus set, when he was "delivered up" to the "sanhedrin" (10:17) and taken before the "governor . . . to bear testimony . . ." (10:18), was consistent with what Jesus taught the Twelve to do when this happened to them.

> "He who does not take his cross and follow me is not worthy of me" (10:38).
> "Do not fear those who kill the body but cannot kill the soul" (10:28).
> "A disciple is not above his teacher . . . it is enough for the disciple to be like his teacher" (10:24–25).
> "He who endures to the end will be saved" (10:22b).

The effect of these words was to embolden those who identified with the Twelve to persevere under persecution, inspired by the example of their crucified and resurrected Lord.

The words of Jesus in 10:5–42 and the example of Jesus' passion (26:1—27:54), are united in Matthew's Gospel by his "passion prediction" passages. So the reader who accepts Matthew as Scripture is led to conclude that Jesus' instruction to the Twelve destined them to make a witness before the authorities (both Jewish and gentile) "like" that made by their "teacher."

In Matt. 10:32–33, Jesus says to the Twelve: "Everyone who confesses me before men, I will acknowledge before my Father who is in heaven; But whoever denies me before men, I will deny before my Father who is in heaven." In the community which was to live out of the inclusive vision of Matthew's Gospel, those who felt called to be "confessors" in the apostolic tradition of the Twelve would be constrained to steel themselves to make public confession of their faith, even if that meant death. "Have no fear of them; . . . What I tell you in the dark, utter in the light; and what you hear whispered, proclaim openly" (10:26–27).

These "confessors" had not only the words of Jesus to the Twelve in 10:5–42 and the example of his passion. They also had his general instruction (5:3—7:27) by which, as disciples, they were to be disciplined along with the rest of the church. Therefore, their witness could never be strident. Even in fearlessly making their "confession" they would be constrained to remain "meek" and "poor in spirit." They would not rail against their persecutors and tormentors, reminding them of the terrible divine retribution which awaited them.[101] Even while bringing down the awful sword of their confessions upon the temporal authority of their oppressors, they would be "peacemakers" no less than their brothers and sisters who were not called to be "confessors." When the persecutions would end and the community faced the problem of what to do with those "confessors" who had broken and denied their Lord, those who had "endured" (10:22) would be constrained by Matthew's Gospel not only to be forgiving of their persecutors, but advocates of mercy for their "apostate" brethren.

This would prove to be a form of "martyrdom" that eventually would break the back of imperial persecution and bring the emperors of Rome to their knees before that Savior at whose name "every knee should bow, in heaven and on earth and under the earth, and every tongue confess that Jesus Christ is Lord, to the glory of God the Father" (Phil. 2:10–11).

Why then did the evangelist include Matt. 10:5–42 in his Gospel? One reason was because this tradition was essential to his understanding of the meaning of the death of Jesus. Jesus had not only died "for us," as Paul taught, but he died to show those who confess him before the world (Matt. 10:33, Phil. 2:11) how to make their confession and, when necessary, *how to die* while making their confession.

As far as we know, this was an original contribution of the evangelist. Nevertheless, it is thoroughly in keeping with Paul's exhortation: "Have this mind among yourselves, which you have in Christ Jesus, who, though he was in the form of God, did not count equality with God a thing to be grasped, but emptied himself, taking the form of a servant . . . and became obedient unto death, even death on a cross" (Phil. 2:5–8).

After Paul's martyrdom, his words, "Be imitators of me, as I am of Christ" (1 Cor. 11:1), could only have encouraged others to think in terms of the martyrdom of Jesus, of Paul, and of the other apostles. This inevitably raised the question in deutero-Pauline circles whether to be "in Christ" did not entail a readiness to die *like* Christ. Those who stood in the tradition of Ignatius, Polycarp, Irenaeus, Hippolytus, and Origen decided that it did. Many of the Gnostics decided that it did not.

After the martyrdom of Paul and after the collection of his letters (which could have been occasioned by his martyrdom), the Gospel of Matthew and other gospels based on it, because of the narration of Jesus' death, could be united with Paul's letters to form the essential core of a distinctively Christian corpus of scripture. This Scripture would feature martyrdom as one valid option for at least those in the church who were called, in the "apostolic" tradition of Jesus' instruction to the Twelve in Matt. 10:5–42, to be "confessors." The need for such a distinctively Christian corpus of scripture may at first have been felt almost anywhere. Antioch, Ephesus, Smyrna, Corinth, or Rome are cities that come quickly to mind. Certainly, the need for such a corpus of scripture would have been felt by the time Ignatius met with Polycarp, Onesimus, and other bishops of Asia Minor in Smyrna, while he was on his way from Antioch to Rome around A.D. 110. Wherever that first compilation of Paul's letters and the Gospels as normative Christian scriptures took place—after the meeting of bishops in Smyrna and following the martyrdom of the bishop of Syria in Rome—all Christians who were to follow this "martyr" tradition of Jesus, Paul, the evangelists, Ignatius, and Polycarp would henceforth be united by their adherence to this new canon of scripture. The meal that Jesus shared with the Twelve on the night he was handed over to the authorities to be whipped and killed would have been central to the fellowship of these Christians.

Christians were reminded regularly in their worship of his body "broken for them," and his blood "shed for them." These words would have had special meaning for them in times of persecution. All who endured persecution in this tradition would have been united by the one cup. To drink from this cup would be to identify with the crucified and resurrected Jesus. This was to be the cup of their salvation. United by their participation in his death and resurrection, many would endure to the end and be saved (Matt. 10:22).

SON OF GOD CHRISTOLOGY AND THE PASSION OF JESUS

Although the evangelist is undoubtedly working with earlier tradition as he composes the passion narrative, this part of his Gospel definitely reflects the influence of his own hand and purpose. He foreshadows what he perceives as God's rejection of the Jewish nation in A.D. 70 by placing upon the lips of the crowd in Jerusalem the fateful words, "His blood be on us and on our children" (Matt. 27:25).

Indeed, the whole story of Jesus' death is told from the point of view of a gentile-oriented Christianity which adheres to a "Son of God" Christology.[102] Viewed in this way, the passion narrative is to be regarded as a continuation and culmination of the historicizing narrative concerning the triumph of faith over unfaith, which constitutes the central section of this gospel (Matt. 13:53—17:20).

1. Peter doubts, but is saved by the risen Christ; the disciples confess Jesus as "Son of God" (Matt. 14:33);

2. Peter confesses Jesus as "the Christ, the Son of the living God" (Matt. 16:16);

3. Peter, James, and John finally see "Jesus only," greater in authority than Moses and the Prophets (Matt. 17:8);

4. The high priest asks Jesus whether he is "Christ, Son of God," and Jesus responds so as to confirm in the high priest's mind the charge of blasphemy, that is, that he claimed to be "Son of God" (Matt. 26:63–66);

5. The crowd says "He claims to be the Son of God" and asks for proof (Matt. 27:43);

6. The centurion and those with him (in contrast to the crowd) make the same confession that the disciples had made earlier, that is, that Jesus is "Son of God" (Matt. 14:33 and 27:54).

Setting forth Jesus as publicly crucified, accompanied by testimony concerning the cosmic consequences and meaning of his death, is represented in Matthew as having the power to evoke faith. Jesus stood before the united representatives of imperial Rome and the established world of Jewish piety. Although they whipped, mocked, and killed him, he endured to the end and gained the victory. One of the representatives of the "principalities and powers" against which he was contending recognized at the end that he was "Son of God."

This representation of the way in which Jesus stood in death exercised great power over the imagination of people who were suppressed by the power of Roman provincial authority that was working hand in hand with the submissive leadership of their inherited religious institutions. Morally sensitive persons of all classes and races within the boundaries of the *oikoumene,* who longed for a cosmic salvation that would bring down righteousness like "mighty waters" with all the social reversals that would entail, had little difficulty appreciating the momentous implications of this event. Nor would they miss recognizing in their own local societies those persons of authority who played the roles of Pilate, Caiaphas, and the other principals involved. With the Gospel of Matthew, the church obtained a powerful new instrument for social and religious liberation through the propagation of faith in Jesus as the Christ, "Son of the living God," who had been given all authority in heaven and upon earth for the salvation of all nations (Matt. 28:16–20).

It is not surprising that further literary effort based upon this model was called for. This was necessary in order to adapt this "divine" instrument for more effective and, in some respects, quite different use among churches which were even more predominantly gentile oriented than were the churches for which the Gospel of Matthew had been composed.

LUKE-ACTS, MARK, AND JOHN

The authors of Luke-Acts, Mark, and John followed Matthew in composing popular religious biography featuring Jesus' martyrdom. When studied apart from all other examples of gospel literature, the four canonical Gospels appear in many respects to be quite different from one another. When they are studied in relation to all extant examples of gospel literature, however, Matthew, Mark, Luke, and John are in fact all strikingly similar. What distinguishes them is their consistent emphasis upon the flesh and blood existence, passion, and martyrdom of Jesus Christ as Son of God. There is no mystery as to why these four Gospels were selected to be included in the Christian canon of scriptures. All other extant gospel literature failed to feature the flesh and blood martyrdom of Jesus. Had there been a fifth "apostolic" gospel, which featured the earthly martyrdom of the Son of God, the church would no doubt have included it. Five gospels would have found obvious scriptural precedence in the fivefold Mosaic canon. The reason there are only four canonical Gospels is because only these four met the requirements of the anti-Gnostic church. Irenaeus's theory of four gospels to match the four corners of the earth is an obvious *theologumenon.*

The author of Luke-Acts makes it clear in the prologue to his first volume that, at the time he wrote, others had already taken in hand the task of drawing up a narrative of those matters which had been fulfilled among Christians. He does not disclose the fact that he has modeled his first volume after the work of a particular predecessor. The model the author of Luke used was the Gospel of Matthew or a common proto-model that has been lost. The reason for affirming some literary dependence between Matthew and Luke is that although each is strikingly different, both are even more strikingly similar. It is not difficult to explain the literary and theological differences. These are natural to the different authors. What is difficult to explain is the manner in which the Gospels according to Luke and Matthew resemble one another at points where both are unlike all other documents. The similarities are too striking to be accidental. It would seem likely that one has served as a literary model for the other. That Luke copied and altered the pattern of Matthew and not vice versa is suggested by Luke's prologue and supported by tradition and historical-critical considerations.[103]

It is noteworthy that in placing upon the lips of Jesus the words from the cross, "Father, forgive them; for they know not what they do," the text of Luke only makes explicit what is already implicit in Matthew.[104] Readers of Matthew knew implicitly from the Sermon on the Mount that if they wanted to imitate Jesus faithfully, they would be obligated to forgive their enemies even while undergoing the most cruel form of torture and death. Jesus' request of his Father that he forgive those crucifying the Son and the petition of the first Christian martyr, Stephen, in behalf of his persecutors—"Lord, do not hold this sin against them" (Acts 7:60)—represents a literary development of a martyr tradition fully present in the *imitatio Christi* doctrine of the Gospel of Matthew.

The primary justification for the Gospel of Luke seems to have been twofold. First, there was a place for a work which would meet the needs of certain western-oriented gentile churches better than the Gospel of Matthew could. Second, there was available to the author of Luke extremely valuable tradition which could be substituted for corresponding but, for his purposes, less suitable tradition in Matthew.

It may not be possible to argue convincingly that the birth stories and resurrection stories in Luke are more valuable than those in Matthew. However, no one has ever denied that the large body of parabolic tradition in Luke is more valuable to gentile Christians than the corresponding parabolic tradition in Matthew. This judgment is no doubt influenced by the fact that the church has preserved in its canon of scriptures not only the Gospels, but also the letters of Paul. By the theological criteria of those letters, the parables preserved in Luke clearly afford credible access to the mind of Christ. There are no parables in Matthew, for example, that have exercised such power over the mind and life of gentile Christians as those of the Prodigal Son and the Good Samaritan.

The Lucan parabolic materials seem to have achieved written form at a very early date.[105] The provenance of this material reflects the topography of Judea and more particularly the environs of Jerusalem.[106] From some Christian community in Judea, these materials passed at a very early period into the hands of a Christian community with strong commitments to the Gentile mission. Such modifications as have been made in the text of these parables reflect the interests of this mission. This is the explanation generally offered for the additional invitation at the end of the parable of the Great Supper, which is taken to refer to the mission to the Gentiles that followed and supplemented the mission to the lost sons of Israel (Luke 14:23). Taking the parable this way, readers of Luke's Gospel would understand that the mission to the Gentiles was definitely in the mind of Jesus from the time of his earthly ministry. Thus from its beginning it was grounded in the eternal purpose of God.

It is interesting to note in this connection that the Gospel of Luke has no trace of the tradition that the keys to the kingdom were given by Jesus to Peter, or that Jesus commanded the twelve disciples not to go into the ways of the Gentiles nor to enter any city of the Samaritans. In fact, in this Gospel Jesus is represented as explicitly sending his disciples into Samaria (Luke 9:52). It seems obvious that the author of Luke intended his Gospel to take the place of the Gospel of Matthew.

This means that after the Gospel of Luke was written and once it began to circulate, it created potential difficulty wherever its adherents came in contact with adherents of the Gospel of Matthew. If the ecumenical developments that led to the writing of Matthew and Luke-Acts were to continue to develop and not to lose force over the divisive potentialities inherent in the sharp differences between the Gospels of Matthew and Luke, then some reconciling form or forms of the gospel were called for in the church at large. The authors of Mark and John may be understood as supplying these forms. John carries the church beyond any impasse over the literary and historical discrepancies between Matthew and Luke by spiritualizing and resymbolizing the Jesus tradition. While the author of John is clearly working within the same overall gospel framework as reflected in Matthew and Luke, he does so with the greatest degree of freedom, creatively restructuring his portrait of Jesus along quite a new and different line.

This new line of development, however, had vital seeds in Matthew and Luke. For example, in Matthew there is the theological discourse of Jesus which reads:

> I thank thee, Father, Lord of heaven and earth, that thou hast hidden these things from the wise and understanding and revealed them to babes; yea, Father, for such was thy gracious will. All things have been delivered to me by my Father; and no one knows

> the Son except the Father, and no one knows the Father except the Son and anyone to whom the Son chooses to reveal him (Matt. 11:25–27).

Later, Luke's prologue refers to Jesus as the "Word," of whom the disciples and apostles had been eyewitnesses and ministers from the beginning. Such key ideas and germinal theological concepts and constructs, so subdued in Matthew and Luke that they tend to escape notice, are developed and written large in John.[107]

Although it is generally understood that John is a "spiritual" Gospel and that the fourth evangelist has freely reused and developed his gospel tradition, it is not generally understood that Mark was written after Matthew and Luke or that Mark represents a development of the gospel tradition that presupposes these earlier compositions. The late nineteenth- and early twentieth-century view of Mark is that it represents the earliest and least-developed form of the gospel tradition. Form-criticism has implicitly challenged that view by indicating that the earliest form of the gospel tradition was well represented in certain parts of early tradition that are unique to Matthew and Luke. This early tradition is not earlier than that attributed to Q, but is generally regarded as equally early.[108] Recent criticism has also raised questions concerning the view that Mark represents the gospel tradition in an early and relatively undeveloped form.[109]

The great importance of Mark as a theological contribution to the literature of the early church is increasingly emphasized today.[110] That Mark is a reliable repository of the earliest forms of the gospel tradition, however, has increasingly come into doubt, particularly as progress in the understanding of the traditioning process has improved.

The late nineteenth-century view that Mark is the earliest gospel is still widely held today. This view arose in response to a particular set of historical and theological circumstances. The evidence and arguments appealed to by critics who proposed Marcan priority cannot be regarded as decisive. Careful analysis of the evidence and of these nineteenth-century arguments has shown them to be inconclusive or circular, that is, capable of leading to an opposite conclusion once all the relevant evidence is taken into account.[111]

The evidence appears to some experts to favor the view that Mark was composed after Matthew and Luke. I will now give special attention to how Mark can be understood or explained according to this view.

CANON CRITICISM OF MARK

I am convinced that the evangelist Mark, in a very intelligent, vivid, clear, and pastoral manner, combined those parts of Matthew and Luke which best served his intention to compose a new form of the gospel adapted to popular missionary use. The Gospel of Mark is pedagogically well designed not only for use in preaching, but also in teaching.[112] As a teaching tool, its purpose and function was to awaken interest in the essentials of the faith. Pedagogically, Mark is introductory not only to Matthew and Luke, but to the larger Christian curriculum in the church for which it was composed. That curriculum almost certainly included Acts, Luke, and Matthew, most likely also Romans, and possibly other letters of Paul. It also included the oral tradition coming from the apostles, as that tradition had developed in the church for which Mark was writing. To what extent Mark actually drew upon that oral tradition in composing his Gospel is less important than the realization that, as he wrote, that oral tradition was a living reality guiding him in ways that often would not be readily evident if we were to think in simplistic either/or terms. To think of Mark as based either on oral tradition or on written tradition is to think in abstract and unreal terms. Oral and written tradition are not mutually exclusive, and the relationship between them is close and complex.[113] Both kinds of tradition, oral and written, must be kept in mind as we seek to understand Mark. To view Mark as having been composed after Matthew and Luke does not rule out the importance of oral tradition; on the contrary, it prepares the way for a better understanding of the influence of oral tradition upon Mark.

The Shape and Content of Mark

If Mark knew and used Matthew and Luke, it may be asked why he omitted so much of these Gospels. To explain why an author has omitted items from sources available to him is very precarious. Sometimes the reason for omission is clear, but often it is obscure. All we can say is that it is characteristic of authors who are working with closely related sources by different authors to produce works which are often shorter than the sources used. Thus, on the basis of known literary analogies, we should not be surprised at all that Mark is shorter than Matthew and Luke. And if shorter, by definition Mark would have omitted material from his longer sources.[114]

It is helpful to begin with a general observation: both Matthew and Luke contain large amounts of tradition that is very Jewish and even Palestinian in origin. It would be good pedagogical practice for Mark to spare his readers (presumably gentiles, and possibly far removed from Palestine) a great deal of what in Matthew and Luke was peculiarly Jewish and/or Palestinian.

A supplementary consideration is this: the purpose of Mark, in the view that it was written after Matthew and Luke, is not to displace Matthew and Luke, but to show that (despite appearances to the contrary) they basically tell the same gospel story. Thus, *both* should be retained and used in the church. Mark commends to his readers both Matthew and Luke by virtue of the fact that those who read Mark must also read each of these Gospels in order to gain the fuller account to which Mark witnesses by his action of uniting Matthew and Luke. Mark's Gospel made it possible and necessary to keep *both* Matthew and Luke. Mark's Gospel complements and supplements Matthew and Luke, not so much in terms of content, but of function. In sum: a church that accepts Mark has a theological instrument which can prepare the way for the church to accept *both* Matthew and Luke. Mark's work helped make possible the mutual recognition of these quite different and sometimes contradictory and inconsistent Gospels.

In an important essay, David L. Dungan has shown that the Hellenistic world in which the church existed placed great importance on the ability of the adherents of the several philosophical schools and religions to prove that they did not advocate contradictions and inconsistencies. It was necessary to be able to show that their body of beliefs was consistent and harmonious.[115] Against the background of Dungan's discoveries, then, it is possible to explicate the inner dynamic of the development of Matthew, Luke, and Mark as follows.

First, *Matthew is characterized by the inclusion of conflicting traditions*. As examples, we may compare the teaching "Blessed are the peacemakers"[116] with the saying "Do not think that I have come to bring peace on earth; I have not come to bring peace, but a sword."[117] Or the tradition "not an iota, not a dot, will pass from the law. . . . Whoever then relaxes one of the least of these commandments and teaches men so, shall be called least in the kingdom of heaven"[118] with the story about Jesus and his disciples breaking the sabbath law, and Jesus' claim that "the Son of man is lord of the sabbath."[119] Or the admonition "Judge not, that you be not judged"[120] with the condemnatory words "woe to you scribes and Pharisees, hypocrites! because you . . ."[121]

Second, *Luke is internally self-consistent, but often inconsistent in comparison with Matthew.* As examples of inconsistencies between Matthew and Luke, compare the story in Matthew where Jesus admonishes the disciples not to go into the way of the Samaritans[122] with the passage in Luke where Jesus is represented as sending his disciples into Samaria.[123] Again, where Matthew represents the last appearance of Jesus to his disciples as having taken place in Galilee,[124] Luke represents the last appearance of Jesus as having taken place in Judea.[125] The differences in the genealogies, birth narratives, and passion narratives of Matthew and Luke are well known.

Third, *Mark is basically an internally self-consistent version of Matthew and Luke,* free from contradictions with either one or the other. We are not necessarily to think that the evangelist consciously set himself the task of producing a gospel of this nature. We are rather to think of an author who recognized the need for a gospel which was suitable for use in a community whose air was charged with dissonance created by conflicting gospel traditions.

The evangelist Mark was aided in his purpose by following Luke where Luke followed Matthew, by taking nothing from Matthew that conflicted with Luke, and by taking nothing from Luke that conflicted with Matthew. Thus he produced a gospel that was free from contradictions with either. Mark is the only one of the three that has the advantage of being both internally self-consistent *and* externally free from contradictions with either one of the other two.

This character of Mark can easily be explained if Luke used Matthew, and Mark was third. But unless there was a close literary relationship between Matthew and Luke and unless Mark was third, it would be difficult to explain how Mark could be essentially free from contradictions with Matthew on the one hand and Luke on the other, and generally neutral in matters where Matthew and Luke contradict each other.

How could Mark have produced such a gospel without being

acquainted with the texts of both Matthew and Luke? Until this question is satisfactorily answered, the neutral and consistent character of Mark vis-à-vis Matthew and Luke constitutes a reason for thinking that it was written *after* Matthew and Luke. This is not a conclusive argument, but a consideration that, in balance, argues for the tertiary character of Mark.

The fact that Mark has accomplished an apologetic purpose while also demonstrating the essential unity of Matthew and Luke helps explain why Mark got into the canon. Mark paved the way for Matthew and Luke to be perceived as basically supplementing rather than contradicting each other. The composition of Mark thus represents an important stage in the development of the Christian canon.

To conclude that Mark was well adapted to serve an apologetic purpose is not inconsistent with holding that Mark was pedagogically well designed as a text for use in teaching and preaching. It is intrinsically probable that every gospel had more than one purpose. And it is a merit of Mark that it would have been useful in meeting different needs in the churches. Naturally, its original importance would have been lost after it was published together with Matthew, Luke, and John as one part of a fourfold Gospel canon. Once that fourfold Gospel canon was formed, with Mark as a bridge between Matthew and Luke, the primary purpose for Mark was achieved. Thereafter it would be taken for granted by all who accepted this canon that Matthew and Luke belonged together, and that for any church to follow any single gospel was to take a path leading to heresy.

The Canonical order, which positions Mark as a bridge between Matthew and Luke, witnesses to Mark's original purpose and is consistent with the view that it was written after Matthew and Luke to unify the two.

Peter and the Gospel of Mark

Testimony of the early church fathers, especially Papias, Irenaeus, Clement, and Origen, consistently associates Peter with the Gospel of Mark. Because of the lack of adequate historical controls, it is difficult to sort out the historical probabilities and to reconstruct the actual relationship between the author of this Gospel and the apostle Peter.

There probably was some justification in the early church for this memory of a close relationship between the Gospel of Mark and the apostle Peter. But what was it? Was the author of Mark's Gospel (granting that his name was Mark) the same Mark mentioned in 1 Peter? If so, what was his relationship to the Mark mentioned in Acts? These are questions that were pondered in the early church when the matter of authorship became acute because of the need to appeal to apostolic authority to combat heresy.

The conclusion reached was that Mark, who is referred to in 1 Peter as "my son Mark," was probably the author of the Gospel "according to Mark." But was this more than a conjecture? If so, what more could it have been? Could there have been a tradition that the Gospel of Mark was written by an associate of Peter—a tradition which actually emanated from the fact of such authorship? That question cannot be answered apart from the answers given to methodologically prior and less difficult questions, such as the question of the dating of Mark and the question of its relationship to Matthew and Luke.

If Mark had been written first and can be dated before A.D. 70, the probabilities of the authenticity of early tradition which associates the Gospel of Mark with a companion of Peter are immeasurably increased. In addition, if Mark had been written after Matthew and Luke, but can be dated before A.D. 70, the probabilities are still strong that this early tradition is to be trusted. For in this case Matthew and Luke would have been even earlier and presumably available to the author of Mark. The difficulty would be to explain the very clear literary connection of Mark and Matthew—Luke in relationship to a dependence of Mark upon the *preaching* of Peter. If, however, a postwar date for the Gospels is assumed and if the presupposed sequence places Mark after Matthew and Luke, then the following considerations would be of central importance in any comprehensive approach to this very important question.

Regardless of what view one takes, the form of the Gospel of Mark remains peculiar. On the view that Mark was written before the other gospels, its form is unexplained. On the view that Mark was third, an explanation of its form is less difficult to find. For if the author of Mark had been preceded in his work by the authors of Matthew and Luke, he presumably would have had access not only to these two Gospels (as well as earlier tradition), but also to Acts, the companion volume of the Gospel of Luke. The Acts of the Apostles explains the peculiarities of Marcan form and content and affords an explanation for the development of the later Papias tradition, which associated the Gospel of Mark with the name of the apostle Peter.

It should be noted that although the Matthean tradition in which Peter is given the keys to the kingdom is omitted in Luke, Peter continues to play an important role. For example, in Luke there is a reflection of the same tradition as is preserved in Paul that Peter was the first of the apostles to whom Jesus appeared after his resurrection (Luke 24:34).

Moreover, in Acts, Peter is the first of the apostles to speak. He took the lead in the first official act of the church following the ascension, calling for a replacement for Judas. In so doing he specified that the replacement should be chosen from the men "who have accompanied with us during all the time that the Lord Jesus went in and out among us, *beginning from the baptism of John* until the day when he was taken up from us" (Acts 1:21–22). Peter thus designates "the baptism of John" as the beginning of the decisive period of time. Thus, any gospel written under the influence of Petrine authority, as that authority could be discerned through the tradition preserved in the speeches of Peter in Acts, would have justification for beginning "the Gospel of Jesus Christ, the Son of God" with the baptism of John.

Similarly, in a speech at Pentecost, Peter is represented as saying (Acts 2:22–24):

> Men of Israel, hear these words: Jesus of Nazareth, a man attested to you by God with mighty works and wonders and signs which God did through him in your midst, as you yourselves know—this Jesus, delivered up according to the definite plan and foreknowledge of God, you crucified and killed by the hand of lawless men. But God raised him up. . . .

At Solomon's porch, Peter is represented as saying (Acts 3:13–15):

> The God of Abraham and of Isaac and of Jacob, the God of our fathers, glorified his servant Jesus, whom you delivered up and denied in the presence of Pilate, when he had decided to release him. But you denied the Holy and Righteous One, and asked for a murderer to be granted to you, and killed the Author of Life, whom God raised from the dead. To this we are witnesses.

Again, in Peter's speech before the rulers, elders, and scribes in Jerusalem, it is mentioned that a healing had been accomplished "by the name of Jesus Christ of Nazareth, whom you crucified, whom God raised from the dead. . . ." (Acts 4:10; see also 5:30).

Finally, there is Peter's remarkable programmatic speech given in Caesarea on the occasion of issuing his apostolic blessing to a mission to the Gentiles. A gentile, Cornelius, had concluded his address to Peter with these words: "Now therefore we are all here present in the sight of God, to hear all that you have been commanded by the Lord." Peter responded as follows (Acts 10:34–43):

> Truly I perceive that God shows no partiality [in Gal. 2:6, Paul makes this same point in relationship to those who were "reputed to be something"], but in every nation any one who fears him and does what is right is acceptable to him. You know the word which he sent to Israel, preaching good news of peace by Jesus Christ (he is Lord of all), the word which was proclaimed throughout all Judea, beginning from Galilee after the baptism which John preached: how God anointed Jesus of Nazareth with the Holy Spirit and with power; how he went about doing good and healing all that were oppressed by the devil, for God was with him. And we are witnesses to all that he did both in the country of the Jews and in Jerusalem. They put him to death by hanging him on a tree, but God raised him on the third day and made him manifest; not to all the people but to us who were chosen by God as witnesses, who ate and drank with him after he rose from the dead. And he commanded us to preach to the people, and to testify that he is the one ordained by God to be judge of the living and the dead. To him all the prophets bear witness that every one that believes in him receives forgiveness of sins through his name.

On the basis of these speeches, it would be simple to determine in general what could be included in any gospel designated to represent the apostolic witness according to Peter's testimony. Such a gospel would begin with an account of John baptizing; then it would tell of Jesus' baptism in terms of an anointing by the Spirit. This would be followed by a preaching and healing ministry beginning in Galilee and including the country of the Jews (that is, on both sides of the Jordan—Judea and Peraea), and climaxing in Jerusalem where Jesus would be delivered up. There he would be denied before Pilate, who would have preferred to release him. Instead, the Jewish authority would prefer Barabbas so that "by the hands of lawless men" Jesus would be crucified, and would be raised from the dead on the third day. In this gospel, Jesus would be approved by God unto Israel by mighty works and wonders and signs. He would go about doing good, healing all who were oppressed of the devil. If such a gospel included an account of postresurrection happenings, Jesus would be made manifest unto the disciples, whom he would charge with preaching the gospel to the people and proclaiming that everyone who believes shall receive remission of sins. Finally, he would be taken up into heaven.

It is clear that both the outline and content of this "Gospel according to the Apostle Peter" is very similar to the outline and content of the Gospel of Mark, even leaving open the question of Mark's ending. This is so not only with regard to what is included in the Gospel of Mark, but also with regard to its omissions. For example, Peter's speeches make no reference to Jesus' preexistence, to his genealogy, or to any of the marvelous things that happened at or following his birth. There is no reference in the speeches of Peter in Acts to Jesus as a teacher. Thus, while Mark shows Jesus as teacher and includes some sayings, his omission of the larger part of the sayings material corresponds to a lack of emphasis on teaching in the speeches of Peter in Acts. Everything tends to be reduced to its strongest kerygmatic form, with a preponderant interest in presenting a highly dramatic portrayal of Jesus' approval by God through "mighty works and wonders."

It follows that the tradition of the early church, which associates the Gospel "according to Mark" with Peter, can be explained in terms of the author of this Gospel deriving authority for its shape and content from the apostolic speeches of Peter as recorded in the Acts of the Apostles. What would be distinctive in this Gospel, warranting its apostolic status, would be its faithfulness to the form and content of this preaching of Peter. In any church which accepted the authority of Luke-Acts, the Gospel "according to Mark" would have been viewed as being in close relationship to the apostolic authority of Peter, just as Luke was viewed as being in close relationship with the apostolic authority of Paul.

Mark as Theologian

It is at the point of Mark's theology that difficulties arise with viewing Mark as a later Gospel, written after Matthew and Luke. The common bond that unites contemporary theologians is not so much what Mark contains as what is not found therein or is diminished therein in comparison with the other Gospels. Each generation has used Mark to its own end. Albrecht Ritschl found "historical" ground for the doctrine of grace in the miracle stories of Mark and, on the basis of the shift to the Gospel of Mark as the earliest and most reliable source for Christian theology, he was able to leave behind the "critical" theology of Ferdinand Christian Baur and move back to a more conservative "evangelical" theology. On the other hand, Ritchl's contemporary, Bruno Bauer, having accepted Mark as the earliest and best authority for the Christian religion, decided that Jesus had not existed as a historical figure. This inaugurated the Christ-myth school of German theology.

So it has gone until today. Out of Mark can be brought almost anything fancy desires. Karl Barth, of course, reacted against the whole enterprise of nineteenth-century liberal theology. Bultmann, under Barth's influence, shifted from the synoptic Jesus to John and Paul. But the fascination with Mark continues today with ever-varied interpretations. If in fact Mark was composed with Matthew and Luke at hand, the exegete has some control over his imagination. The permutations and combinations of theological speculation are radically reduced. Mark often followed the text of his sources, and one can write about Mark's special interests with much greater precision and confidence because one can actually see what Mark is doing with the Gospel tradition, that is, how it is developing in his hands. But what can one say?

As for the question, What sort of theologian does Mark turn out to be if his account is based on Matthew and Luke? the answer is not hard to find: a church theologian. Mark is doing his theology in and through the traditions that came to him in Matthew, Luke-Acts, and Paul (as the latter is represented in Romans). Mark represents the growing strength of the mediating tendencies which had originated in the historical Peter and that eventually led to the rejection of Marcion and all attempts to base theology on a single tradition. Mark represents an important stage in the development between Matthew and Irenaeus. Irenaeus speaks for Mark as well as for Matthew and the less polemical Paul of Romans. Mark is an "irenic" theologian. That is a better way to state his purpose than to say with the Tübingen school that he was "neutral." Mark, in essence, is active, positive, and dynamic. But as he advances the *cause of Jesus,* he does so in an irenic manner, not hindering it by unnecessarily alienating any important sector of the church in and for which he labored. In his own way and for his own time he was carrying forward the reconciling tradition worked out by Peter and Paul and the other apostles during the controversy over the admission of gentiles into the church. This reconciling tradition reached a unique literary form in Matthew and historical justification in Luke-Acts. Mark's peculiar literary contribution was his success in reconciling the discrepancies between Matthew and Luke and in demonstrating the essential unity that was present in their very real diversity.

Mark was almost certainly written for gentile Christians. It was possibly written in one of the provincial capitals of the empire. It may have been written in Rome itself. It no doubt fits a Roman provenance. Rome was certainly the place where diverse traditions flourished. In such a context Mark holds high the possibility of unity. To bring the most important of the diverse traditions of his day together into a powerful new synthesis was Mark's chief theological contribution.

If the Gospel of Mark was written in Rome, it was composed for a Christian community which, either in recent memory or in an earlier period, had been profoundly torn by persecution and the martyrdom of the apostles Peter and Paul. It is wrong to assume that all Christians in Rome were in agreement on how to cope with persecution or that all agreed that martyrdom was a commendable way for Christians to follow. That both Peter and Paul had accepted martyrdom was a powerful inducement for the deutero-Pauline and deutero-Petrine groups in Rome to unite against any proto-Gnostic Christians who would discount the importance of *imitatio Christi.*

After the martyrdom of Paul, his letters would have been read by Christians in Rome in the light of that example of "obedience unto death." That Paul's martyrdom was to be understood as an example of *imitatio Christi* would have seemed self-evident to many Christians who read his letters. Paul's exhortation, "Be imitators of me, as I am of Christ" (1 Cor. 11:1) would no longer have been read simply in the apocopated sense: "empty yourselves of all claims to privilege and assume the role of obedient servants." Now the full meaning would have been: "Assume the role of the obedient servant of God who is willing to be obedient *even unto death.*" After his martyrdom, Paul's words would have been understood by many in Rome in the sense: "Be imitators of me through obedience unto death even as I have imitated Christ, who himself was obedient unto death."

In this way a developed tradition of Pauline doctrine would have come full circle to unite with the tradition of Palestinian doctrine as developed in the Gospel of Matthew. The words of Jesus to the Twelve—"And you will be hated by all for my name's sake. But *he who endures to the end will be saved*" (10:22)—were reinforced in his messianic sermon from the Mount of Olives: "Then they will deliver you up to tribulation, and put you to death; and you will be hated by all nations for my name's sake. . . . But *he who endures to the end will be saved.* And this gospel of the kingdom will be preached throughout the *oikomene*, as a *martyrion* to all nations; and then the end will come" (Matt. 24:9–14). For Mark "this gospel of the kingdom" that must be preached everywhere to all the Gentiles was none other than "the gospel" (used absolutely) proclaimed by Paul: "And *the gospel* must first be preached to all nations . . . and you will be hated by all for my name's sake. But *he who endures to the end will be saved* (Mark 13:10–13).

Mark takes this particular "gospel," which he believed Paul had been sent to proclaim to all the Gentiles, and makes it the watchword of his gospel: "The beginning of *the gospel* of Jesus Christ . . ." (1:1).

Mark then conceptually unites this Pauline kerygma, subsumed under the watchword "the gospel" (used absolutely only by Paul and Mark), with the Palestinian tradition *at exactly those key points which undergird martyrdom.* "Whoever loses his life for my sake *and the gospel's* will save it" (8:35). "There is no one who has left house or brothers or sisters or mother or father or children or lands, for my sake *and for the gospel,* who will not receive a hundredfold now in this time, houses and brothers . . . with persecutions, and in the age to come eternal life" (10:29–30).

Certainly, the omission of the birth narratives, which assume such an important role in Matthew and Luke but to which Paul never refers in his letters, fits Mark's concern to shape his gospel to conform to the Pauline kerygma. His decision to reduce attention to discourse material may have been influenced by Paul's lack of preoccupation with words of Jesus. Such words of Jesus as are needed by Mark are generally drawn from that great reservoir of narrative-discourse material *common* to Matthew and Luke. When this is not the case, as with the saying "he who endures to the end will be saved" (found in Matthew and not in Luke), it is because such sayings are especially suitable for Mark's purpose.

In Rome within circles where this particular deutero-Pauline tradition (featuring the *imitatio Christi*) prevailed, the Gospel of Matthew and the two-volume work Luke-Acts would have found ready acceptance for their realistic portrayal of "Jesus Christ publicly crucified" (cf. Gal. 3:1). At this point the Gospels of Matthew and Luke are at one with the apostolic witness of Peter in his sermons in the Acts of the Apostles. The author of 1 Peter clearly unites the tradition of the passion of Jesus in the Gospels with the tradition of Peter's sermons in the Acts of the Apostles in his doctrine of *imitatio Christi*: "Christ also suffered for you, leaving you an example, that you should follow in his steps. He committed no sin; no guile was found on his lips. When he was reviled, he did not revile in return; when he suffered, he did not threaten; but he trusted to him who judges justly. He himself bore our sins in his body on the tree, that we might die to sin and live to righteousness. By his wounds you have been healed" (1 Pet. 2:21–24).

Taken together, these Christian writings would have provided an extensive textual basis and convincing scriptural support for a positive interpretation of the final witness of Peter and Paul. This combined apostolic witness would have stood over against any Gnostic-like tendency to discount the necessity the gospel places upon Christians to engage the world by publicly proclaiming the gospel and enduring persecution to the end for the sake of Jesus and for the sake of his gospel, wherever that became necessary.

Seen in this way, the purpose of Mark was to inspire and unify the whole Christian community in Rome in the face of renewed persecution, on the basis of that "gospel of Jesus Christ" for whose sake Peter and Paul had suffered martyrdom.[126]

Like the author of Ephesians in the East who may have preceded him, Mark was one of the great deutero-Pauline architects of the New Testament canon. Both he and the author of Ephesians understood well that by his death Christ had made all things clean, removed the great dividing wall between Jews and gentiles, and intended that his house be a house of prayer *for all nations*.

PART III

The Development of the New Testament Canon

The moment we bring the concept "New Testament Canon" into our discussion of the gospel tradition and the development of the gospel genre, we introduce a factor which requires a special task of historical reflection. How did the tradition concerning Jesus come to be enshrined within the New Testament? Unless we understand the answer to this question, our interpretations of this tradition are going to be naive and misleading regardless of whether we live in a society which is constituted by a doctrine of separation of church and state or in an older society where the Christian church continues to function legally as a privileged institution within the established order of the state.

There were three basic factors that contributed to the shaping of the New Testament canon. First, there was state persecution of Christians. This not only evoked martyrdom, but also stimulated a whole set of responses by the church to strengthen the faith and discipline of its members. Second, there were diverse systems of Christian theology. This doctrinal diversity, especially where it affected the question of martyrdom, tended to weaken the collective witness of Christians in the face of state persecution by denying them the added support that comes from ecclesiastical and doctrinal unity. The only state that could sustain a prolonged and widespread persecution of the church was the Roman Empire, and the only authority that could assure the church widespread protection from such persecution was the emperor. Thus, the third major factor that contributed to the shaping of the New Testament and especially to its acquiring official function as a set body of documents (a closed canon) was the establishment of the Christian religion in the Roman Empire under Constantine the Great.

THE FINAL PHASE: THE CLOSING OF THE CANON

When we speak about the closing of the canon, we should make a distinction between the Chalcedonian and the non-Chalcedonian churches. "The closing of the canon" is a topic that has primary reference to the final phase in the development of the New Testament as it is accepted in those branches of the Christian church which acknowledge the validity of the Council of Chalcedon. This distinction does not rest on any known decision or finding of that council, but rather on the fact that the earlier, pre-Constantinian diversity in the number and names of the New Testament books continues among the non-Chalcedonian churches into the present. For example, the official New Testament canon of the Syrian orthodox churches, specifically the so-called "Jacobite" churches, is that of the Peshitta—a Syriac version of the New Testament dating from about the fifth century.[127] This is a twenty-two book canon and does not include the Book of Revelation, 2 Peter, 2 or 3 John, or Jude. In modern translations of the New Testament prepared for use in Syrian Orthodox churches in India, all of these books have been given a place. This is for ecumenical reasons. But the authorities in these churches would never agree that their briefer official canon is "deficient." In fact, they realize that their briefer twenty-two book canon is closer to the "undisputed" list of New Testament books acknowledged in the pre-Constantinian period than is the twenty-seven book canon of the post-Constantinian, Chalcedonian churches.

It is of the greatest importance to recognize that the New Testament, as it is generally accepted in all branches of the Christian church which accept the Council of Chalcedon, was not finally agreed upon until the time of Constantine or shortly thereafter. De facto, of course, all the books finally included in this New Testament were recognized as Scripture in many if not most parts of the church long before. But the status of Hebrews, Revelation, 2 Peter, James, Jude, 2 and 3 John was still being disputed in some important churches until the time of Constantine.

Three factors—(1) response to persecution, (2) combating heresy, and (3) accommodation to the Constantinian settlement—decisively served to shape the New Testament writings into a canon for the church. This canon of Christian scriptures in turn served to provide a doctrinal and legal basis after Constantine for the sociopolitical reality known as "Christendom." We live at a time when the Constantinian establishment of the church is being dismantled. Many interpreters speak of the post-Constantinian age. Nonetheless, our thinking and feelings about the New Testament are still largely determined by the profound and fateful understanding that was reached under Constantine. For this reason it is best to begin an analysis of the essential developments of the New Testament canon by giving some attention to Constantine. But before we approach Constantine and his interest in Christian scripture, we must consider his prototype, Alexander the Great. In Constantine, the gospel tradition of Jesus of Nazareth and the heritage of Alexander the Great came together in an uneasy alliance that remains the single most dynamic force for integrating human society and unifying the human race that the world has ever known.

Alexander the Great

F. E. Peters, in *The Harvest of Hellenism: A History of The Near East from Alexander the Great to the Triumph of Christianity,* has written:

> The *oikoumene* created by Alexander carried within itself the twin implications of universalism and localism. . . . In the end, however, it was the universalism and not the particularism within the *oikoumene* that triumphed. A state, Rome, and a religion, Christianity, both originally local phenomena in the *oikoumene,* moved onto the terrain already conceptually plotted by the Stoics, and the promise of Alexander's achievement was fulfilled: one state, one culture, one God.[128]

The heritage of Alexander the Great remains alive in the world as we know it today, above all in three of the most powerful forces presently at work in shaping the future of the world. Their emphasis upon unity conceptually unites all three: the *United* States of America; the *Union* of Soviet Socialist Republics; and the *United* Nations. The ideal representative for any country to send to the United Nations is a man or woman who shares the vision of a world free from racial hatred and from war that is inspired by mistrust and misunderstanding between peoples of different nations, races, and cultures—a world united in its commitment to policies that will foster the welfare of all peoples of all nations, races, and cultures.

Constantine the Great

Policies of state, ostensibly aimed at establishing the unity and brotherhood of mankind, can be oppressive against recalcitrant minorities like Jews and Christians. When states establish and maintain oppressive policies by force, they can and do become demonic and tyrannical.

This was the situation in the Roman Empire before Constantine's conversion. The policies of the state seemed to fluctuate. At one time Christians were being tolerated, at another time they were being forced to conform. At this place they were under local persecution, at other places they were left alone. As pressure on the state to keep Christians in line with imperial policy and practice increased, so the will of the Christians to withstand persecution strengthened and spread. Something had to give. Constantine's "conversion"[129] saved both state and church from a final cataclysmic confrontation.

The importance of the Scriptures in the persecutions of Christians is unmistakable. As with the Jews, Christian resistance was perceived by state authorities as rooted in the Christians' loyalty to their sacred writings.

Eusebius has preserved a story that carries us to the very heart of the matter.

> A man at Caesaerea in Palestine, called Marinus, honored by high rank in the army and distinguished besides by birth and wealth, was beheaded for his witness to Christ, on the following account. There is a certain mark of honor among the Romans, the vine-switch, and those that obtain it become, it is said, centurions. A post was vacant, and according to the order of promotion, Marinus was being called to this advancement. Indeed, he was on the point of receiving the honor, when another stepped forward before the tribunal, and stated that in accordance with the ancient laws, Marinus could not share in the rank that belonged to Romans, since he was a Christian and did not sacrifice to the emperors; but that the office fell to himself. And the judge was moved at this, and first of all, asked what views Marinus held; and then, when he saw that he was steadfast in confessing himself a Christian, gave him a period of three hours for consideration.

We can imagine the conflicting feelings that stirred in the breast of Marinus as he stepped outside the courtroom building.

> When he came outside the court, the local bishop, Theotechus, approached and drew him aside in conversation, and, taking him by the hand, led him forward to the church. Once inside, he placed him close to the altar itself, and, lifting his cloak a little, he exposed to the soldier's view a sword in his waistband; at the same time, he brought and placed before him the book of the divine gospels, and bade him choose which of the two he wished. Without hesitation Marinus stretched forth his right hand and took the divine book. "Hold fast then," said Theotechus to him, "Hold fast to God; and, strengthened by Him, mayest thou obtain that thou hast chosen. Go in peace."

Marinus had ample time to ponder his alternatives. Near the end of the three-hour period, he started back to the courtroom.

> As he was returning thence, immediately a herald cried aloud, summoning him before the court of justice. For the appointed time was over. Standing before the judge he displayed still greater zeal for the faith; and straightway, even as he was, was led away to death, and so was perfected.[130]

This story makes it clear why those predecessors of Constantine who persecuted Christians "ordered the divinely-inspired scriptures to be destroyed and consumed by fire."[131] One can also understand why, after his conversion, Constantine "resolved to apply himself to the reading of the divine books."[132]

After his decision to favor Christianity, Constantine looked to certain Christian bishops for counsel. Some of these bishops in turn looked upon the first Christian emperor with favor. Through the eyes of one of these bishops, Eusebius of Caesarea, we learn the following:

> He constituted a church as it were, within the imperial palace; and, with diligence and cheerfulness, lead in worship himself, those who assembled within that church. Moreover, he took the Bible into his hands, and with an attentive mind meditated upon those divinely-inspired oracles. After which he recited the usual prayers, together with the whole assembly of his courtiers.

Even today, on ships of the United States Navy, the captain has the right to ordain a time for divine worship and to appoint chaplains or others to conduct the services. The captain himself may lead the assembled in prayer and reading from the Bible. This is an unbroken tradition that reaches back through the British Royal Navy to Europe's medieval imperial armed forces and, ultimately, to Constantine himself.

Eusebius's account of Constantine continues:

> He ordained that a day should be set aside as convenient and fit for prayers; that day namely, which really is the chief and first of the other days, and which is truly the Lord's; and the salutary day. Moreover, he appointed deacons and ministers consecrated to God, who were graced with integrity of life and all other virtues, to be the keepers of his whole house. Lastly, the protectors and trusty guards, furnished with the arms of good affection and faith, acknowledged the emperor himself as their instructor in the practice of piety; and they themselves, in the same manner, honored the salutary and the Lord's day, whereon they poured forth (to God) prayers that expressed their gratitude to the emperor. And this blessed (emperor) incited all other men to practice the same thing; since his highest desire was that by degrees he might make all persons worshippers of God. And for this reason, he issued out a precept to all those who lived under the Roman empire, that they should keep holy-day on those days which had special significance from the life of our Saviour; as likewise, that they should honor the day before the Sabbath: in memory (as I think) of those things said to have been performed on those days by the Saviour, whose benefits could be shared by all.

Constantine instructed the whole army to honor Sunday diligently, and he allowed time and lèisure to Christians for attending church functions and participating in Christian worship.

> But to them who as yet had not embraced the doctrine of the divine faith, he issued out a precept in a second law, that on Sundays they should go out into a pure field in the suburbs, where, after a given signal they should all together power forth a prayer to God, which they had learnt before: that they ought not to place their confidence in their spears, nor in their armor, nor in their strength of body: but were to acknowledge the supreme God, the giver of every good thing, and of victory itself; and, that to Him the solemn prayers were to be performed; lifting up their hands on high toward heaven; but raising the eyes of their minds higher, as far as the celestial king himself: and that in their prayers they ought to call upon him as the giver of victory, the saviour, the preserver, and the assistant. Further, he himself gave all his soldiers a

form of prayer, ordering all of them to recite these words in the Latin tongue:

> We acknowledge Thee to be the only God:
> We declare Thee to be King:
> We invoke Thee as our assistant.
> 'Tis Thy gift, that we have gotten victories.
> By Thee we have vanquished our enemies:
> To Thee we pay our thanks for past blessings:
> And from Thee we expect more in the future.
> We are all Thy humble supplicants.
> Keep our emperor Constantine (together with his most pious children), in safety amongst us,
> And continue him a victor during the longest space of time,
> We humbly beseech Thee.

These things Constantine ordered his military companies to do on Sundays, and taught them to utter these expressions in their prayers to God.

At this point Eusebius relates how Constantine assimilated Christian features into his families' ancestral worship of the sun, performing himself "the office of prelate or pontif."

Eusebius continues:

> In this manner he himself performed the office of a priest to his own God. But to all persons who lived under the Roman empire, as well as to the civilian population, as to the militia, the doors of idolatry were shut, and every sort of sacrifice was prohibited. A law also was transmitted to the presidents of provinces, that they likewise should venerate the Lord's day. Which (presidents) by the emperor's order did in like manner honor the feast days of the martyrs, and gave due reverence to the times set aside for festivals of the church. All these matters were taken care of in a manner that brought the greatest joy and satisfaction imaginable to the emperor.
>
> Wherefore, when on one occasion, while entertaining the bishops, he expressed himself as being of the following mind: namely, that he himself was also a bishop: the words he made use of in our hearing, were these: "You are bishops in those matters transacted within the church; but in those done outside the church, I am a bishop, constituted by God."[133]

It is of the greatest importance to recognize that no ecumenical council voted to elect Constantine to this "episcopal" office. Like the apostle Paul before him, he was breaking new ground, and Eusebius and others accepted the validity of this new revelation.[134]

It was in this period that the New Testament of the later Chalcedonian churches first achieved its definitive form and began to achieve its present "legal" status. Henceforth ministers within Christendom, who were to read these Scriptures and preach the gospel, were to be regarded as "legal" ministers of the state empowered, for example, to enter the prisons and visit the prisoners. They had behind them the authority of the New Testament with the gospel command of Christ to visit those in prison. In case of a showdown, however, they also had behind them the authority and military force of their "bishop" (the emperor) who, standing outside the church, "governed all his subjects with an episcopal care."[135] The principles upon which the revolutionary new system was to work are made very clear by Eusebius:

> Constantine confirmed those decrees of bishops which were promulgated in synods, by his own authority: in so much that it was not in the power of the governors of provinces to rescind the bishop's determinations. For the priests of God (said Constantine) were to be preferred before any judge whatever. He promulgated a vast number of laws of this nature. . . .
>
> And on the churches of God he conferred innumerable gifts, in a manner that was extraordinary and transcendent; sometimes bestowing lands; at other times food supplies for the sustenance of the poor, fatherless children, and widows. Lastly, he took all imaginable care, that unlimited numbers of garments should be provided for the naked and such as were in want of clothing.
>
> But, above all others, he vouchsafed the highest honor to those who had wholly addicted themselves to the divine philosophy. Indeed, he paid little less than a veneration to those who had taken the vows of celibacy for the sake of God, since he was fully persuaded that that very God, to whom they had consecrated themselves, had taken up his habitation within the minds of such persons.

Thus began the Constantinian settlement of the conflict between church and state. The Christian religion became established. Christians were henceforth to occupy a privileged place within the imperial household and within the empire.[136] All idolatry was to be abolished as were all cultic sacrifices, certainly including those of the emperor cult.

All religious practices that could not be assimilated to Christianity were thus directly or indirectly suppressed. Judaism, though it retained a certain legal status, was henceforth to be treated as a religion of lower value. Constantine made it a law that no Christian should serve Jews. For it was, he said:

> A thing not to be permitted, that those who had been redeemed by our Saviour, should be reduced under the yoke of slavery to those who were the murderers of the prophets of the Lord. But, if any person professing the Christian religion should be found to be a slave to a Jew; (his order was) that he should be set at liberty; but that the Jew should be punished with a monetary fine.[137]

Thus was created an anti-Jewish bias in the state which inevitably was to draw out, exaggerate, and institutionalize certain anti-Jewish features of the New Testament. In addition, this bias was to obscure the far more fundamental truth that the pre-A.D. 70 Jewish origin of Christianity made Christianity a sister religion to Mishnaic and Talmudic Judaism which developed after and partly in response to the catastrophic events of A.D. 66–70 and A.D. 135.

Eusebius relates that Constantine

> prohibited all persons from sacrificing to idols; from a curious consulting of diviners and soothsayers; from erecting images; from performing secret initiations; and from polluting the cities with the bloody shows of gladiators.[138]

In brief, Constantine was a religious reformer who had access to power, both religious and military. He never relinquished confidence in the sword, only in ultimate trust in its final authority. As for the new constitution of things, this was provided by the Christian scriptures which he perceived not as a secret code, but as public documents to which new converts like the emperor himself should have ready and fitting access.[139]

All that has been said thus far about Alexander and Constantine has been set forth for this one purpose: to help the reader appreciate the significance of what Eusebius next relates about Constantine. The essentials of what we have learned are that Constantine inherited the responsibility of governing a world that had come into being, at least partly, in response to Alexander's dream of unifying humankind and establishing a fellowship based upon love.[140] All efforts to realize this dream had failed, and yet the dream would not die.[141] Now at last there was hope through faith in Christ that this dream might be realized. Here were men and women who, placing their faith in the Gospels rather than in the sword, were willing to die rather than deny their new faith.

Constantine's Commission to Eusebius

Alexander the Great kept a copy of Homer with him on his campaigns. His descendants provided for the education of humankind by establishing in Alexandria, the city named after him, a famous school and library where copies of the Hellenistic canon of writings could be edited, copied, and published. Now Constantine, in the city named after him (Constantinople) and in the Alexandrian tradition, wrote to Eusebius for the sake of the education of those committed to the universal religion that was to help save the world.

> Victor Constantinus Maximus Augustus,
>
> To Eusebius
>
> In that city which bears my name, by the assistance of God, our Saviour's providence, a vast multitude of men have joined themselves to the most holy church. Whereas, therefore, all things do there receive a very great increase, it seems highly requisite, that there should be more churches erected in that city. Wherefore, do you most willingly receive that which I have determined to do. For it seemed fit, to signify to your prudence, that you should order fifty copies of the divine scriptures (the provision and use thereof you know to be chiefly necessary for the instruction of the church) to be written on well-prepared parchment, by copyists most skillful in the art of accurate and fair writing; which (copies) must be very legible, and easily portable in order to their being used. Moreover, letters have been sent off to the chief financial officer of the diocese, giving instructions that he should take care for the providing of all things necessary in order to finishing of said copies. This, therefore, shall be your responsibility, to see that the written copies be forthwith provided. You are also empowered by the authority of this, our letter, to have use of two public carriages, to aid in their transport. For, by this means, those which are transcribed fair, may most commodiously be conveyed even to our sight; to wit, one of the deacons of your church being employed in the performance hereof. Who, when he comes to us, shall be made sensible of our bounty.
>
> God preserve you, dear brother![142]

Eusebius relates that the commission was carried out to the full satisfaction of Constantine.[143] Constantine would have had the opportunity to see the results of his commission, and to hold these copies in his hands and examine them before they were made available for distribution to the churches of his "new Rome." Eusebius says that these fifty copies of the Christian Bible were "magnificently adorned."[144] But we may be certain that Constantine's attention to the adornment of these Bibles did not distract him from more practical matters. Was the parchment well-prepared, was the script completely legible, and what measures had been taken to assure the accuracy of the copies? Now we come to our central question. What Christian books were contained in these copies? Did all copies contain the same books? We have no reason to doubt that the Christian writings in these copies of the Bible were precisely those in our present New Testament.

How can we be so confident of this? The answer is clear. We know that until this time the question of which books to include in the New Testament canon had not been finally settled in the church. We also know that after this time, within the Roman Empire where Constantine and his successors had the power to influence developments, uniformity prevailed more and more until the question, at least for the Chalcedonian churches, was virtually settled without further dispute.

The New Testament Lists of Athanasius and Amphilochius

The New Testament canon that prevailed within the Chalcedonian churches can be traced back as far as Athanasius, whose list carries us back to the decades following Eusebius' carrying out of the commission given him by Constantine. That list reads as follows:

Four gospels:

- According to Matthew
- According to Mark
- According to Luke
- According to John

The Acts of the Apostles

- Catholic letters of the apostles (7)
  - James
  - Peter (1, 2)
  - John (1, 2, 3)
  - Jude

Letters of Paul the apostle (14)

- Romans
- Corinthians (1, 2)
- Galatians
- Ephesians
- Philippians
- Colossians
- Thessalonians (1, 2)
- Hebrews
- Timothy (1, 2)
- Titus
- Philemon

The Revelation of John

These are precisely the books that have been universally accepted in the Chalcedonian churches and, except for the place of Hebrews which eventually was put after Philemon and for the reversed order of the catholic letters and the letters of Paul, this is the exact arrangement of these books that eventually prevailed.[145]

The list of Amphilochius of Iconium (died 394) includes the same books listed by Athanasius. But Amphilochius arranged these books in the order that eventually prevailed—Hebrews after Philemon, and the catholic epistles after Paul.[146]

Amphilochius recognized that there was some question about Hebrews and listed it at the end of the Pauline corpus. He, however, rejected the view of those who regarded it as uncanonical. Of the catholic letters, Amphilochius recognized that not all church fathers agreed on the number: some said seven, others accepted only three, that is, one of James, one of Peter, and one of John. Amphilochius knew that some accepted the Revelation of John, but that the majority called it unacceptable. In short, he was obviously working with a list identical to the one that eventually achieved unquestioned acceptance in the vast majority of Chalcedonian churches. But it was a list he knew was still being questioned (as, for example, in the case of the Revelation of John). What other list could Amphilochius have been working with than that set by Eusebius for the copyists who were engaged to carry out Constantine's commission?

Goodspeed observes: "Only gradually in the centuries that followed did it [the Revelation of John] make its way into acceptance as a part of the canon of the Greek church, and to this day Greek Christianity has no readings from the Revelation in its church lessons."[147]

It is clear that the New Testament canon that eventually prevailed in Chalcedonian churches can be traced back to lists that can be dated in the decades following the Constantinian settlement. But what evidence is there that this list of New Testament books was the list Eusebius set rather than some earlier list? The evidence comes from Eusebius himself.

Eusebius's Witness on the Canon

In his *Ecclesiastical History,* Eusebius documented the state of the New Testament canon that prevailed in his own day as follows.

> We must set in the first place, the holy quaternion of the gospels; after which comes the writing of the Acts of the Apostles. After this should be reckoned the Epistles of Paul. Following them should be recognized the Epistle of John, called the first, and likewise, the Epistle of Peter. In addition to these we should list, if it seem appropriate, the Revelation of John, the arguments concerning which we will set forth at a proper time. These writings belong to the Recognized Books.
>
> Of the Disputed Books, which are, nevertheless, known to the majority (and therefore can hardly be said to be "inauthentic"), there is extant, the Epistle of James, as it is called; and that of Jude, and the second Epistle of Peter; and the so-called second and third Epistles of John which may be the work of the evangelist or some other of the same name.
>
> Among the books which are (not only "disputed" but should be counted as clearly) "inauthentic," are the Acts of Paul; the work entitled the Shepherd; the Apocalypse of Peter; and, in addition to them, the Epistle of Barnabas; and the so-called Teachings of the Apostles. And, in addition, as I said, the Revelation of John, if this view prevails. For as I said, some reject it, but others give it a place among the Recognized Books.

Eusebius notes that among the "inauthentic" books some Christians reckoned also the Gospel of the Hebrews. He then continues:

> Now, all these would be included among the Disputed Books; but nevertheless, we have been constrained to list them also, distinguishing between those writings which, according to the tradition of the church, are true, genuine and recognized (that is, the Recog-

nized Books), and those which differ from them in that though they are not canonical—but rather, are disputed—yet are, nevertheless, recognized by most writers in the church. (And this we have done) in order that we might be able to know these "disputed" writings as well as the writings which the heretics put forward in the name of the Apostles, namely gospels like those attributed to Peter, and Thomas, and Matthias, and others as well; or Acts such as those of Andrew and John and the other Apostles. None of these latter books has been deemed worthy of any kind of mention in a writing by a single member of successive generations of churchmen. Moreover, the type of phraseology differs from apostolic style, and the opinion and tendency of their contents is widely dissonant from the true orthodoxy and clearly shows that they are the forgeries of heretics. For this reason, this latter group of writings ought not even to be reckoned among the books that (as designated above) are categorized as (merely) "inauthentic," but rather, should be shunned as altogether wicked and impious.[148]

Later in the same book, Eusebius writes in a summary statement:

We have now described the facts which have come to our knowledge concerning the apostles and their times; (1) the sacred writings which they left us; (2) those books which are disputed yet, nevertheless, are publicly read by many in most churches; (3) and those which are altogether "inauthentic" and foreign to apostolic orthodoxy.

This summary statement clarifies the somewhat ambiguous grouping of books that Eusebius has made. He is clearly thinking in terms of three categories. The first includes books that are accepted in all or most of the churches which he regards as holding the apostolic and orthodox faith. The third clearly is made up of books that are *not* cited in the writings of churchmen who stand in the succession of apostolic orthodoxy. The second category is less homogeneous. The books it includes are publicly read in apostolic and orthodox churches yet, for some reason, are disputed. Among these are certain books that are sometimes grouped with those in the first category. Eusebius will not say that they are altogether "inauthentic." Yet they are unquestionably "disputed," a less pejorative designation. These books include James, Jude, 2 Peter, and 2 and 3 John. As for the Revelation of John, Eusebius is willing to grant that it is not only "disputed," but may be as some claim, "inauthentic." Other "inauthentic" books that are being publicly read in apostolic and orthodox churches include the Acts of Paul, the Shepherd of Hermas, the Apocalypse of Peter, the Epistle of Barnabas, and the Teachings of the Apostles.

Hebrews, interestingly enough, is not specifically mentioned here by Eusebius. We know for a fact, however, that Hebrews was definitely a "disputed" book, widely rejected in the West both before and after Eusebius. Just how unsettled some of these questions were may be gauged from another citation from Goodspeed's discussion:

> In the west, on the other hand, the uncertainty attached not to Revelation, but to Hebrews. We have seen that in the middle of the third century, when Roman Christianity began to use Latin, it still omitted Hebrews from the Letters of Paul, and accepted only three Catholic letters—1 Peter and 1 and 2 John . . . Jerome, the great reviser of the Latin Bible, included it (Hebrews) in his famous Vulgate version undertaken in 382, but repeatedly mentions the Latin suspicion of it: "The custom of the Latins does not accept it." "Among the Romans, to this day, it is not considered Paul's." Augustine at first considers it Paul's, but later calls it anonymous. Yet, he does not question its place in the canon, and acknowledges that the example of the eastern churches has influenced him to accept it. He, in turn, influenced the North African Councils of Hippo (393) and Carthage (397, 419) to include it in their New Testament lists. . . .
>
> The eastern list of seven Catholic letters came even more slowly into general acceptance in the west. . . . Jerome is careful to observe that 2 and 3 John are ascribed not to John the Apostle, but to John the presbyter of Ephesus. But as with Hebrews, his inclusion of them in his Vulgate version outweighed these halting reservations. . . . His revised New Testament of twenty-seven books undertaken at the instance of Pope Damasus, and thus having behind it the prestige of the Roman church, completed the victory of Hebrews and the longer list of Catholic letters in the west.[149]

The order and content of Eusebius's New Testament, including its uncertainties, can be represented as follows:

Four Gospels:

According to Matthew
According to Mark
According to Luke
According to John

The Acts of the Apostles

Letters of Paul (14?)

- Romans
- Corinthians (1, 2)
- Galatians
- Ephesians
- Philippians
- Colossians
- Thessalonians (1, 2)
- Hebrews (?)
- Timothy (1, 2)
- Titus
- Philemon

Catholic letters of the apostles (2 or 7)

- Epistle of Peter 1 (2?)
- Epistle of John 1 (2 and 3?)
- (James?)
- (Jude?)

(Revelation of John?)

The order of these books is important. Paul's letters follow Acts and come before the catholic letters, as in the arrangement of the New Testament canon that finally prevailed. Since Athanasius places the catholic letters before the letters of Paul and since there is strong manuscript support for this arrangement going back to fourth-century Egypt,[150] the reverse arrangement, where the letters of Paul are given pride of place among the letters of the apostles, seems significant. The prominence given to Paul certainly served the theological interests of Eusebius and Constantine. Eusebius accorded to Constantine an authority which supplemented the apostolic authority of bishops and which rested upon direct revelation from God through Jesus Christ. It was an authority which corresponded to that enjoyed by Paul. Eusebius specifically alludes to this "Pauline" precedent for Constantine's unparalleled authority in the church by paraphrasing a pertinent passage in Galatians where Paul claims that his apostolic authority has come directly from God through his Son, Jesus Christ, and was not mediated through any church authorities.[151] If Eusebius instructed copiers to follow this order in carrying out his commission from Constantine, we have a possible explanation why the order of the catholic epistles and

Pauline corpus that eventually prevailed in the Chalcedonian churches was the reverse of that of Athanasius and of very important Egyptian manuscript authority going back to the fourth century.[152]

It is very clear that the uncertainties concerning the content of the New Testament canon which existed in the church when Eusebius wrote continued for some time. It is also clear, however, that with regard to the question of which books to include there was steady movement toward a consensus represented by the post-Constantinian lists of Athanasius and Amphilochius—lists which are virtually identical with those Eusebius regarded as "undisputed" and supplemented by some "disputed" books which Eusebius knew to be "recognized by most writers in the church."

So we repeat our question. Given the unsettled state of the New Testament canon in Eusebius's day and recognizing that by the time of Athanasius a list of New Testament books had been made which (at least as far as content is concerned) eventually became normative, what alternative is there but to conclude that Athanasius's list was very close to the list Eusebius followed in carrying out Constantine's commission?

No doubt Eusebius followed a list which had already developed in the Alexandrian school. It seems likely, however, that he also participated in the further development of that list. It is highly probable that he took pains to consult others, and that he sought to make a list that would include as many of the disputed books as he thought worthy of being canonical (and, for whose inclusion, he was able to find effective support from fellow bishops). Constantine would have expected Eusebius to produce a list on which there would have been as much consensus as possible.[153]

Since the New Testament canon was in dispute, there was no list Eusebius could settle on that would not be subject to criticism from some important part of the church. However, these fifty copies were being prepared for the emperor to be used in newly formed churches in a city that had no tradition of its own. Here was an opportunity to develop a canonical model in the "new Rome." Here was an opportunity to settle what otherwise might go on in endless dispute. Once these copies had passed the emperor's personal inspection, they would go forth with his official approval. In an expanding church-state bureaucracy opening up a vast new empire-wide world of ecclesiastical opportunity, it would only be natural that deviation from this "authorized" list would gradually diminish until eventually rival lists (at least within the Roman Empire) would become obsolete or inoperative.

The chief virtue of this "authorized" list, if indeed Eusebius did set it down to be followed by the copyists concerned, is that it is prudently inclusive. The inclusion in the same list of both Hebrews (accepted in the East), *and* of the Revelation of John (accepted in the West) would have been a compromise solution hopefully acceptable in both parts of the church.

The fact that "new Rome" was to be a meeting place between east and west was sufficient reason to seek an inclusive solution. The decision to include the Revelation of John no doubt pleased Constantine.[154]

In due time this book, which had been largely rejected in the East, gave Byzantium its most glorious and distinctive religious symbol—the "Pantocrator," that arresting and majestic figure of the divine ruler of the whole of creation. Moreover, the Bible, which began with the story of creation, had its fitting end with the vision of the new Jerusalem.[155]

Summary Statement

The birth of Christendom and the closing of the New Testament canon took place within the context of humankind's search for unity and concord. When Alexander the Great prayed "that the peoples of his world might live in harmony and in unity of heart and mind, he proclaimed for the first time the unity and brotherhood of mankind."[156] But until the time of Constantine, that prayer and that proclamation had remained unfilled. "Alexander . . . did undoubtedly afford a model to imperial Rome, and official propaganda even went as far as to allow a miraculous conception (as with Alexander) both to Caesar and Augustus."[157] However, neither the emperor cult nor the imperial legions had been able to unite the *oikoumene* in harmony of heart and mind. Constantine stepped into the breach. Perceiving the folly of persecuting the Christians, he became one of them.

The unity and salvation of the human family was the chief responsibility of all Roman emperors who wielded ecumenical and imperial power in the tradition of Alexander. Though Christians, following Jewish tradition, discounted Alexander, it is clear that if the world has ever known an Alexander *redivivus,* it is Constantine.[158]

The difference between these two great inescapable figures of the past is the Christian religion. Constantine knew, as Alexander did not, a new race of human beings made up of people from all racial, economic, and social groups. They had found social and religious unity and concord through their faith in Christ. This unity and concord was manifest in their love for one another and in their capacity to resist unto death all outside efforts to integrate them into the empire by force.

Constantine's conversion to Christianity may have been genuine.[159] Whether it was or not, it need not have entailed his rejection of Alexander's dream. In fact, Christianity may have provided Constantine with an instrument for unity and concord. The Christian church was a dynamic force before which Roman emperors had to give way. In resisting imperial persecution, the catholic church had demonstrated the near indestructible nature of its spiritual unity. If this unity could be maintained and manifested in the new era when the church had the support of the emperor, perhaps the church could serve to help the emperor in his efforts to unify the broken humanity of his divided empire. Our conjecture is a simple one: Constantine believed that the unity of the church was important for the sake of the unity of the empire and perhaps of the world.[160] The dream that could not be implemented by the sword alone was to come into reality through a gospel for which people were ready to die. For this reason Constantine insisted on unity of creed and practice within the church, and he used his power to banish dissidents to achieve this end. In a moment of frustration and impatience, he wrote some bishops:

> You know me, your fellow-servant, you know the pledge of your salvation which I have in all sincerity made my care, and through which we have not only conquered the armed force of our foes, but have also enclosed their souls alive to demonstrate the true faith of the love of man. But at this success, I rejoiced most of all because it resulted in the renewal of the *oikoumene*. And, indeed, it is a thing to wonder at that so many peoples should be brought to the same mind—peoples which but yesterday were said to be in ignorance of God. And think of what they might have learnt if no shadow of strife had come upon them. Why then, my beloved brothers, tell me, why do I bring a charge against you? We are Christians, and yet we are torn by pitiable disagreements.[161]

Whether Constantine's "charge" was made explicit or not is of little matter. Implicit in his commission (that is, to prepare fifty new copies of the Bible for the expanding churches of his expanding "new Rome") was a charge for Eusebius to make sure that these new copies would foster unity among Christians and reduce to a minimum "pitiable disagreements."

We conjecture, therefore, that Constantine was himself, along with others, concerned to resolve the question of the New Testament canon, and that his commission to Eusebius provided the occasion for a *fait accompli* unparalleled in the history of the canon. There was no compulsion to comply. Nevertheless, as soon as those fifty magnificently adorned copies of the Bible left the emperor's hands, every bishop would have understood the implications of what had happened. Eusebius must have consulted wisely because, as far as is known, the matter never became a cause of conciliar dispute. Objections in the church to Hebrews, James, 2 and 3 John, 2 Peter, and the Revelation of John continued to be voiced. But these objections were increasingly muted until the Reformation.[162] Only during the Counter-Reformation did it happen that a council claiming to be ecumenical undertook to decide and pronounce on the New Testament canon.[163]

According to this way of perceiving the matter, the reason no one knows when or whether the New Testament canon was closed is because of the way the matter was handled. In principle it was closed when Constantine and his associates decided it was important that it should be. In fact, however, it was closed whenever and wherever bishops standing in the tradition of the Constantinian settlement decided that the church had no stake in keeping it open. The reservations of theologians like Augustine and Luther, standing within the Chalcedonian tradition, and the diversity in the scriptural canons of the non-Chalcedonian churches remind us that every bona fide effort to reappraise the question of the closing of the canon can find support in the tradition.

THE CLASSICAL PHASE: THE FORMING OF THE CANON

In opening the discussion of the classical phase of the development of the New Testament canon, it is of the greatest importance that the reader recognize we are moving back in time into the pre-Constantinian period of church history. Such concern for unity as prevailed in the pre-Constantinian church was spiritually, theologically, and ecclesiastically motivated. In this period there was no Christian emperor to use the power of the state to encourage doctrinal or ecclesiastical unity within the ranks of Christians. In fact, the state not infrequently used its power to persecute the church and force individuals and churches to apostacy, which in turn created division among Christians. At the same time such state persecution, especially when it became empire-wide, encouraged churches, which in more peaceful times could afford the luxury of a relatively isolated and provincial existence, to reach out to the wider Christian fellowship which could provide trustworthy intelligence on developments that were taking place elsewhere within the empire. In this way Christians in one place could learn from the experience of persecution of Christians in other places. Thus, they could sometimes anticipate developments, prepare themselves, and effectively stiffen their resistance to the state.

When Christians in North Africa who were facing persecution shared the cup of Christ, they were conscious that fellow Christians in Asia Minor and other parts of the empire were sharing the same cup. In this way all communicants were mystically bound together in Christ. They were united into one body by his blood shed for them and their salvation. This was a unity that prevailed in spite of the state, not because the state willed it. The New Testament that was formed in the classical period was a canon of Scripture which both resulted from and inspired and sustained this unity.

We now turn our attention to the forming of this pre-Constantinian canon, which still unites all Christians. Granting Eusebius's uncertainty about some books, it cannot be denied that the New Testament canon had already reached its essential form before his time. When did that happen? What were the basic causative factors at work at this penultimate stage of canon formation?

To answer these questions, we first need to consider the form and content of that canon which was not in dispute when Eusebius took his survey of scriptural opinion and practice in the great church. This "undisputed canon" consisted of the fourfold Gospel canon; the Acts of the Apostles; the Pauline corpus, including the pastorals; and 1 Peter and 1 John. Harnack and Goodspeed both noticed that the main parts of this canon consisted of two collections of writings organically united by the Acts of the Apostles, that is, a collection of the gospels and a collection of apostolic letters united by Acts.

This New Testament canon first appeared with Irenaeus, who also included two apocalypses—the Revelation of John and the Shepherd of Hermas.[164] Between Irenaeus and Eusebius, however, stands the great biblical scholar Origen. If we seek to trace the origin of the scholarly and ecclesiastical tradition that lay immediately behind the New Testament canon and that was recognized by Eusebius and Athanasius, we are first led back to Alexandria and especially to the most important head of the Christian school founded there, namely, Origen.

The Alexandrian School

Origen's New Testament canon is very close to that adopted by Eusebius and Athanasius. But if we go behind Origen in the Alexandrian school to his predecessor Clement, we find a significantly different situation. Clement knows gospels and Paul's letters as well. He makes little use of the Acts of the Apostles, and his attitude toward Scripture is much less systematic and structural than Origen's. Clement's Christian writings do not provide the prototype for the New Testament of Origen. Between Clement and Origen something has happened that cannot be explained by developments simply internal to the Alexandrian school. To understand what happened between Clement and Origen, we must consider the contribution of Irenaeus.

We shall first, therefore, consider the views of Origen to see the evidence indicating that his scholarship has directly influenced the thinking of Eusebius and Athanasius. Then we shall consider Clement's views on Christian scripture to establish the point that Origen's New Testament did not come simply from that source. In this way, then, we will be in a position to understand and appreciate the important contribution made by Irenaeus to the formation of the New Testament canon.

Origen

It can hardly be an accident that the number of books in Irenaeus's New Testament is very close to, if not exactly, twenty-two. Josephus counts the books of the Hebrew canon as twenty-two. Origen also lists the number of books as twenty-two and notes that this is the number of the letters in the Hebrew alphabet. He then proceeds to distinguish the twenty-two books he regarded as apostolic, that is, written by apostles or disciples of apostles.

Something very important happened in the church that transformed its perception of its scriptures. Gospels and apostolic letters were not simply to be added to an expanded canon received from Judaism. These distinctively Christian writings were to be considered as a coherent whole in relationship to, but distinguishable from, the scriptures of the Jews.

A consideration of the different ways in which the New Testament canon *might* have developed proves that the eventual form that it *did* achieve was not a foregone conclusion. Harnack concluded that there were "seven different starting points of development that could have led to collections of works competing with the growing New Testament." Furthermore, he was able to show that "in part, these developments did not only start, but actually took definite form." Harnack refers to these seven starting points as seven "embryonic collections" and lists them as follows:

1. A collection of late Jewish and Christian prophetic-messianic or prophetic-hortatory books inserted in the Old Testament—thus, an expanded and corrected Old Testament. As examples of books to be thus inserted into the "Christian" version of the scriptures inherited from the synagogue we have the Book of Enoch, Apocalypse of Ezra, and the Assumption of Moses.

2. A collection of late Jewish and Christian prophetic books standing independently side by side with the Old Testament. The Revelation of John, Harnack points out, was meant to stand side by side rather than inside the Old Testament.

3. A simple collection of sayings of the Lord standing side by side with the Old Testament.

4. A written gospel or a collection of several gospels containing the history of the crucified and risen Lord together with his teaching and commands standing side by side with the Old Testament.

5. A gospel (or several) together with a more or less comprehensive collection of inspired Christian works of the most different character and graded prestige, standing side by side with the Old Testament. Harnack notes that:

> The characteristic of this form is that, although the idea of a collection of books of the "New Covenant" in addition to the gospel [the gospels] has at last been realized, yet no clearness prevails as to the principle, according to which further authoritative books are to be added to the gospels. The second half of the collection is still quite formless and is therefore destitute of boundaries, nor is it closed against other works . . . This is the condition of things presupposed by Clement of Alexandria. . . .

6. A systematized "Teaching of the Lord" administered by the "Twelve Apostles," of the character of the "Apostolic Canons, Constitutions, etc.," which also included "Injunctions of the Lord" side by side with the Old Testament and gospel. We find the beginning of such an embryonic collection in the "Didache," that is, "The Teaching of the Lord by the Twelve Apostles."

7. A book of the synthesis or concordance of prophecy and fulfillment in reference to Jesus Christ, the apostles, and the church standing side by side with the Old Testament. Collections of messianic passages from the Old Testament were made by Jews. First attempts toward working out a comprehensive Christian synthesis of messianic prophecies and fulfillment can be seen in those parts of the Epistle of Barnabas and the writings of Justin Martyr and Tertullian that deal with such concordance.[165]

To these seven we should add:

8. A collection of Paul's letters standing independently side by side with the Old Testament. This presumably would have been the situation in some Pauline churches.

9. A collection of Paul's letters together with a gospel and a systematic work showing the contradictions between the scriptures of the Jews and the Christian scriptures. This was the form of Marcion's canon.

All of these nine embryonic Christian canons are written. None of them rules out the importance of an oral tradition, particularly "words of the Lord." This oral tradition would have existed side by side with the Old Testament and any one of these embryonic New Testaments. Only Marcion, who rejected the Old Testament, seems to have had a canon that was independent of such an oral tradition.

Even if one or more of these nine embryonic collections were to be questionable, it would still appear highly probable that in the period before the middle of the second century the New Testament canon was in an archaic state. The womb of Christian scripture was pregnant with alternate possibilities. No one could have said with certainty what particular form the eventual Christian canon would take.

As we consider Origen's New Testament, it becomes clear that a particular form of the New Testament canon has at last emerged. Origen does not set forth a systematic scheme for classifying New Testament books. But he does reject some books outright. He also makes a distinction between books that are unquestionable, such as

Matthew, Mark, Luke, and John, and books that are doubted, such as 2 Peter, 2 and 3 John, and Hebrews.

A very important consideration for Origen is whether a book was written by an apostle. Thus, Peter wrote 1 Peter and possibly 2 Peter. But 2 Peter is doubted. John wrote, in addition to a gospel, the Apocalypse of John and the First Epistle of John. He may also have written 2 and 3 John. But Origen knew that not all churches accepted these letters as coming from the apostle. As for Hebrews, its style was not that of Paul even though its thoughts and teaching were worthy of the apostles. And churches that accepted it as coming from Paul were to be commended. Thus Origen, on balance, came down on the side of regarding Hebrews as apostolic.

The first gospel was written by the apostle Matthew; Mark was written in accordance with the apostle Peter's instructions; Luke wrote the gospel that the apostle Paul praised. He also wrote Acts. Thus, the books which Origen regarded as authoritative were written by apostles or persons closely associated with apostles.[166]

Taking Origen's explicit statements about the authenticity of New Testament books together with his practice of citing them as Scripture, we can reconstruct the *content* of Origen's apostolic and (except for Hebrews) undisputed canon as follows:

Four gospels:

- According to Matthew
- According to Mark
- According to Luke
- According to John

The Acts of the Apostles

Letters of Paul the apostle (13)

- Romans
- Corinthians (1, 2)
- Galatians
- Philippians
- Ephesians
- Colossians
- Thessalonians (1, 2)
- Timothy (1, 2)
- Titus
- Philemon
- (Hebrews?)

Catholic letters of the apostles

Peter (1)
John (1)

The Revelation of John

Origen *does not arrange any of these books in sequence* except the four gospels. Even so, the close affinity of Origen's views with those embodied in the lists of Eusebius and Athanasius is obvious.

Origen's New Testament canon seems to include twenty-two books. This presumably reflects an interest in correlating an equal number of the most important Christian scriptures with the twenty-two books of the Hebrew canon. It also appears to be a quite conscious act of canon making.

These twenty-one undisputed books (Hebrews making the total of twenty-two), however, do not really exhaust Origen's list of Christian writings that could possibly qualify as apostolic. Origen regarded the Epistle of Barnabas as apostolic and also, possibly, the Shepherd of Hermas and the First Epistle of Clement. He clearly thought it possible that 2 Peter and 2 and 3 John were apostolic.[167] However, each of these books was disputed in one or more places.

Origen explicitly rejected the Gospel of Thomas, the Gospel of Mathias, the Gospel of the Twelve, and the Gospel of the Egyptians. He did not explicitly reject the Gospel of the Hebrews. He doubted the Preaching of Peter. In some cases, Origen seems to have changed his mind. At first he tended to accept the Acts of Paul, but later he rejected it. There is some evidence that he changed his attitude toward the Didache, the Shepherd of Hermas, and the Epistle of Barnabas after he left Alexandria and moved to Caesarea.[168]

Clement of Alexandria

When we move back to Origen's teacher, Clement of Alexandria, there is much less evidence of systematic reflection on the question of canon. Clement appears to make use of most of the New Testament books later accepted as indisputably apostolic by Origen. However, he knows others that he does not distinguish from these: James, Jude, and 2 John. Clement accepts as Scripture the First Epistle of Clement, the Epistle of Barnabas, the Revelation of Peter, and the Shepherd of Hermas. He also cites the Preaching of Peter as coming from the apostle Peter. Clement once quotes the Didache as Scripture.[169]

What distinguishes Clement from Origen is not so much the Christian literature each recognizes as Scripture, but the lengths to which Origen was willing to go in recognizing within this relatively undifferentiated body of Christian writings a particular category of "undisputed" books.

The Influence of Irenaeus

The New Testament of Irenaeus probably included twenty-two books.[170] Irenaeus gives these books (except for the gospels) no particular arrangement. For ease of comparison, they may be listed as follows:

Four gospels:

- According to Matthew
- According to Mark
- According to Luke
- According to John

The Acts of the Apostles

Letters of Paul the apostle (13)

- Romans
- Corinthians (1, 2)
- Galatians
- Ephesians
- Philippians
- Colossians
- Thessalonians (1, 2)
- Timothy (1, 2)
- Titus
- (Philemon?)[171]

Catholic letters of the apostles

- Peter (1)
- John (1) (2?)

Revelations of the apostles (2)

- John
- Hermas (?)[172]

Origen's understanding of the New Testament canon appears to bridge that of Irenaeus and that of Clement. Origen knows the larger corpus known to Clement. Within this larger corpus he knows an undisputed group of writings. Origen's undisputed category of New Testament books is almost identical with the New Testament canon recognized by Irenaeus.

Summary Conclusions

Two conclusions may be drawn from our survey thus far. First, we have been able to trace the prevailing New Testament canon at least as far back as Origen. Origen's views appear to represent a coalescence of two earlier traditions—those represented by his teacher Clement and those represented by Irenaeus. Origen began the particular mediating tradition within which Eusebius and those of his school lived and moved and had their being.[173] The second conclusion that we can draw is that Origen's chief model for his New Testament canon appears to have been the New Testament of Irenaeus rather than that of his teacher Clement.

Irenaeus and the Church of Gaul

Heresy and Persecution

In order to set the stage for understanding the formative influence of Irenaeus, it will be helpful first to consider two documents preserved by Eusebius in his *Ecclesiastical History*.

The Factor of Heresy

Serapion, who became bishop in Antioch in A.D. 191 and died in A.D. 210, composed a book that was ostensibly addressed to the church at Rhossus, about thirty miles from Antioch. But this book could have been used by anyone who needed to be warned about the "heretical" Gospel of Peter.

> For our part, brethren, we receive both Peter and the other apostles as Christ, but the writings which falsely bear their names, we reject, as men of experience, knowing that such were not handed down to us. For I myself, when I came among you, imagined that all of you clung to the true faith; and, without going through the gospel put forward by them in the name of Peter, I said; If this is the only thing that seemingly causes captious feelings among you, let it be read. But since, from what has been told me, I have now learnt that their mind was lurking in some hole of heresy, I shall

> be diligent to come again to you; wherefore, breathren, expect me quickly. . . . We were enabled to go through it and discover that most of it was in accordance with the true teaching of the Saviour. But that some things were added. . . . [174]

This letter is important for showing how decisions regarding authoritative gospels were made. In the church there was an awareness of the "true teaching of the Saviour" as well as of the "true faith." Apparently, Bishop Serapion was aided in making his "discoveries" about the Gospel of Peter by comparing it with older gospels which had been "handed down" in the church. When the Gospel of Peter was first written, it was permitted to be read in the church because, for the most part, it conformed to the true faith. But as time went on, those who wrote the Gospel of Peter were succeeded by others who built on the docetic character of this gospel and began to lead some of the faithful astray. Since these "false" teachers were able to justify their "docetic" views by appeal to the text of a gospel which the good bishop had at first approved for being read, it was necessary for him to refute the false teaching in this gospel and to explain the circumstances under which he once had unwittingly given it his approval.

The point to note is that *canon presupposes heresy*. At first there was no operational distinction that dictated the use of some gospels and the rejection of others. Then came individuals and groups that used one or more of these gospels to turn aside the faithful into heterodox teachings. To combat these "heretics," it was necessary to discredit the apostolic authority of the scriptures that justified their teaching. The concomitant effect of refuting the books of the "heretics" was to accord a special "canonical" status to those books that were accepted as "apostolic." Books which earlier had been perceived as scriptures that were permitted to be read in the churches were now perceived as books that had the added function of serving as a written canon or measure of the rule of faith. Before, they had been read in church because they were in line with the true faith. Now they were read in church for an additional reason: they were "apostolic." They did not, like the rejected gospels, falsely bear the names of apostles. They were in accord with the true teaching of the Savior, as the Gospel of Peter was not. As written expressions of that true teaching they could be read in church when other gospels could not. They were now quite distinctive.

They stood out from all the rejected gospels. If one of them could not be said to have been written by an apostle, it could at least be associated with a disciple of an apostle. Gospels that had been handed down in the church, were to be kept together and read and studied together. In this way, the faithful would be mentally prepared to defend the true faith against all the dangerous new interpretations based on gospels that had not been handed down from the earlier period.

We can now understand clearly the way in which "heresy" was a formative factor in the shaping of the New Testament. There was no single "heresy" that contributed to the forming of the New Testament. Nor was there a single gathering of the bishops of the churches to decide which books to accept and which to reject. There was, rather, a generation of practical-minded bishops like Serapion of Antioch. These were bishops who were disposed to be inclusive in their approach to ecclesiastical problems, but who had both the courage to change their minds in the face of new evidence and the scholarly resources to back up their theological and administrative decisions. The greatest of these Christian theologians was Irenaeus, bishop of Lyons.

Before we proceed to consider the formative contribution of Irenaeus, it will be helpful to consider a second document from this same period. For this document makes clear that, in addition to "heresy," there was another formative factor at work, namely imperial persecution of Christians.

The Factor of Persecution

Christians had suffered persecution at the hands of state officials at different times and at different places in the Roman Empire long before Irenaeus.[175] About A.D. 178 under Emperor Antoninus Verus, however, persecution against Christians broke out anew in different parts of the world. We are able to form a vivid mental picture of the effect of this persecution on Christians in the Province of Gaul, where Irenaeus was a presbyter, from a treatise preserved by Eusebius at the beginning of Book V of his *Ecclesiastical History*. This is a most remarkable document and of the greatest importance in illuminating the historical processes that contributed to the formation of the New Testament canon.

After some introductory comments, Eusebius justifies his inclusion of this document with the following observation:

> Other writers of historical works have confined themselves to giving accounts of victories won in wars, and conquests of enemies, of the exploits of generals and brave deeds of soldiers, men stained with the blood of countless numbers of those they killed for the sake of children and fatherland and other possessions; but our history of those who order their lives according to God will inscribe on everlasting monuments the record of most peaceful wars waged for the very peace of the soul, and of those who in such wars have been valiant for truth, rather than for fatherland, and for religion rather than for the dearest members of their families; our history will proclaim for everlasting remembrance the struggles of the champions of religion and their deeds of bravery and endurance, conquests of demons and victories over unseen adversaries, and crowns gained when all was accomplished.[176]

According to this perception, the Christians were engaged in a peaceful war and were contending valiantly for truth. In this war the Christian martyrs were champions of God. Their deeds of bravery and endurance brought victory over devils and invisible adversaries. It was the bravery and endurance of these Christian martyrs that eventually brought the Roman Empire to its knees and that taught the Roman emperors both the folly of persecuting Christians and the value to the state of according divine honors to the God who sustained this new race in the face of all adversity. As we follow the text of the letter cited by Eusebius, we are looking especially for what we can learn about the import of New Testament scriptures for this peaceful war against devils and invisible adversaries. What role did Christian scripture play in bringing the Roman imperial authority to bay? How was the struggle of Christian martyrs related to the ideals of the *oikoumene*—the need for concord and the unity of all races?

Eusebius continues:

> Gaul was the country in which was prepared the stage for these events. Its capital cities . . . were Lyons and Vienne, through both of which passes the Rhone river, flowing in an ample stream through the entire country. Now, the most illustrious of the churches of this country circulated an account of their martyrs among the churches of Asia and Phrygia. . . . I will quote their words: "The servants of Christ sojourning in Vienne and Lyons in Gaul to the brethren in Asia and Phrygia, who have the same faith and hope of redemption as you. Peace and grace and glory from God, the Father and Christ Jesus, our Lord."

> Then, after other prefatory remarks, they begin their account in the following way: "The greatness of the persecution here, and the terrible rage of the heathen against the saints, and all that the blessed martyrs endured is beyond the power of pen to narrate accurately. For, with all his might the adversary attacked us, giving us a foretaste of his coming which is shortly to be. He tried everything, training and exercising his adherents to act against the servants of God, to the end that we were not merely excluded from houses and baths and market place, but they even forbade any of us to be seen at all in any place whatsoever. But, against them, the grace of God did act as our captain; rescued the weak, and set up over against the foe steadfast pillars able by their endurance to draw upon themselves the whole attack of the evil one."

According to 1 Tim. 3:15, the church is the pillar and bulwark of truth. In Gal. 2:9, the apostles Peter, James, and John (martyrs all) are referred to as pillars of the church. In this letter, the imagery of the warrior hero who drew all the spears of the enemy line into his own body—making himself a living sacrifice so that victory could be achieved by those who rushed through the resulting gap in the opposing line—has been combined with scriptural imagery to forge a powerful new image of the Christian martyr. The Christian martyr is, indeed, the champion of truth. Through the sacrifices of Christian martyrs, victory will come only if they can endure the attack of the evil one. They must expect the most demonic form of torture and destruction to fall upon them. These dedicated men and women will join together to forge an invincible defense of peace, concord, and love. They will acknowledge no race and answer to no name but "Christian." The letter continues:

> These indomitable pillars closed ranks, enduring every kind of reproach and punishment; yea, regarding their many trials as virtually nothing, they hastened to Christ and did, indeed, prove *that the sufferings of this present time are not worthy to be compared with the glory which shall be revealed to us.*

This citation from the apostle Paul's letter to the Romans (8:18), though not identified as such, would not have gone unnoticed in Asia and Phrygia. Paul's letters had long since been collected and were circulating throughout the church. These were the words of one who had suffered imprisonments and countless beatings, and was often near death. He had been stoned, shipwrecked, placed in all kinds of danger, spent many a sleepless night in hunger and thirst, in cold and exposure (2 Cor. 11:23–27). He was a man in

Christ. Paul exhorted others to be imitators of him as he was of Christ. Like his crucified Savior, Paul had died a martyr at the hands of the Roman authorities. This affords a glimpse of something very important. *The New Testament* (where the Gospels of Christ are united with the letters of Paul by the Acts of the Apostles) *is the book of the covenant of Christ* to all who stand in the martyrological tradition of Jesus and the apostles—above all, the apostles Peter and Paul who had made their final witness and had received their crown of martyrdom in the very seat of authority of the "evil one."

Irenaeus and the Martyrs of Gaul

Later, some of the surviving Christian martyrs in Gaul gave Irenaeus a letter of commendation and addressed it to the bishop of Rome:

> Once more and always, Father Eleuthesus, we greet you prayerfully in God. We have asked our brother and comrade Irenaeus, to bring this letter to you and we beseech you to hold him in esteem, for he is a zealot for the covenant of Christ. . . . [177]

More than any other, Irenaeus is said to have been responsible for the shaping of the New Testament. As we shall see, he did not speak and write only for himself. After the martyrdom of his bishop, he was made bishop of Lyons. He went as a presbyter to Rome with the backing of the martyrs of Gaul. He returned to Gaul to become a spokesman for the whole church. But Irenaeus never forgot who he was. Irenaeus was the martyr's bishop. And his New Testament embraced the scriptures of the martyrs. The gospels reminded all Christians of the martyrdom of Jesus. The epistles reminded them of the martyrdom of the apostles. Acts reminded them of the martyrdom of Stephen. The Revelation of John reminded them of the martyrdom of the saints. Virtually the whole of what Irenaeus championed as New Testament scripture reminded the church of the central role of martyrdom in the life of God's people.

Persecution and Heresy Interrelated

Gospels without the passion of Jesus Christ (like the infancy gospels or the Gospel of Thomas) were of little interest to Christian martyrs. Moreover, docetic gospels which suggested that Jesus Christ had not really suffered on the cross or had not suffered the death of crucifixion (like the Gospel of Peter) had to be repudiated as subversive among the ranks of those engaged in the "peaceful" life and death struggle with the "evil one."

In this way the factor of "heresy" was joined with the factor of persecution. The two are not to be thought of as entirely separate. In the processes forming the New Testament, these two factors were intimately interrelated. It is no accident that the greatest tract against "heresy" that the church has ever known was written by the bishop of Lyons, brother and comrade of the martyrs of Gaul.

The Martyrs of Gaul

During the persecution in Gaul, Christians had been accused of the most inflammatory deeds: eating their children and practicing incest. As such rumors spread, the whole populace was infuriated at them. Even those who had hitherto behaved with moderation on the grounds of kinship now turned against their own friends and relatives who had become Christians, and cooperated with their persecutors. We resume the account in the letter from the martyrs of Gaul at this point:

> The entire fury of the mob and of the governor and of the soldiers was raised beyond measure against Sanctus, the deacon from Vienne . . . and against Blandina (a slave), through whom Christ showed that things which are mean and obscure and contemptible in the eyes of men are accounted worthy of great glory with God because of the love towards him, a love which showed itself in power and did not boast of itself in appearance.

Blandina's mistress was a Christian woman who was herself facing martyrdom. She and all those around her were faltering out of fear that they would not be able to make confession because of weakness. Yet Blandina

> was filled with such power that she was released and rescued from those who took turns in torturing her in every way from morning until evening, and they themselves admitted that they were beaten, for they marveled that she still remained alive, since her whole body was mangled and filled with gaping wounds, and they testified that any one of these tortures was sufficient to destroy life, even when these tortures had not been multiplied and intensified. But the blessed woman, like a noble champion, kept gaining in vigor in her confession, and found comfort and refreshment and freedom from pain from what was done to her by repeating: "I am a Christian woman and no foul thing happens amongst us."

Sanctus also endured with noble and surpassing courage all the torture that could be inflicted upon him:

> For, though the wicked hoped through persistence and the rigor of his tortures to wring from him some admission of wrong doing, he resisted them with such firmness that he would not even state his own name, or the race or the city whence he came, nor whether he was slave or free. To all questions, he answered in Latin, "I am a Christian." This he repeated for name and city and race and for everything else, and no other word did the heathen hear from him.

What eloquent testimony to the fact that Christian faith had the power to give people a new identity. They were no longer Romans, Phrygians, or Jews. By race they were Christians, members of a new covenant. Each person was a new creation with a new superhuman and almost divine capacity to withstand the demonic wiles of the "evil one." This may have been a surprising answer to the quest for unity and concord pioneered by Alexander the Great. But it was without doubt a powerful witness to the fact that in Christ there was neither Jew nor gentile, neither slave nor free. And to the extent that both slave and free women and men made these confessions, it pointed to the fact that to be a Christian was to be a member of a race of people in which spiritual unity included being "neither slave nor free . . . neither male nor female; for (we) are all one in Christ Jesus" (Gal. 3:28). As the letter continues, it is related that the authorities even went so far as to suspend the gladiatorial contests, substituting the spectacle of hanging Blandina on a stake and offering her as a prey to the wild beasts that were let in:

> She seemed to be hanging in the shape of a cross, and by her continuous prayer, she greatly encouraged those around her who were contending. For, in their torment, they beheld with their outward eyes in the form of their sister, him who was crucified for them. The effect was to persuade those who believe on him that all who suffer for the glory of Christ have eternal fellowship with the living God. And as none of the wild beasts then touched her, she was taken down from the stake and cast again into prison. . . .

Here again there is every reason to think that the gospels, with the dramatic foreshadowing of the death of Christ and the events of passion week followed by the resurrection stories, and Paul's letters, with their emphasis upon the cross of Christ, must have had a formative influence upon the minds of those who would record an event like this in such terms if not, indeed, upon the minds of those who actually withstood such tortures.

The effect of this faithfulness was to move many who had at first given in to their persecutors to change their minds and decide that they too wanted to join their brothers and sisters in making their confession. The governor accordingly examined these persons again, sending all who confessed their faith as Christians to their death.

After copying out a great deal more of the letter, Eusebius pauses to comment:

> Such things happened to the churches of Christ under the emperor mentioned, and from these things, it is possible to form a reasonable conclusion as to what was done in other provinces. It is worthwhile to add other statements from the same document, in which the gentleness and the kindness of the martyrs already mentioned, have been set down in these very words: "And they carried so far their zeal and imitation of Christ . . . that for all their glory, and though they had testified not once or twice, but many times, and had been taken back from the beasts and were covered with burns and scars and wounds, they neither proclaimed themselves as martyrs, nor allowed us to address them by this title; nay, they severely rebuked any one of us who so styled them in letter or conversation. For, they gladly conceded the title of martyr to Christ, the faithful and true martyr. . . . They conceded that those who had given their lives in faithful witness were martyrs, but that those who did not actually depart this life are not—they are only 'confessors.' "

Eusebius writes that a little farther on in the letter it is said:

> They humbled themselves under the mighty hand, by which they are now greatly exalted. At that time, they made defense for all men, against none did they bring accusation; they released all and bound none; and they prayed for those who had inflicted torture, even as did Stephen, the perfect martyr; *Lord, lay not this sin to their charge.* And if Stephen prayed thus for those who were stoning him, how much more (should we pray) for the brethren (who have lapsed.)[178]

This is the earliest clear example of the influence of the Book of Acts in the life of the church. The example of Stephen as the perfect martyr taken together with the imprisonments of the apostles and other hardships inflicted on the first Christians recounted in Acts and such sayings as "we must obey God rather than men" (Acts 5:29) must have turned the Book of Acts into a scripture of special interest and importance to churches under persecution.

Eusebius skips over other parts of the letter and then picks up the narrative again:

> For their greatest contest with the beast (that is, the "evil one"), through the genuineness of their love, was this; that the beast should be choked into throwing up alive those whom he had at first thought to have swallowed down (that is, they sought the redemption of their Christian brothers and sisters who had denied the faith). For they did not boast over the fallen, but from their own abundance supplied with a mother's love those that needed. And, shedding many tears for them to the Father, they prayed for life, and he gave it to them, and they divided it among their neighbors, and then departed to God, having in all things carried off the victory. They ever loved peace; peace they commended to us; and with peace they departed to God; for their mother (the church) they left behind no sorrow, and for the brethren no strife and war, but rather glory, peace, concord and love.[179]

To emphasize the forgiving attitude of these martyrs toward those who had lapsed in contrast to the recalcitrant attitude of some of his own contemporaries like the Donatists and Novatians, Eusebius adds:

> This record of the affection of those blessed ones for the brethren who had fallen, may profitably be set forth, in view of the inhuman and merciless temper displayed by those who afterwards behaved so harshly towards members of Christ.[180]

A Martyr's Canon of Scripture

The apocalyptic imagery of the "beast" of Revelation is obvious. But this scripture is not by itself a norm for the martyrs of Gaul. In the background, in addition to the conciliatory words of "the perfect martyr" Stephen, there are the norming words of the martyred apostle Paul: "If I deliver my body to be burned, but have not love, I gain nothing" (1 Cor. 13:3). Above all, there looms the magisterial norm of the apostolic gospel with the example of "the faithful and true martyr" who was remembered to have prayed: *Father, forgive them; for they know not what they do.* In addition, the true martyr taught his disciples to seek out the lost and to forgive those who had sinned against them: *not . . . seven times, but seventy times seven* (Matt. 18:22).

We see emerging not simply a martyr's canon of Christian scripture, but a *particular* martyr's canon.[181] This canon featured the Revelation of John, the Acts of the Apostles, the Epistles of Paul—all normed by the fourfold apostolic Gospel. The martyrs who lived by this norm would not only risk their lives for the sake of Christ and his gospel, they would refuse to condemn those who did not become martyrs with them and would, in all matters, strive to achieve concord and peace as they sought to reunite the family of God.

By this divine path, the human family had opened up to it one possible way it might find the elusive "concord" and "unity" for which, since Alexander the Great, so many had longed. With this divinely constituted community—a community formed by the Spirit of Jesus; a community rich in faith; a community that produced a host of Christian saints, confessors, and martyrs—we are in touch with the same Spirit that breathes through the New Testament as a whole.

There is a remarkable kinship between the text of the letter from the martyrs of Gaul and the New Testament. No fewer than seventy-three citations or allusions to the books of the New Testament have been noted in this letter in the Lawlor-Oulton edition of Eusebius's *Ecclesiastical History*. There are seventeen citations or allusions noted for the gospels; twelve for the Acts of the Apostles; thirty for the Pauline epistles, including the pastorals; two for 1 John; three for 1 Peter; four for 2 Peter; and five for Revelation. The remaining identifiable scriptural citations or allusions are: two for Ignatius; three for the Psalms, two for Isaiah; one for Ezekiel; one for 2 Maccabees; and two for Daniel.

It is striking that the only New Testament books neither cited nor alluded to in this remarkable document are James, Jude, 2 and 3 John, Titus, and Philemon. Except for Titus and Philemon, which would be included in the Pauline corpus, the books either not alluded to or not cited in this document are also not included in the twenty-two book New Testament canon of Irenaeus, or in the twenty-two book "undisputed" category of New Testament writings of Origen.

To state the matter positively, the New Testament books which are not in dispute in the church after Irenaeus are almost without exception books which had special meaning for certain known churches that had experienced persecution.[182] Furthermore, the very close relationship between the New Testament books cited or alluded to in this document (coming from the Rhone Valley) and the New Testament scriptures acknowledged by Irenaeus (bishop of the church in the Rhone Valley), strengthens our contention that the New Testament canon of Irenaeus has been profoundly influenced by the factor of persecution and martyrdom. Irenaeus makes no mention of 2 Peter, whereas it may be alluded to four times in this document. This document does not allude to the Shepherd of Hermas, which Irenaeus cited as Scripture. With these exceptions, the correspondence between the New Testament books alluded to in this letter and the canon of Irenaeus is truly striking.

One could and should note, of course, that all New Testament books cited and alluded to in this document existed long before the persecution that broke out in A.D. 178. So we have not necessarily answered the question, Whence came the New Testament? by identifying and clarifying the importance of Christian martyrdom. We have only put our finger on an important reason why this set of Christian writings, rather than some other, emerged as the canon of the church. This reason is persecution. It is only one reason, but a major one.

The New Testament of the church serves the needs of Christians under persecution in a most adequate and inspiring manner. It does not encourage blind fanaticism, nor does it sustain self-righteousness. It has the power, however, to nourish and guide not only Christian saints, but Christian confessors and martyrs as well. For churches that have experienced persecution, these scriptures would be known as sacrosanct books—books of God, books that make the difference between life and death. These are books that churches will cherish and hand down with love and affection. They will be holy books, consecrated by the blood of martyrs.

Some Ecclesiastical Consequences of Martyrdom

Following his extensive quotations from this letter to the Christians in Asia and Phrygia, Eusebius records further information about the activities of the martyrs from Gaul.

> Just at that time, the party of Montanus and Alcibiades and Theodotus, in the region of Phrygia, were winning a widespread reputation for prophecy (for the many other wonderful works of the

> grace of God which were still being wrought, up to that time in various churches, caused a widespread belief that they also were prophets). And when dissention arose, about Montanus and the others, the brethren in Gaul again formulated their own judgment, pious and most orthodox, concerning them, subjoining various letters from the martyrs who had been consecrated among them, which letters they had composed, while they were still in prison, for the brethren in Asia and Phrygia, and also for Eleutherus, who was their bishop of the Romans, negotiating for the sake of the peace of the churches.[183]

It is clear that during the persecution the church in Gaul had been an underground church. Christians in prison for the sake of the gospel, like the apostle Paul before them and countless Christian prisoners since, redeemed the time by writing letters. Some of these letters were to be carried great distances, even greater distances than any known letter that Paul had sent. It is clear that the authorities in Gaul had imprisoned not simply some zealous Christians who were eager to win the crown of martyrdom, but leaders of the church who had a vision of its organic and visible unity. Other Christians needed to be informed about what was happening to the church of God in the Rhone Valley. No doubt the Christians in that remote province needed outside contacts with Christians in other parts of the empire. Thus, we may be confident that there grew up an informational and inspirational network of correspondence and oral communication between Christians who identified with one another and who provided mutual support whenever persecution broke out.

The weak links in the chain of mutually supporting churches that united Christians within the empire would have been the churches under Gnostic influence. These churches tended to question the value of martyrdom.[184] In addition, these churches found in the Christian scriptures, especially the letters of Paul, grounds for a quite different spirituality—one that did not move Christians into positions of opposition to the state, thus not posing the same need for mutual support from Christians in other parts of the empire or for disciplined episcopal leadership and interregional consultation.[185] Outstanding men like Valentinus might journey to Rome. But their goal was to propagate their new doctrine in the capital of the empire, not to consult with the bishop of Rome to find that common ground on which all Christians could unite in their defense of the faith against an opposition from the state that threatened the extinction of apostolic Christian belief and practice.

In the hands of Irenaeus, a bishop of a uniting Christian church, the catholic tendencies of the apostles came to fruition. The goal of the catholic revolution had been agreed upon in principle. It was to establish the apostolic tradition handed down through Peter, Paul, Ignatius, Polycarp, and the bishops in apostolic succession in the great Christian centers of the Roman Empire. Irenaeus, with grass roots support from the churches in Gaul (providing him with a solid power base of zealous evangelical piety), faced the greatest theological challenge the church had known since the days of the apostle Paul. However, Irenaeus was in no sense limited to a provincial outlook. He had come to Gaul as a missionary from Asia Minor, where he had been a student of the venerable Christian martyr Polycarp.

The persecution experienced by the church in Gaul was shared by other churches in other parts of the empire. Irenaeus knew all about this and understood very well what was at stake. The blood of the martyrs, beginning with Jesus, was the seed of the church. This church was now threatened by a seemingly uncontrolled plethora of theological and exegetical speculation, which sapped the strength of the church in its resistance against the wiles of the "evil one." Therefore, to do battle against this immediate and long-term threat, Irenaeus undertook his *magnum opus.*

One hundred years later, during the great empire-wide persecutions of A.D. 303–312, the church in the province of Gaul (where Constantine's father governed) was spared. In order to appreciate what was at stake in what Irenaeus was about to undertake, we will reflect on this "Great Persecution of 303–312" through the eyes of a modern historian.

> One final trial awaited the Christians. . . . For nineteen years Diocletian had been emperor and the Christians had been left in peace. . . . high positions in the emperor's court were occupied by them, and his own family seems to have favored them. . . . Successively the army, provincial administration and currency were overhauled, and new life was put into the cities of the empire. This involved the rebuilding of temples and the revival of pagan cults. Indeed, the whole spirit of the Diocletianic reform was religious-conservative, harking back to the traditional virtues of Rome. The inscription on the obverse of the new, "people's" coinage read, "To

> the Genius of the Roman People." The empire was placed under the patronage of the Roman gods, Jupiter and Hercules.
>
> Conservative religious values and a desire to secure a minimum of conformity from the "whole race of the Romans" were clearly among the reasons that led Diocletian and his colleagues to try conclusions with the Christians. The fear of foreign-inspired religious innovations sapping the "immemorial customs" was real enough and was shown by Diocletian's rescript to Julian, proconsul of Carthage, proscribing the Manichees for doing this very thing. It laid down a whole series of penalties for those found guilty of belonging to the sect and ordered their books to be handed over and burnt.
>
> Six years later, it was to be the Christians' turn. . . . between 298–302, a series of incidents in the army of Syria and North Africa sowed fears in Diocletian's mind that the Christians might not be reliable. He ordered his commander-in-chief, Veturius, to purge the army of them. . . .[186]

It is only to be expected that Christians serving in the armed forces of a Roman emperor bent on these reactionary policies might have begun to have second thoughts about where their ultimate loyalties lay. "The genius of the Roman people," the "patronage of the Roman gods," and the "whole race of the Romans" were concepts that certainly represented a dangerous relapse of great magnitude when considered from the point of view of every community within the empire which had a vision of the future that transcended the interests of any one race or culture or temporal order.

> On 23 February 303, there was posted an edict in Nicomedia ordering all copies of the scriptures to be surrendered and burnt, all churches to be dismantled, and no meetings for Christian worship to be held. Next day, a supplementary edict deprived Christians of all honors and dignities, making them all liable to torture and debarring them from being plaintiffs in any legal action. . . .

The news of this persecution of Christians was received badly in some of the eastern provinces.

> Revolts were reported in Syria and Melitene, the provinces on the headwaters of the Tigris. Both were sensitive areas in the Roman defense against Persia. Fires broke out in the emperor's palace, and, as a reprisal, a second edict went out ordering the arrest of all bishops and clergy. . . . In November, he (Diocletian) issued a third edict ordering that the clergy should be constrained to sacri-

fice and then be freed. No effort was spared to compel them to do so. Indeed, all over the empire, magistrates took delight in the recantation of Christians. This was becoming a matter of life and death for the empire. . . .

Withholding the Scriptures

Frend continues:

In Africa . . . measures were far more thorough. It was in the last fortnight in May that the first edict arrived in both pro-consular Africa (roughly, modern Tunisia) and Numidia (roughly, east and central Algeria). It was acted upon by the city magistrates without any hesitation. The fact that the Christian bishop may have been a well known figure did not save him from a summons to surrender the scriptures. At Cirta, the capital of Numidia, the immediate reaction of the Christians was either flight to the hills south of the town or apostasy. The curator (mayor) came to the "house where the Christians used to meet," and the following scene took place.

The Mayor to Paul, the Bishop: Bring out the writings of the law and anything else that you have here, according to the order, so that you may obey the command.

The Bishop: The readers have the scriptures, but we will give you what we have here.

The Mayor: Point out the readers or send for them.

The Bishop: You all know them.

The Mayor: We do not know them.

The Bishop: The municipal office knows them, that is, the clerks Edusius and Junius.

The Mayor: Leaving over the matter of the readers, whom the office will point out, produce what you have.

We can feel the tension mount as Frend, using primary source material, reconstructs the scene before our very eyes.

The Mayor then continues his examination in order to receive the copies of the scriptures. Successively, the sub-deacons and readers were questioned. There was a certain amount of argument and prevarication, as each tried to shield the other, but, in the end, the Mayor got his way. The copies of the scripture were quietly given up. . . . [187]

What can we learn from this? We can learn that by the end of the third century withholding or giving up the Scriptures was recognized on both sides as the nub of the matter, and that the bishop himself was not to have custody of the Scriptures. Moreover, we can see that to name those who had the Scriptures in their custody was to be avoided, if at all possible. Not to give in, in the last analysis, would mean incarceration. And, in that case, bishops and clergy could expect to be released only after they had offered sacrifice to the emperor. Such sacrifice was only the final apostasy. The withholding of the Scriptures was the first line of defense. To give them up became a form of apostasy. To withhold them was to make confession. Some did. Some did not. Those who did not withhold but surrendered the Scriptures were betrayers of the faith.

In this way, to withhold the Scriptures from persecuting authorities became a matter of life and death. The community recognized the significance of the act of withholding the Scriptures under these circumstances. Therefore, the question of which books were worth going to prison for would have been a pressing one for every local church. Since bishops were recognized by the magistrate as spokespersons for the Christians, this was a matter on which, at least on a regional basis, they could have taken counsel. But often it would have come down to a local decision to be enforced by a bishop and the clergy of a particular city or metropolitan area. Thus, a decisive test would have been the witness of the Spirit within churches in particular places and at particular times of local crises. Above all, it would have involved the witness of the spirit to those members of the church who were chosen to speak and act for the church vis-à-vis the authorities, when the moment of truth arrived. These would be the bishops, priests, deacons, subdeacons, readers, and the families of these persons whose lives were being placed on the line by the decisions being reached as each church asked the question in turn, Can this book be withheld? This meant, Is this book worth dying for? Books that were regarded as "not worth dying for" after such a process of community decision making naturally assumed a different status. They might still be regarded as edifying to read. But the process of deciding that a particular scripture need not be withheld would have marked it as one that had not inspired a defense of its sacred character. Certainly docetic scriptures, which left in doubt the "human element in the Saviour and his suffering, death and resurrection,"[188] under these circumstances would have failed to inspire the verdict: "To be withheld."

Summary Conclusions

In analyzing the effect of state persecution upon Christians, we have been able to identify a decisive element in the process of the formation of the New Testament canon that fully justifies the tradition that the church was guided by the Spirit in the choice of books for the New Testament canon. What but a Spirit-filled and Spirit-guided church could decide that a particular codex or scroll was worth the life of a single member? That such a codex or scroll was a copy of something that was or was not written by an apostle could not, by itself, have been sufficient reason to render the judgment: "It should be withheld." Otherwise, the New Testament should include a representative number of books bearing the names of apostles who were not martyrs.[189] Except for Jude, however, all of the books in the New Testament either bear witness to the example and teaching of the primal martyr, Jesus (Matthew, Mark, Luke, and John), or they bear the names of apostles who were themselves martyrs (Peter, James, John, and Paul), or they feature the careers of apostles who became martyrs (Peter and Paul in the Acts of the Apostles). That the reality of Christian martyrdom in the early church and the selection of Christian writings for the New Testament canon stand in some vital relationship to one another is as certain as anything that can be conjectured on this complex historical question. Irenaeus was commended to the bishop of Rome by the martyrs of Gaul, and himself succeeded a Christian martyr as bishop of Lyons. These are facts that help us understand how and why Irenaeus was enabled to strengthen the church in the face of its greatest challenge since the time the apostles had hammered out a solution for the problem of admitting gentiles into the church.

Irenaeus: *Against Heresies*[190]

Books One, Two, and Three

Irenaeus begins his work *Against Heresies* with an analysis of the works of the Valentinians and especially their use of the Scriptures (Book 1, Chapters 1–9). He then takes up the subject of the church and asserts that the faith once given to the apostles has been handed down through the church until his own time. He intends neither to add to it nor to diminish it (Chapter 10). Irenaeus then returns to his attack. He considers the views of numerous Christian writers, refuting their use of the Scriptures which had been handed down in the church and discrediting their new "spurious" scriptures (Chapters 11—31).

In Book 2, Irenaeus continues his refutation in great detail and claims to have been able to trace the origin of all heresy to its father Simon (Chapters 1—35).

In Book 3, Irenaeus takes up the Christian scriptures and strengthens his case against those he opposes by building a historical and scriptural defense of what he understands as the true and apostolic faith. In Chapter 1, he writes:

> We have learned from none others the plan of our salvation, than from those through whom the gospel has come down to us, which they did at one time proclaim in public, and, at a later period, by the will of God, handed down to us in the scriptures, to be the ground and pillar of our faith.[191]

Irenaeus draws upon the Acts of the Apostles for the story of Pentecost and the apostolic preaching mission. Then comes his famous tradition concerning the authorship and provenance of Matthew, Mark, Luke, and John.

As to the "heretics' " point that truth concerning the faith was not delivered by means of written documents, but viva voce, well, there is the viva voce of the tradition that originated with the apostles!

If the apostles had known hidden mysteries, which they were in the habit of imparting privately to "the perfect," apart from the other Christians, they certainly would have delivered them to those into whose hands they were committing the churches they had founded.

Since we can trace the succession of bishops in the major churches from the apostles to the present, we can be sure that in the faith handed down to us in these churches, we have the true apostolic faith. This is confirmed by the fact that the faith adhered to in all these churches is the same. We can go to the heart of the matter by taking up the tradition as it has come down to us from the apostles of the very great, ancient, and universally known church founded and organized at Rome by the two most glorious apostles, Peter and Paul. Having founded and built up the church in Rome, they committed the office of bishop into the hands of Linus. From Linus until now, it is possible to name in succession all twelve bishops of the church in Rome. With Valentinus, Marcion, and the other heretics, the situation is quite different. None of them can trace his authority back through any episcopal line to an apostle. Each claims he has the authority to say what the truth is by interpreting the scriptures according to some private understanding or some secret revelation. But these scriptures, when rightly read, only serve to refute the views of these heretics and confirm the apostolic faith that is taught in all the churches (Chapters 2—25). This, in brief compass, is Irenaeus's fundamental line of reasoning.

Chapter 18 is of special interest because in it, Irenaeus treats the subject of persecution and martyrdom, and we are provided the opportunity to see how he viewed the matter.

Irenaeus begins with a series of passages from the letters of Paul to establish the point that Jesus Christ truly lived, suffered, and died. Rom. 14:9, "For to this end Christ died and lived again, that he might be Lord of both the dead and of the living." 1 Cor. 1:23, "But we preach Christ crucified." 1 Cor. 15:3, "For I delivered to you as of first importance what I also received, that Christ died for our sins. . . ." Irenaeus concludes: "It is plain, then, that Paul knew no other Christ besides him alone, who both suffered, and was buried, and rose again, who was also born, and whom he speaks of as man. . . . And everywhere, when referring to the passion of our Lord, and to his human nature, and his subjection to death, he employs the name of Christ, as in that passage: 'Destroy not him with thy meat for whom Christ died.' "

Irenaeus, then, without referring to the Gospels by name, turns to Matthew and Luke and argues as follows: "After Jesus asked his disciples, 'Who do men say that I am?,' it is said that 'he began to show to his disciples, now that he must go to Jerusalem and suffer many things of the priests, and be rejected, and crucified, and rise again the third day.' Jesus went on to say, 'If any man will come after me, let him deny himself, and take up his cross, and follow me. For whosoever will save his life, shall lose it; and whosoever will lose it for my sake shall save it.' "

Irenaeus concludes this stage of his argument with these words:

"For these things Christ spoke openly, he being himself the Saviour of those who should be delivered over to death for their confession of him, and lose their lives."

Next, taking up the view that Christ was not to suffer and therefore left the body of Jesus on the cross, Irenaeus asks rhetorically, "Why, then, did he exhort his disciples to take up the cross and follow him?" He notes that Jesus said to the Jews: "Behold, I send you prophets, and wise men, and scribes: and some of them you shall kill and crucify." This implies, reasons Irenaeus, that Jesus expected his disciples to suffer for his sake. To his disciples Jesus had said: "Ye shall stand before governors and kings for my sake; and they shall scourge some of you, and slay you, and persecute you from city to city." Jesus knew his disciples would suffer persecution and would be killed, and he did not speak of any other cross than of the suffering which he himself should first undergo, and his disciples afterwards. For this reason, he also said: "Fear not them which kill the body, but are not able to kill the soul; but rather fear him who is able to send both soul and body into hell." Thus, he exhorted them to hold fast to those professions of faith which they had made concerning him.

> For He promised to confess before His Father those who should confess His name before men; but declared that He would deny those who should deny Him, and would be ashamed of those who should be ashamed to confess Him. And, although these things are so, some of these men have proceeded to such a degree of temerity, that they even pour contempt upon martyrs, and vituperate those who are slain on account of the confession of the Lord, and who suffer all things predicted by the Lord, and who, in this respect, strive to follow the footprints of the Lord's passion, having become martyrs of the suffering One. . . . And, from this fact, that He exclaimed upon the cross, "Father, forgive them, for they know not what they do," the long-suffering, patience, compassion, and goodness of Christ are exhibited, since He both suffered, and did Himself exculpate those who had maltreated Him. For the Word of God, who said to us "love your enemies, and pray for those that hate you," Himself did this very thing upon the cross; loving the human race to such a degree, that He even prayed for those putting Him to death.[192]

Irenaeus concludes by assuming, for the sake of argument, that if there were two Christs—one who suffered on the cross and another who flew away—the truly good one would have been the "one, who, in the midst of His own wounds and stripes, and other cruelties inflicted upon Him, was beneficent, and unmindful of the wrongs perpetrated upon Him," rather than, "he who flew away, and sustained neither injury nor insult."

As for the similar view that Jesus only "seemed" to suffer, Irenaeus has this to say:

> If he did not truly suffer, no thanks to Him, since there was no suffering at all; and when we shall actually begin to suffer, He will seem as leading us astray, exhorting us to endure buffeting, and to turn the other cheek, if He did not Himself before us in reality suffer the same; and as He misled them by seeming to them to be suffering when He was not, so does He also mislead us, by exhorting us to endure what He did not endure Himself.[193]

Summary Conclusions

In Irenaeus's theological system, the Scriptures function in two ways. They have been handed down in the church and witness to the faith of the apostles. But they also provide an excellent basis for refuting "heretics," because it can be shown by appeal to these scriptures that the "heretics' " views are mistaken.

As Justin Martyr in an earlier period disproved the views of the Jews by appealing to their scriptures, so Irenaeus, as the apologist for the catholic faith, disproved the views of the "heretics" by appealing to their scriptures. And as in the dispute with the Jews it became necessary to distinguish the books each side would accept as Scripture, so also in the dispute with the "heretics" it became necessary to distinguish the books that each would accept as Scripture. From the side of Irenaeus, this required discrediting the "new" scriptures of the "heretics." The Gospel of Peter, Valentinus's Gospel of Truth, and Marcion's Gospel are examples of new scriptures that needed to be discredited. With Irenaeus, Matthew, Mark, Luke, and John have a new status. These scriptures bear witness to the gospel or the rule of faith that was given to the apostles by Christ. They also serve as a written canon, norm, or measure of the faith by which it is possible to disprove the views of the "heretics," and thus to prove that their new gospels are not reliable.

More than any other church father, Irenaeus helped the Christian community sort out its thinking about its scriptures. After Irenaeus, there was never again any serious thought given to rejecting the Old Testament. The fourfold Gospel canon of Matthew, Mark, Luke, and John thereafter was firmly placed at the head of all lists of New Testament books. Acts, which had been used by the martyrs of Gaul, at the hands of Irenaeus, emerged for the first time as an important scripture of the church.

Marcion and Valentinus had made much of the apostle Paul. Irenaeus embraced Paul fully, but insisted that there were other apostles. Peter was of special importance. For the teaching of the apostle Peter, Irenaeus relied primarily on the speeches of Peter in the Acts of the Apostles. For this reason, Acts was indispensable for Irenaeus. Moreover, Irenaeus used the Acts of the Apostles along with Paul's letters (including the pastorals) for his sources for the teaching of Paul. Formally speaking, Acts united the fourfold Gospel canon with the epistles of Paul, and Paul with those disciples of Jesus who had been apostles before him. Finally, Irenaeus, with the help of John's Apocalypse, "reaches right to the consummation of history in the millennial kingdom."[194]

With Irenaeus, the church had all the essential parts of what came to be its New Testament canon. There was the fourfold Gospel, Acts of the Apostles, letters of apostles, and the Revelation of John. Moreover, with Irenaeus, the church had a way of perceiving these New Testament scriptures in relation to the Old Testament scriptures as one book with a universal plan of salvation for the human family. Certain Christian scriptures had been consecrated by the blood of the martyrs. By his creative genius, Irenaeus formed these scriptures (with the Old Testament scriptures) into a comprehensive and coherent Christian canon.

How did the tradition concerning Jesus come to be enshrined within the New Testament? The answer, in part, is that this tradition, as it was formed into the Gospels of Matthew, Mark, Luke, and John, together with other Christian scriptures, helped the church remain faithful to its Lord in times of crises. It helped the church pass through the fiery ordeal of imperial persecution and check the debilitating internal spread of Gnostic influence.[195]

To appreciate Irenaeus's contribution more fully, we must not only consider the importance of persecution and "heresy" in his own immediate background, but also what had happened in Rome and other parts of the church during the two previous generations.

This has to do primarily with the formation of the fourfold Gospel canon and the earlier collection and publication of Paul's letters, and with the need of the church to find some way to unite these two collections into a more inclusive canon of Scripture that would support and guide the church in fulfilling its mission to preach the gospel and make disciples of all the Gentiles. This carries us back into the archaic phase of canon making where the New Testament that eventually emerged in the church had its beginnings.

THE ARCHAIC PHASE: THE BEGINNINGS OF THE CANON

The Protology of the Christian Canon

What are the protological realities that lie behind the developed textual appearance of the New Testament? We ask not about the deeper theological matters like faith in the God of Israel and belief in the saving benefits of the death of Jesus Christ. These, of course, are basic. We focus rather on the earliest relation of "scripture" to these primal matters of faith and belief.

Scripture and "Spirit"

For those steeped in the Jewish scriptures, there was in the beginning the Spirit of the Lord. The scriptures of Israel witnessed to the reality of this Spirit working in history and in creation. Jesus and his disciples read these scriptures. The premise for all reflection on the earliest beginnings of what is normative in the Christian canon is this: the Spirit of the Lord was in Jesus and gave him the authority to interpret the scriptures and, when necessary, to supersede them with new revelation. In Jesus, the authority of the scriptures was united with the authority of the Spirit of the Lord.

Jesus spoke with an authority that was direct from God. Among his disciples and later within the church, this authority was seen as transcending the authority of the rulers of the synagogues and the high priests.

The Spirit of the Lord that was in Jesus was also in the midst of his disciples whenever they met in his name. This Spirit witnessed to the spirits of Christians that they were sons of God. Some of these Christians were inspired by the Spirit to speak in the name of the Lord. Thus, the sayings of Jesus remembered from his earthly ministry were augmented by new sayings from Christian prophets who, in the Spirit of Jesus and in his name, gave the church new life-giving sayings. Some of these were also remembered and handed down with the other remembered sayings as "words of the Lord."

This developing corpus of an oral tradition of sayings of the Lord was handed down in different churches in ways that reflected the different interests and needs of these churches. There never was one single uniform and set body of oral tradition that was handed down unaltered in all churches. However, the evidence provided by the Gospels, in which a great deal of this oral tradition has been preserved in written form, does indicate that along with variation there was an abiding consistency in the character of these remembered "words of the Lord." The simplest explanation for all the relevant facts concerned indicates that the Spirit of the Lord (that was in Jesus and that was in the midst of the disciples when they gathered in his name) acted in conformity with the church's memory of the gospel Jesus preached.

It is this gospel that normed the tradition. As new situations developed in the church, which required new sayings of the Lord, there was a norm by which the church could distinguish between true and false prophets. The church that remembered Jesus could recognize the Spirit of the Lord when it spoke through Christian prophets. When the words spoken were not in accord with the Spirit of Jesus, as he was remembered and known in the church, they were forgotten or rejected on the spot, and thus not handed down as "words of the Lord."

The words of the Lord that were most influential were those that were most often recalled and repeated. In this way, selection resulted according to the differing needs of the respective churches. These differing needs also necessitated different words being spoken by Christian prophets in different churches. Thus, without doubt, the oral tradition developed in different ways. However, the same Spirit and the same original memory of Jesus remained alive in many churches. Otherwise it would be impossible to explain, granting all the diversity that was inevitably and necessarily introduced, how these churches could recognize each other as one church, even after several generations had passed and quite new social and cultural differences had grown up to distinguish these churches from one another.

Until such time as the need arose for these words of the Lord to be written down, the only scriptures in the churches were those that from the beginning had been recognized as such by Jesus and his disciples. The first evident need for writing down the words of the Lord would have been in connection with the need for this oral tradition to be translated in a reliable way into languages other than that spoken by Jesus or other than that spoken by Christian prophets in the Spirit and name of Jesus.

It is difficult to find the exact words to express in a second language a saying that was originally created in a first language. Different translators working on the same saying will produce translations that sometimes have significantly different meanings. This is a common experience in all translation work. Thus, to assure that a translation is reliable, it is necessary for it to be authorized. Some agreement needs to be reached that the meaning of the saying in the new language is as near as possible to the original meaning it had in the original language.

This means that whenever the oral tradition of the sayings of Jesus was being rendered into Greek, authorization was necessary from those who were in the best position to remember as accurately as possible what Jesus had said. It was also important that these authorities know the circumstances under which Jesus had spoken —for the circumstances under which words are spoken are often decisive for their proper understanding and correct translation. This process of authorization could best be met by reducing the tradition in the new language into an authorized written form. The reason for this follows.

The exact wording of the tradition in Aramaic or Hebrew need not be written. It could be retained in oral form because the sayings had been carefully crafted, as a poet crafts a poem.[196] The task of rendering these sayings into Greek, so that as much as possible of their original beauty and meaning could be retained, required great care and skill. We may suppose that this entailed the production of written documents in Greek. Thereafter, these documents could be authorized by the church for use in preaching and teaching in Greek-speaking circles and, when needed, utilized as aids to accurate and reliable oral memorizations of these sayings in their new Greek form.[197]

We conjecture that scriptures which are distinguishable from those the church had inherited from Judaism were first born in some such way as this. These new written materials would have been regarded as Scripture because they contained "words of the Lord." As oral tradition, they already had the authority of Scripture in the church—even higher authority than existing scripture. Until they received an authorized written form, however, they could not properly be thought of as Scripture since scripture is, by definition, written.

Once these words of Jesus that were written in Greek were incorporated into Greek gospels, the gospels in turn became Scripture for Greek-speaking Christians, *since they contained written "words of the Lord."* The distinction, however, between the written words of the Lord contained in the gospels and the written narrative accounts of the evangelists was well understood in the early church. As late as Irenaeus, the "words of the Lord" were cited from the Gospels without acknowledging that that is where they could be found. At the same time, "words of the Lord" were cited by church fathers that are not in any Gospel. This further confirms the fact that these words had a separate existence in the church that was distinguishable from their presence in one or another of the Gospels.[198]

Of course, new words of the Lord created by Christian prophets in the Greek language would, at first, have been handed down orally. There is every reason to believe that oral tradition in Greek continued to develop until conditions in the church associated with Montanism began to work against this development and in favor of an episcopally-regulated traditioning process favoring the authority of a written canon.

This does not mean that oral tradition in Aramaic or Hebrew could not have been written down and used in the traditioning process. Nor does it preclude the use of such written materials in the process of rendering the words of Jesus into Greek. It only means that the argument that there was no need for the words of Jesus to be put in written form in Aramaic or Hebrew would not necessarily apply with the same force in answering the question, Was there any need for the sayings of Jesus to be rendered into written form in the Greek language? The very process of translation introduces a qualitative difference into the traditioning process.

One of the most important places where translation and authorization of the oral tradition into Greek could have been carried out under optimum circumstances would have been Jerusalem. No doubt such work of this nature as was carried on there would have been under the general supervision of the apostles, and ultimately of the pillars of the Jerusalem church—Peter, James, and John. James could have spoken with authority as to the meaning of words, expressions, and allusions in the native tongue of Jesus, since that language had been spoken in his own home. Peter and John were two witnesses of the circumstances under which words of Jesus, in the fixed oral tradition, had originally been spoken. By the time of Paul, conditions in the churches had already changed. Words of Jesus fixed in the Aramaic or Hebrew oral tradition were undoubtedly assuming new meanings in these changing conditions. Change and variation in the meaning of Jesus' words would have arisen imperceptively and caused no serious difficulty *until* it became necessary to render them into another language. At that point, it would have become especially important to reflect on what Jesus had meant whenever different interpretations were being given to particular sayings in the fixed oral tradition. In this way the memory of Jesus' disciples was put to the test, and an important rationale for an apostolic college would have certainly been felt.

This does not mean that translation of the words of Jesus into Greek could not or did not take place outside Jerusalem. We may presume that the work of translation did occur also in Galilee, southern Syria, and elsewhere. But this cannot gainsay the fact that Christians looking to Peter, James, and John, and wishing to stand in the apostolic tradition they represented, would have found it convenient to benefit from whatever authorizing process may have been carried out at the center of Jewish culture and religion. In Jerusalem, above all, were to be found the linguistic resources and the apostolic authority for such a process.

We are not to think that there was some comprehensive project of rendering the oral tradition of the words of Jesus into Greek on some large and uniform scale. Missionary work of this kind may sometimes be so envisioned by a dreamer. But the hard realities are different. The work progresses as it is prompted by the Spirit.

Missional priorities vary from time to time in the same place, and from place to place at the same time. The work proceeds in a practical way—first this saying and then that; first these sayings and then those. Translations of certain sayings into Greek made elsewhere and brought to Jerusalem would be valuable assets in the process. The changing situations in the mission field must be born in mind. So has it always been in the missionary translation work of the church.

The earliest beginnings of a distinctively Christian canon would have consisted of the writings of the prophets and other Jewish scriptures handed on by Jesus and his disciples, plus the "words of the Lord," both oral and written. Once the Gospels were written, they would have been regarded as books to be added to the already existing scriptures because, like the scriptures inherited from Judaism, they too contained "words of the Lord."

It is important to realize that as far as the first Christians were concerned there was no need for a new set of scriptures. From the beginning, the books of Moses, the books of the prophets, and the other Jewish scriptures were read christologically in the church, that is, on the premise that the voice of the Lord could be heard in all scripture addressing itself to the messianic present of the reader. Jesus Christ as Lord spoke in all these writings. So these scriptures were no less Christian than anything written by a Christian.

Not everyone who read these scriptures agreed with the way they were understood by Christians. It is clear, therefore, that something besides these scriptures was at work among the Christians that enabled them to read these writings as they did. This is the gospel faith that originated with Jesus and his disciples and which, following his death and resurrection, developed into what Paul sometimes refers to as "the faith," but generally calls "the gospel." This "faith-gospel" preceded all distinctively Christian writings. It did not, of course, precede in time the first Christian scripture, that is, the part of our present Christian Bible referred to as the Old Testament. This "faith-gospel" also was the source of the Christian's interpretation of the writings of Moses, the prophets, and the other Jewish scriptures. There was, however, a reciprocal relationship between these scriptures and the "faith-gospel" that precludes speaking in strict terms of priority. It is really impossible to know to what extent the gospel Jesus preached was a product of his reflection on the meaning of the scriptures and to what extent it was a special revelation. The two appear to have been inextricably bound up together.

Scripture and Apostolic Presence

Paul and the Scriptures

Like the other apostles, Paul received the Jewish scriptures that had been received by Jesus and his disciples. However, as the apostle to the Gentiles, when he was working in Greek-speaking circles, Paul no doubt accepted these scriptures as they had developed in the Greek-speaking Jewish diaspora. In carrying out his mission to the Gentiles, Paul found scriptural authority for his special mission above all in the story of Abraham and in the Book of Isaiah.

In his letter to the Romans, there is a central section (9:19—10:21) in which he provides scriptural justification for his gospel. He artfully weaves into the text of his argument a catena of fourteen references to the Jewish scriptures: Isa. 29:16; 45:9; Hos. 2:23, 1:10; Isa. 10:22–23; 1:9; 28:16; Joel 2:32; Isa. 52:7; 53:1; Ps. 19:4; Deut. 32:1; Isa. 65:1; 65:2. The catena begins and ends with texts from Isaiah, and texts from Isaiah form the backbone of the whole into which are interspersed texts from other scriptures.

We may take Isa. 65:1, which occurs near the end of this section, to illustrate the way in which the text of Isaiah, read messianically, functions as a scriptural canon for Paul. When Paul read the words of the Lord in Isaiah "I was ready to be sought by those who did not ask for me; I was ready to be found by those who did not seek me," he did not take these words to refer to apostate Israel, but understood them to refer to the Gentiles. Read in this way, Paul could be certain that it was God's will that the Gentiles be saved. Or, at least, it was God's will that they should have the gospel preached to them. Why else would the Lord show himself to those who did not seek him?

The earthly Jesus himself may never have engaged in a mission to the Gentiles. But for Paul, the crucified and resurrected Jesus was the Lord, and the Lord could also be heard speaking through the prophet Isaiah. When read christologically, what is found in Isaiah is normative. We are not to think that the words in Isaiah initiated Paul's work with gentiles (though this possibility cannot be strictly ruled out). We are rather to imagine, I think, that Paul's experience of the fact that gentiles were being saved, quite apart from a conscious and deliberate mission to them, opened his eyes to what was there in the scriptures to be seen by those who had eyes of faith. Clearly it was the Lord's intention that gentiles be saved!

Paul's call to engage in a mission to the Gentiles became a part of the norm for his gospel. It was the will of God that this mission proceed in spite of any difficulties it might cause. Beatings, shipwreck, exposure, imprisonment were all as nothing compared to the privilege of witnessing to the glory of God that had shown forth in the face of Jesus Christ.

Thus arose the conflict over the law. It was a conflict over what was to norm the corporate life of the church. For Paul, preaching the glorious gospel of Jesus Christ was inseparable from preaching to the Gentiles. Yet the law required that Jews remain separate from gentiles. Beneath this conflict over the law was a far deeper consciousness and feeling of the love of God that had been shed abroad by Jesus Christ in the heart of both Jews and gentiles.

The fact remains, however, that it was not Jesus but the apostles who worked through the problem of the law so that gentiles could be admitted into the church without circumcision. Or, perhaps, we can say that this was accomplished by Jesus *and* the apostles. Or, to be more precise, it was the achievement of "the Word of the Lord" and the apostles. In other words, in this instance, a new problem had arisen for which there was no "word of the Lord," and Christian prophets had to speak for him in the apostolic councils where this question was eventually resolved. This underscores that there have been an untold number of life-giving "words of the Lord" spoken in the Spirit of Jesus that have made decisive contributions to expediting the gospel, but which have not been handed down in the church.

Nevertheless, the fact that the achievement of full admission of the Gentiles was worked out with the decisive participation of the apostles meant that *any canon of scriptures adequate for the needs of the Gentile church could only be a canon that made clear the role of the apostles in carrying on and extending to the Gentiles the work begun by Jesus and his disciples.*

The Apostolic Presence of Paul

While Paul never envisioned a new canon of scripture that would feature a collection of his letters, his churches knew that his letters carried his apostolic presence. Paul wrote to the church in Corinth that he did not want to appear to be frightening them with his letters. He explains that his opponents were saying, "His letters are weighty and strong, but his bodily presence is weak, and his speech of no account." He then proceeds to warn the Corinthian Christians: "Let such people understand that what we say by letter when absent, we do when present" (2 Cor. 10:11). This means that Paul's letters, at least those that were written with this purpose in mind (and all that have been preserved appear to meet this standard), represented his apostolic presence.[199]

One reason Paul was able to accomplish so much was that it was not necessary for him personally to visit every church that needed his guidance. His letters had the power to represent his presence. For those who would accept them as such, Paul need only write letters, thus saving the time and energy required to travel and make personal visits.

A collection of Paul's letters would have served to make Paul's presence powerful in the churches that possessed them if only they could be properly edited and placed in the hands of people who remembered the apostle and could authoritatively interpret their meaning. It was virtually assured, once these letters were collected and began circulating as a corpus, that any new canon of Christian scripture adequate for the use of gentile churches would include these writings. They made clear the decisive contribution of the apostles; above all, of the apostle to the Gentiles.

For the gentile church, Jesus without the apostles was meaningless. For these churches, only Jesus *and* the apostles would be adequate. The earliest apostolic writings that have been preserved in the church are letters of Paul. *Paul's letters, along with the "words of the Lord," constituted the embryonic beginnings of what eventually emerged as the New Testament canon.*

The Gospels, Paul's Letters, and the Motif of Martyrdom

Paul's way of expressing his conviction that it was God's will that the Gentiles be saved was to assert that Christ died for all—Jew and gentile alike. Thus for Paul, the death of Christ or the cross of Christ meant an end to the normativity of the law God had given Moses on Mount Sinai (at least as far as the church is concerned). Through Christ there came a new creation: neither Jew nor gentile, neither slave nor free, neither male nor female. Salvation is open to all who by faith trust in the righteousness of God, who justifies the sinner—both Jew and gentile.

All of the Gospels that have been included in the canon of the Christian church embrace this Pauline doctrine of salvation for gentiles apart from the law. The words of Jesus are incorporated into Gospels that feature not only the teachings of Jesus as "words of the Lord," but also his passion, death on a cross, resurrection, and exaltation as the messianic Son of God.

The Gospels already presage the uniting of the two basic elements of the New Testament, that is, the "words of the Lord" and the witness of the apostles to the death and resurrection of Jesus for the salvation of all who enter into the new covenant of faith. The Gospels invite and call for discipleship. They are apologetic missionary writings proclaiming the good news of God's salvation for all. Once they are brought into relationship with the letters of Paul, however, they will become something more. They will provide the model for imitation. When Paul writes, "Be imitators of me, as I am of Christ" (1 Cor. 11:1), he had in mind the self-emptying love of Christ.[199a] But by the time Paul's letters were collected, he had imitated his Savior by undergoing martyrdom at the hands of the Roman authorities. Ignatius, who is the first to base his teaching on both the letters of Paul and the Gospels, concluded that imitating Christ meant above all imitating the passion and martyrdom of Jesus.

Ignatius and Polycarp, both profound students of Paul's letters and the Gospels, establish the tradition that to imitate Paul as Paul imitated Christ one must read both Paul's letters and the Gospels. From these sources persons can learn how to be faithful martyrs. *In a tradition that honors the memory of the martyred apostles (Peter, Paul, James, and John), to read the Gospels and Paul's letters together is to move decisively, even if inadvertently, in the direction of a martyr's canon.* The purpose of these martyrdoms is to rekindle apostolic faith and keep alive the "apostolic presence."

With Ignatius and Polycarp we have the authentic root of the particular tradition of martyrdom that strongly influenced the formation of the New Testament. Irenaeus not only was a disciple of Polycarp, but also regarded Ignatius as a model for Christian martyrdom. In *Against Heresies* (V. 28.4), Irenaeus wrote:

> As a certain man of ours said, when he was condemned to the wild beasts because of his witness to God: "I am the wheat of Christ,

and am ground by the teeth of the wild beasts, that I may be found the pure bread of God."

This use of Ignatius's words in his letter to the Romans (Chapter 4) removes all doubt concerning the origins of the tradition of martyrdom received and handed on by Irenaeus. It came from the east, from Asia Minor and Syria. It was embodied in Polycarp of Smyrna and Ignatius of Antioch. As we see clearly in the example of Ignatius, however, this was a tradition that was oriented toward Rome and the martyrdom there of the apostles Peter and Paul.

The Conceptual Importance of Luke-Acts

The Necessity for "Acts of the Apostles"

One thing the Gospels do not and cannot do is make explicit a particular matter that is implicit in them. The Gospels do not make explicit the decisive circumstance under which gentiles were admitted into the church apart from the works of the law. This means that the Gospels themselves, while representing the apostolic witness to the death and resurrection of Jesus, cannot do justice to the full importance of the apostles. Without the "apostolic presence," the Gentiles would never have heard the gospel of Christ. The fact that an adequate Christian canon must make clear the decisive contribution of the apostles was well understood by the author of Luke-Acts.[200]

John Knox has argued convincingly that the author of Luke-Acts must have known of the letters of Paul. According to Knox, the fact that the author of Acts makes no mention of Paul as a letter writer and, as far as we can tell, shows no evidence of dependence on these letters indicates that he has chosen to ignore them. This is best explained if we imagine the author of Luke-Acts living at a time and in a church where Paul's letters were being used in a way that rendered them of dubious value for his purposes.[201]

The author of Luke-Acts was not prepared to allow his church to be dependent on Paul's letters for its understanding of the apostolic contribution to salvation history. Any tendency to exalt the contribution of a particular apostle above all others was to be corrected by the work of this author. Above all, any tendency to exaggerate the conflict between Peter and Paul or Paul and the apostles in Jerusalem was to be corrected. The unity of the church was to be underlined. The author of Luke-Acts brought together the two chief apostles, Peter and Paul. Acts especially shows how the gospel was carried first to the Jews and then to the Gentiles. It also clarifies for the gentile reader how the Gospel of Jesus Christ, which began with Jesus and his disciples in Judea and Galilee, was connected with the gospel that had been preached to them by the apostles.

The Pre-Marcionite Roman Canon

Luke-Acts was especially useful to the Christian church in Rome, because it showed how the apostle Paul reached Rome. It also explained Paul's relationship to those who were apostles before him. From these earlier apostles had come those who first preached the gospel in Rome. Any church that knew Paul mainly through his letter to the Romans and that remembered his martyrdom in Rome would have appreciated Luke-Acts. The emphasis upon the importance of concord within the church at the end of Romans accords well with the overall position of the author of Luke-Acts.

The Acts of the Apostles was never, as far as we know, of any scriptural importance outside of Rome until after the middle of the second century. Its first explicit use is in the letter from the Rhone valley to the churches of Asia concerning the martyrs of Gaul. It was not cited or acknowledged as Scripture in the east until Clement. Origen, presumably under the influence of Rome or the writings of Irenaeus, acknowledged it as a part of the New Testament canon in the third century. If the Gospels were written after A.D. 70 and if the external evidence for a Roman provenance for the Gospel of Mark is reliable, then the use of the speeches of Peter in Acts by the author of Mark affords the best explanation both for the tradition closely associating the apostle Peter with the Gospel of Mark and for the shape and content of Mark.[202]

Assuming the reliability of the scholarly consensus dating Matthew and Luke after A.D. 70 and the reliability of the common authorship of Luke-Acts, and assuming the reliability of the external evidence supporting a Roman provenance for Mark (if, as appears probable, Mark was written after Matthew and Luke-Acts), then Mark's use of Acts would be the earliest external evidence for the date and provenance of Luke-Acts. We conclude that Luke-Acts was known in Rome at the time the Gospel of Mark was written.[203]

After the Gospel of Mark was written, there was in Rome an early canon of Christian scriptures including at least the Gospels of Matthew and Mark, the two-volume work Luke-Acts, and Paul's Epistle to the Romans. What other "canonical" writings may have been circulating in Rome at this time is difficult to conjecture. But even these books alone make up one-half of the eventual New Testament canon that finally developed. *These books constitute a very important core of writings that could easily have developed into the list of books included in Irenaeus's New Testament.* All that is needed is the addition of more letters of Paul, letters of other apostles, the Gospel of John, and the Revelation of John.

Marcion

Marcion was born about A.D. 85. When he came to Rome around 140, he was in his fifties and probably had long since worked out the basic essentials of his program. It is presumed that he brought with him to Rome his copy of a collection of Paul's letters. He may also have brought with him the gospel he edited from the Gospel of Luke. The need for his gospel must have been apparent to him for a long time before he reached Rome.

Marcion's Gospel

Based on what we can learn indirectly about Marcion from references to his work by others, it appears that his gospel was as freely edited as had been the Gospels of Matthew, Luke, and Mark. There is no evidence that his gospel included tradition that was not present in either Matthew or Luke. In this regard, Marcion's gospel was similar to Mark. Like Mark, his gospel had no birth narratives and omitted precious "words of the Lord" like the parable of "The Lost Son." Most of the tradition in Marcion's gospel is found in the Gospel of Luke. Tertullian is convinced that Marcion created his gospel out of Luke by making major and unwarranted excisions from Luke. Marcion's gospel is clearly shorter than Luke and also shorter than Matthew. We cannot say, however, that Marcion's gospel is a simple editing of Luke. It appears to have contained some tradition that is found only in Matthew.

John Knox notes that "Marcion's text is undoubtedly nearer Matthew and Mark than is Luke."[204] Harnack suggests that there was a text of Luke in Rome which had been corrected to the text of Matthew and Mark.[205]

All that we can be certain of is that Marcion's gospel was the fourth synoptic gospel. Marcion recognized the distinction between

Matthew, Mark, and Luke on the one hand and John on the other. His decision to compose his gospel as he did was a decision against the Gospel of John. This was an act of courage for the son of a Christian bishop in Asia Minor. The Gospel of John was the Gospel of Asia Minor. This is clear from the debate that arose over the date of Easter. The churches of Asia Minor, following the Gospel of John, celebrated Easter on the assumption that the death of Jesus occurred on the preparation day for the feast of Passover, that is, the fourteenth day of the Jewish month Nisan. The other churches in the Roman Empire followed the tradition of celebrating Easter always on the first day of the week without worrying about conforming this date too exactly to the Jewish calendar. The attempt was made to observe Easter on the first Sunday following the Jewish Passover, since the death of Jesus did indeed occur during the period that Jews were in Jerusalem for the Passover festival. This practice seemed to meet fully the requirements set by the texts of Matthew, Mark, and Luke. The difference that developed between the observance of Easter in Asia Minor and that which developed outside of Asia Minor caused great difficulties in the days of Victor, bishop of Rome, who temporarily excommunicated the churches of Asia Minor on the grounds of this difference.

We may presume that Marcion's gospel, turning its back on the Gospel of John in its overall approach to the gospel tradition, would have made Marcion seem disloyal and rash in Asia Minor. According to legend the leading bishop of Asia Minor, Polycarp of Smyrna, once referred to Marcion as a "son of Satan."

Marcion was a ship owner and merchant. In this capacity he had occasion to travel about the Mediterranean and learn about Christian churches outside his native region. As the ancient Greek geographers and historians had earlier sailed the eastern Mediterranean inquiring about the sources of the great rivers and the origin of religious customs in different countries, so it would appear that Marcion, the second Christian *histor* (the first being, I am assuming, the author of Luke-Acts), made inquiries about Christian origins and sources that led him to remap the world of Christian theology in ways that eventually made him unpopular at home.

There need be no mystery as to why Marcion seems to have chosen Luke as his basic source for his reconstructed gospel. If he were set on finding the truth about Christian beginnings, he was standing in the tradition of the author of Luke-Acts. It would have been in accord with his purposes to begin with that gospel, whose author had avowedly the same end in view. Also, Marcion's preoccupation with the primitive Pauline corpus is explained well in terms of an aim to study the second volume of Luke-Acts in the light of earlier and more original sources.

Since Marcion's father was a bishop of the church (and we know of no question about his father's orthodoxy), it may be presumed that Marcion grew up with a Johannine tradition. It is not unnatural to conclude that Marcion's first departures from that tradition were consequent to theological reflection stimulated by the wider perspective that came with travel, and the affluence to support his private investigations.

We are not to think that when he arrived in Rome it was his first visit to that great Mediterranean city and important Christian church. We are rather to view his arrival around A.D. 140 as Marcion's conscious move as a Christian reformer to actualize change in the church of his fathers.

A date of about A.D. 85 for the birth of Marcion appears quite defensible.[206] Thus, he would have been a grown man by A.D. 105 and well along in life when the renewed outbreak of war between the Jews and Romans took place in Judea in A.D. 135. Many Jews were convinced that bar Cochba was the long awaited messiah. This raised questions for thinking Christians that had never been raised before, at least not with the sense of historical urgency posed by the bar Cochba revolt. It is likely that it was at this time that Marcion became acutely aware of the fact that the scriptures of the Jews could be read as a history of the Jewish nation, and that the traditional way of reading these scriptures in the church was certainly not the only way to read them and perhaps not even the best way.

Marcion was in the prime of life four years later when he consciously moved his base of operations to Rome. Jerusalem, where Paul had laid his gospel before those who were apostles before him, was in ruins. Where was the leadership of the church to which a Paul *redivivus* could appeal if not in Rome? Rome was not only at the crossroads of the empire, but the city where the blessed Paul had made his final witness.

At first Marcion was accepted in Rome. No doubt Rome offered fertile ground for pressing his case against the Mosaic law and against what he regarded as Judaizing interpolations introduced into Paul's letters and the Gospel of Luke. Rome also would have been hospitable to his enthusiasm for the apostle Paul and to his championing of the Pauline corpus which, until that time, probably had not been regarded in Rome as a discreet collection of scriptures. Marcion developed a strong case against regarding the God of the Jews as the God of the Christians. Rome was a city in which this case may at first have been listened to with real interest.

Marcion responded to his acceptance by the church in Rome with a large gift. (Compare Paul's agreement to raise money for the saints in Jerusalem after the acceptance of his gospel by the pillars of the church in Jerusalem.) This gift was in the form of a donation of 200,000 sesterces (well over one million dollars). This sum may be exaggerated, for it is a very large amount of money. We may be confident, however, that it was a substantial gift. As far as is known, it was the largest single contribution ever made to a Christian church until that time. There is every reason to believe that Marcion like Paul before him was making a conscious bid for power in the apostolic church. It is difficult to imagine that this bold move to Rome had nothing to do with the bloody upheaval caused in the eastern Mediterranean world by the messianic uprising of the Jews, only recently suppressed by the Romans.[207] The emperor had unequivocably banished all Jews from Jerusalem. This had resulted in an enormous displacement of the Jewish population which must have created refugee problems throughout the Mediterranean world. Tensions between Jews and the native population of all Mediterranean cities naturally heightened dramatically.

Not since the bloody conflict of A.D. 66–70, which had resulted in the destruction of the Temple in Jerusalem and the dismantling of the Jewish state, had the Pauline gospel (over against the more Jewish interpretations of Christian faith) been so evidently vindicated by the apparent course of historical events. As the fall of Jerusalem in A.D. 70 had resulted in a great resurgence of Paulinism among postwar Christian churches,[208] so also, we may be confident, there was a renewal of confidence in the rightness of Paul's vision following the events of A.D. 135. We must imagine what it meant for an affluent, well-traveled, devoted Paulinist, just turning fifty, to listen to reports about the final crushing blow of the Roman state against the flesh of Abraham, and to hear about the decision to build a Hellenistic temple on Mount Zion. We know that Marcion was absorbed in the question of the relationship between Christianity and Judaism. These events must have riveted his attention and forced him to reflect on their significance. The irrepressible Jewish hope in a messiah and the belief of many that bar Cochba *was* the expected messiah of the Jewish scriptures would have led anyone interested in Christian origins to the deepest kind of reflection, and to ponder the most radical of Christian options. The Jewish scriptures bore witness to the history of the Jewish nation. That nation, all reasonable persons would have been prone to conclude, was now finis.

Marcion went to Rome convinced that the God and Father of Jesus Christ had nothing to do with the God worshipped by the Jews. As a merchant and shipbuilder, Marcion understood very well the benefits of the Pax Romana. The fortune he turned over to the church at Rome was far more than most men were able to earn in a lifetime, let alone save. His business had flourished. He had felt the issues that had been raised by the religious war in Judea not only in his mind and heart, but in his pocketbook. From his head to the soles of his feet, Marcion had been radicalized in midlife, and he had made his decision. His decision was to engage in an all-out effort to persuade the church to disown its Jewish heritage.

A generation later, Marcion's bitterest detractor, Tertullian, was to ask, "What has Jerusalem to do with Athens?" The question Marcion posed for Christians was, "What has the gospel to do with Jerusalem?"

No doubt in the aftermath of the bar Cochba uprising, this was for a time regarded as a discussable question. But in due course it became apparent in the church that the implications of this question, as posed by Marcion, were far too radical. About A.D. 144, after a hearing before the presbytery of the church in Rome, which met at his request, Marcion was expelled. Marcion went on to spend more than fourteen years carrying on missionary activity in the Mediterranean world, not neglecting Rome, which continued to be a fertile mission field for him even after his excommunication.[209]

Marcion's Canon

For the use of his churches, Marcion created a Christian canon that was made up of Christian writings only. Over against the Old Testament, Marcion produced a document called "The Antitheses." This work brought out the conflicts and contradictions between

Christian faith and the Old Testament. We can now appropriately use the term *Old Testament* for the term *Jewish Scriptures* to refer to the Christian scriptures the gentile churches received from the apostles, which had been handed down in the earliest communities from Jesus and his disciples. Now, for the first time, these scriptures were perceived as belonging to the past, as far as the church was concerned. No longer would Christians who had been influenced by the kind of radical rethinking of the question of canon posed by Marcion read these writings as they had been read by the apostles, including the apostle Paul. These writings would henceforth, in the eyes of those who no longer regarded them as "Christian" scripture, refer to the covenant which God made with Israel—a covenant now superseded at best and, in the eyes of Marcionites, invalid for Christians.

It seems likely that Luke-Acts functioned as a model for Marcion's Gospel-Apostle. In place of Luke, Marcion substituted his "improved" version of that same Gospel. In place of the Acts of the Apostles, Marcion substituted his edited version of a collection of Paul's letters.[210] It is *very significant* that at the head of his collection of Paul's letters Marcion placed Galations. In the original form of the collection of Paul's letters, it is believed that Ephesians headed the list. The collection had been made and edited by some Paulinist who was confident about the value of stressing a need for the unity that Christians have in Christ. This unity was to be made manifest in the unity of the church. Marcion saw a different need—the need to stress the freedom that Christians have in Paul's gospel.

There need be little doubt of Marcion's personal and existential identification with the frustrated, defiant, and undaunted Paul of Galatians. There is no reason to think that Marcion any more than Paul was unnecessarily provocative or polemical. He had built up his shipping business because he knew how to plan for the future, organize, and inspire others to work with him toward a common goal. This is one reason he was so successful in founding churches all over the eastern Mediterranean world. Marcion knew how to get along with others. At times, no doubt, the exhortation for concord that Paul makes at the end of his letter to the Romans was an ideal Marcion lifted up for his adherents to follow. But in laying down the constitution of his church, which was to begin a movement of reform among Christians, he made the decision to give a prominent place to Paul's letter to the Galatians.

Like Paul and Luther, Marcion was a man of courage and passion, who had worked out his position carefully and had done the work of scholarship to back it up. This position called for radical change. Understandably, this change was resisted. When Marcion stood his ground, conflict ensued and he was expelled from the church. Where Paul had succeeded, Marcion failed. Marcion did not, in the showdown, carry the leadership of the church with him.[211]

Nonetheless, Marcion has left his mark on the church. The New Testament canon of the great church that expelled Marcion is clearly in part an expansion and development of the pre-Marcion Roman canon, made in response to Marcion's new "Gospel-Apostle."

Justin Martyr and Tatian

Edgar J. Goodspeed opened his chapter on the "Age of Justin" with the following overall picture of the situation in Rome in the period following Marcion's excommunication—at the beginning of the great missionary effort to which Marcion devoted the remainder of his life.

> In the middle of the second century, the Christians in Rome [Goodspeed is referring to those who excommunicated Marcion] would gather on Sunday and listen to the reading of memoirs of the apostles or the writings of the prophets. This is the statement of Justin, who was a member of the Roman church at that time (1st *Apology* 63.3). Justin was born in Palestine. . . . he became a Christian (in Asia Minor). About 140, he became a Christian teacher, and a few years later went to Rome, where Marcion was already established. By the time Justin reached Rome, Marcion . . . had left the church and begun the organization of churches of his peculiar Pauline type. With men at Rome like Valentinus, Cerdo, Marcion, Justin, and Tatian, the years that followed were of great significance there.[212]

Goodspeed is convinced that Justin wrote his famous dialogue with Trypho as "a great counterblast to Marcion's *Antitheses*." He goes on to say, "Marcion maintained that Christianity contradicted the Jewish scriptures; Justin maintained that it fulfilled them."[213] It does appear that Justin's work could have been conceived by Justin and others as a response to Marcion's program to rid the church of doctrinal dependence on the Old Testament.

Justin does not specify the names of the apostles whose "memoirs" were being read in church. But he knows that they were composed by "the apostles and by those who followed them." This distinction suggests that he knew that Mark and Luke were not written by apostles, but by disciples of apostles. However, at one point he refers to a statement that is found only in the Gospel of Mark (3:16–17) and says, with reference to Peter, that it is recorded "in his memoirs" (*Dialogue* 106.3). This indicates that Justin was accustomed to recognizing the Gospel of Mark as one of the "memoirs of the apostles" read in church. There is little reason to doubt that the other gospels he recognized as "memoirs of the apostles" were Matthew, Luke, and John. Justin knows other gospels, but he seldom uses them.

The important point is this: at the very same time that Christians in Marcionite churches were learning to read a *single,* newly reconstructed gospel based conservatively on what Marcion believed to be the most original form of the gospel that Paul read, in the church that had expelled Marcion, no *single* gospel was being read. Justin uses the *plural*—gospels were being read. This church was well aware of the differences between the gospels and of the need for some solution to the problem created by these differences. As long as only Matthew and Luke were involved, Mark could point the way forward for the church at Rome. But the churches in Asia Minor were following the Gospel of John, and this was causing difficulties, as the matter of observing Easter made clear. Though a native of Palestine, Justin had become a Christian in Asia Minor. For him, the Gospel of John was an important apostolic memoir.

The advantage the Marcionite churches had with a *single* gospel that was free of inconsistencies and Judaistic interpolations was very real. The whole problem was, no doubt, discussed in Justin's school in Rome. One of his students, Tatian, after Justin's martyrdom around 165, published in Syria a *single* unified gospel which drew together on an inclusive basis almost all of the traditions contained in the Gospels of Matthew, Mark, Luke, and John. It was called *The Diatessaron* because it was one gospel through four. There is evidence that in Justin's school the words of Jesus were sometimes cited from texts in which sayings found in the gospels of Matthew and Luke had been combined or harmonized.[214]

Justin was the first writer to mention the Revelation of John. He believed that it had been written by the apostle John (*Dialogue* 81.4).

From about the middle of the second century, the Christian churches in Rome had the experience of what might be termed "well organized denominational competition." In this competitive situation, the pre-Marcion Roman canon developed into the first post-Marcion "catholic" canon. If the Gospel of John was not already used in Rome in the earlier period, it now began to be recognized as an apostolic gospel. If the Revelation of John was not used in Rome in the earlier period, it now began to gain recognition as a book written by the apostle John.

By the time of Justin, the Christian scriptures known and used in Rome included about two-thirds of the eventual content of the New Testament. What mainly remained to be done was to (1) separate Luke and Acts; (2) place Luke with Matthew, Mark, and John in a fourfold Gospel canon; (3) embrace Marcion's ten-letter Pauline corpus, expanding it with other letters of the apostle Paul and letters of other apostles; and (4) retain Acts as a bridge between the fourfold Gospel canon and the expanded corpus of apostolic letters.

What was to be the next development? How was it to take place?

Polycarp, Bishop and Martyr of Smyrna

In the Revelation, the Christian prophet John, in response to heavenly instruction, wrote to the church in Smyrna as follows:

> Do not fear what you are about to suffer. Behold, the devil is about to throw some of you into prison, that you may be tested, and for ten days you will have tribulation. Be faithful unto death, and I will give you the crown of life (Rev. 2:10).

"Be faithful unto death, and I will give you the crown of life." What fateful words for a city to hear!

When Ignatius, bishop of Antioch, was on his way to a martyr's death in Rome, he was able to persuade those who held him in protective custody to stop in Smyrna. There he met Polycarp, bishop of Smyrna. Later, from Troas, he wrote a letter to the church in Smyrna in which he greeted the Smyrneans as follows:

> I have perceived that ye are established in faith immovable, being as it were nailed on the cross of the Lord Jesus Christ, in flesh and in spirit, and firmly grounded in love in the blood of Christ, fully

persuaded as touching our Lord that He is truly of the race of David, according to the flesh. . . . Truly nailed up in the flesh for our sakes under Pontius Pilate and Herod the tetrarch. . . .

He suffered all these things for our sakes; and he suffered truly . . . ; not as certain unbelievers say, that he suffered in semblance. . . .

If these things were done by our Lord in semblance, then am I also a prisoner in semblance. And why then have I delivered myself over to death, unto fire, unto sword, unto wild beasts? But near to the sword, near to God; in company with wild beasts, in company with God. Only let it be in the name of Jesus Christ, so that we may suffer together with Him. I endure all things, seeing that He, Himself, who is perfect Man, enableth me.[215]

At the same time, Ignatius sent a letter to his younger episcopal colleague, Polycarp, in which he wrote:

Be sober, as God's athlete. The prize is incorruption and life eternal, concerning which thou also are persuaded. In all things I am devoted to thee—I and my bonds which thou didst cherish.

Let not those that seem to be plausible and yet teach strange doctrine dismay thee. Stand thou firm, as an anvil when it is smitten. It is the part of a great athlete to receive blows and be victorious. But especially must we, for God's sake, endure all things, that He may endure us. Await Him . . . who suffered for our sake, who endured in all ways for our sake.[216]

It was many years later at the advanced age of eighty-six that the bishop of Smyrna was martyred along with other Christians in Smyrna. The church in Smyrna, sensing the great importance of the death of its bishop, drew up a letter that was intended for wide circulation. It reads, in part, as follows:

We write unto you, brethren, an account of what befell those that suffered martyrdom, and especially the blessed Polycarp, who put an end to the persecution by sealing it, so to speak, with his own martyrdom. For nearly all the foregoing events came to pass that the Lord might show us once more an example of martyrdom which is conformable to the gospel. For, he waited to be betrayed, just as the Lord did, to the end that we also might be imitators of him. . . .

So, it befell the blessed Polycarp. . . . he showed himself not only a notable teacher, but also a distinguished martyr, whose martyrdom all desire to imitate, seeing that it was after the pattern of

> the Gospel of Christ. Having by his endurance overcome the unrighteous ruler in the conflict and so received the crown of immortality. . . .[217]

A colophon attached to the end of the extant copies of this letter indicates that we have copies in our possession that go back to a copy of this letter that reached the hands of Irenaeus. This letter was read in the churches of Gaul on a regular basis. According to tradition, Irenaeus was in Rome at the time that Polycarp was martyred.

Before his death, Polycarp made an important trip to Rome. Ireneaus, as a young man, had been a disciple of Polycarp. Whether Irenaeus was with Polycarp during the visit to Rome is not known. But Irenaeus certainly visited Rome from Gaul, and there can be little doubt that between these two native sons of Asia Minor there was also an important Roman connection. Nor can there be any doubt that this Roman connection was important for the development of the New Testament canon.[218]

Fortunately, we have reliable knowledge of Polycarp's choice of Christian scriptures. Not long after Ignatius had written him from Troas, Polycarp received a letter from the church in Philippi. Ignatius had asked the Philippians to write a letter of encouragement to the church in Antioch. The Philippians indicated in their letter to Polycarp that they had written such a letter and that they were sending it by way of Smyrna with the hope that Polycarp would arrange to have it forwarded to its destination. They also asked Polycarp whether he would send them copies of any letters of Ignatius that he might have. In his reply to the Philippians, Polycarp disclaims any expert knowledge of the scripture. But this disclaimer clearly refers to the Jewish scriptures handed down from Jesus and his disciples. His own letter is full of phrases and expressions from New Testament books. According to Bishop J. B. Lightfoot's edition of the *Apostolic Fathers*,[219] there are a total of forty-six New Testament references in the text of Polycarp's letter: Matthew (5), Mark (2), Luke (1), Acts (2), Romans (2), I Corinthians (4), 2 Corinthians (3), Galatians (4), Ephesians (4), Philippians (2), Thessalonians (2), 1 Timothy (3), 2 Timothy (2), 1 Peter (9), 1 John (1).

The frequent references to Paul's letters are notable. This includes Ephesians and 1 and 2 Timothy. 1 Peter gets special attention, and the single reference to 1 John is important. Two possible allusions to Acts are also of importance. It is striking that there are no allusions to any Christian writings that later were rejected as heretical. There can be little doubt that Polycarp's library of Christian writings is the purest touchstone we have of the emerging New Testament canon that is later made evident in the writings of Irenaeus, the critical reflections of Origen, and the literary and historical investigations of Eusebius.

It was in the very period when Justin published his counterblow against Marcion that Polycarp made what was, as far as we know, his one and only trip to Rome. The purpose of his trip was to visit Anicetus, bishop of Rome. The trip was made around A.D. 154–55.

Ernst Barnikol traced the "birth" of the catholic church to this episcopal conference.[220] He noted that before this unprecedented meeting of bishops from East and West, orthodox Christianity had possessed no monarchical episcopate, no New Testament canon, and no creed. It had made no parallelism between the apostles Peter and Paul, but had in fact ignored Paul. Barnikol concluded that the importance of the meeting lay in the probability that the two bishops agreed to make common cause against the threat of Marcion.

The expression "orthodox Christianity" is troublesome in this context, and one might want to take exception to some of what Barnikol claimed. For example, the Acts of the Apostles makes a parallelism of sorts between the apostles Peter and Paul. However, Barnikol's suggestion that the two bishops agreed to make common cause against Marcion appears altogether probable.

Basilides and Valentinus

Before Irenaeus could make his contribution, it was necessary for the church to experience even further challenges than those posed by Marcion or by state persecution. These challenges came from Egypt in the form of Christian-Gnostic theological reflection, writing, teaching, and influence.

Basilides taught in Alexandria during the period when the Jews under bar Cochba were raising the banner of Jewish freedom and sovereignty in neighboring Judea. It must have been touch and go for Christians in Egypt, since Alexandrian auxiliaries were no doubt once more being called upon to shed their blood in putting down a dangerous Jewish threat to the stability and security of the eastern frontier of the Roman Empire. Some of the same pressures that worked upon Marcion were also at work upon Basilides and Valentinus. However, in Alexandria there was the Philonic tradition of allegorizing Moses and the prophets. This prepared the way for a similar approach to the Gospels and Paul's letters. In Syria and Asia Minor, in the figures of Ignatius and Polycarp, we are treated to more than mere glimpses of a Christian tradition of engaging the world, just as Jesus had engaged the authorities in Jerusalem and Paul eventually engaged them in Rome. From Egypt we are exposed to a different early second century Christian tradition, one of nonengagement with the world.

Valentinus traveled to Rome. But unlike Ignatius, Polycarp, Justin Martyr, and even Marcion, all of whom had in mind the dominical and apostolic example of action for God in the world, Valentinus appears to have been in Rome primarily to obtain a wider hearing for his ideas.

Until the recent discovery of the Nag Hammadi materials in Egypt, we have been almost solely dependent upon hostile witnesses to the teaching of the Christian Gnostics. The work of reconstructing the history and significance of Christian Gnosticism on the basis of these documents is still under way.[221] Meanwhile, it is possible to confirm that Basilides and the disciples of Valentinus accepted and used (1) the scriptures handed on to the church by Jesus and his disciples, (2) the Gospels of Matthew, Mark, Luke, and John, plus some others, and (3) the letters of Paul. Moreover, these Christian scholars produced a corpus of exegetical literature based upon these writings. It was this literature that gave scope for the philosophical and theological development of their Gnostic systems.

There is no evidence, however, to indicate that these Christians from Egypt had very much direct influence upon the formation of the "catholic" New Testament. They clearly accepted and used many of the same basic books that circulated as scriptures and Christian writings in the rest of the Christian community. They contributed many of their own books, which were in turn used by Christians of their own persuasion. But their main contribution to the formation of the "catholic" New Testament was providing a challenge to the realistic, action-oriented, world-engaging interpretation of Christian faith championed by Ignatius, Polycarp, Justin Martyr, the martyrs of Gaul, and Irenaeus.

In taking up and overcoming this challenge, it was necessary for "catholic" theologians like Irenaeus to discredit the special books used by these Christian Gnostic thinkers and writers. This resulted in a refining process of selection that eventually had an effect upon the shape of the "catholic" New Testament.[222]

Valentinus had come to Rome in the midst of the conflict over Marcion. At one point, he may have had hope of becoming the bishop of Rome.[223] His scriptural interests in Paul and John no doubt played some part in the deliberations that went on. The fourfold Gospel canon would have been inclusive of his theological interests in John while, at the same time, reminding the church of the importance of the other three—and relegating to a lesser status the plethora of other gospels that had been written and were circulating in the churches (like the Gospel of Thomas, the Gospel of Peter, etc.).

The new "catholic" canon that was emerging in the church should be viewed as both a uniting canon (bringing together East and West) and an excluding canon (shutting out certain individuals and groups with their special books).

Irenaeus

Irenaeus was an immigrant from Asia Minor who had known Polycarp as a young man. It is possible that before settling in Lyons, Irenaeus "had spent time in Rome and had known Justin."[224] Later, as bishop of Lyons, Irenaeus wrote Victor, bishop of Rome, remonstrating with him concerning the excommunication of the churches of Asia Minor over the question of dating Easter. He reminded Victor of how differently his predecessor, Anicetus, had behaved when Polycarp was in Rome. If Irenaeus did spend time in Rome and was there when Justin was, it is quite possible that he was present when his teacher Polycarp arrived, and that he had firsthand accounts of the understandings reached between the parties of Polycarp and Anicetus.

This would help explain why later in his writings as bishop, he championed the apostolic traditions of Asia Minor and Rome and why, when it was threatened, he would attempt to preserve the unity that had been forged between these two traditions in connection with Polycarp's visit to Rome.

But it does not really matter whether Irenaeus was personally in Rome during this crucial period or not. Since he was the bishop of the martyrs of Lyons, he could not have been unmindful of the instances of martyrdom that followed Polycarp's visit to Rome—both in Rome and in Smyrna. Justin was martyred in Rome in 165; Polycarp seems to have been martyred in Smyrna at about the same time.[225]

By far the simplest solution that can be offered to explain the New Testament canon of the martyrs of Gaul, which was so close to that of Irenaeus, is to see it as a united East-West response to Marcion and the docetic tendencies present in Gnosticism. This canon had been negotiated in principle in conversations involving representatives from both East and West in the period between A.D. 150 and A.D. 170. We only know inadvertently about the meetings of the two representative bishops, Polycarp and Anicetus. Had Irenaeus not written his remonstrating letter many years after the event and had Eusebius failed to include what Irenaeus had written in his *Ecclesiastical History,* we would not even know about this conference.

There probably were numerous discussions before certain fundamental solutions were agree upon rather than one dramatic meeting when everything was decided. But there must have been breakthroughs that came with creative ideas, like the fourfold Gospel canon. Could that idea have come from a young *peritus* in the party of the bishop of Smyrna?

In any case, the work was done by men who were inclusive in their approach, but capable of drawing lines when they were convinced that essentials of the faith were at stake.

The Collection of Paul's Letters

The collection of Paul's letters is the one major contribution to the New Testament canon yet to be discussed. This contribution was made in the East, in Asia Minor. It is impossible to appreciate fully the dynamics of what happened in Rome after the arrival of Marcion without considering this topic.[226]

When Ignatius was on his way to Rome and was still some distance from Smyrna, knowing that he would not pass through Ephesus, he sent messengers ahead along an alternate route to inform Christians there that he would stop in Smyrna on his way to Troas. In spite of his advanced age, the bishop of Ephesus decided to make the two- or three-day trip to Smyrna to intercept Ignatius and to assure him of his prayers and brotherly concern.

Ignatius was greatly moved by this particular visitor, as well he should have been. For if John Knox is right, and I am persuaded that he is, this elderly man was none other than the slave about whom the apostle Paul wrote in his letter to Philemon. Moreover, this bishop, Onesimus by name (the same name borne by the slave who is featured in Paul's letter to Philemon), appears to have been the person who collected and published Paul's letters.

The destruction of Jerusalem in A.D. 70 would have provided reason enough for some Paulinist to collect and publish Paul's letters, since they exhibit a form of the faith that is not tied to the Temple in Jerusalem or to the temporal fate of the Jewish nation. For that matter, the martyrdom of Paul in the previous decade could have effected a similar practical result. However, on the basis of traces of widespread use of Paul's letters, including Ephesians, it is conjectured that the collection of Paul's letters, whenever actually first made, began to receive wide circulation during the closing decade of the first century. We cannot say more than that about the date of the collection.

But what are the reasons for thinking that it was Onesimus, bishop of Ephesus, who made the collection?

1. In his letter to the Ephesians written after meeting their bishop in Smyrna, Ignatius clearly alludes to Paul's letter to Philemon and draws analogies between his own situation and that of Onesimus (the slave) and the apostle Paul. Ignatius even plays on the name Onesimus. There appear to be only two real possibilities: (a) Onesimus, the bishop of Ephesus, either was the slave concerning whom Paul wrote in his letter to Philemon, or (b) he was a namesake of that Onesimus, whom Ignatius saw fit to associate by allusion with the Onesimus of the letter to Philemon. In either case, there is a significant connection between Onesimus, bishop of Ephesus, and the Onesimus in Paul's letter to Philemon.

2. A slave who had been brought into the service of Christ through the apostolic ministry of Paul and had risen to a role of leadership in the church would have understood very well the powerful influence of Paul as a letter writer. He would also have had a worthy motive to undertake the collection of Paul's letters and just grounds for insisting that local churches provide copies of any letters from Paul that might be in their custody.

3. Certainly, a bishop of Ephesus would have had the resources in terms of assistants, finances, and influence to see that the collection was properly edited and published by whomever actually made it. That is, he could have arranged for edited copies to be made and circulated in other churches.

4. The best evidence available makes it clear that Paul's letter to Philemon was the only personal letter included in the original collection of Paul's letters. This original list included the letter to the Ephesians, which is often regarded as deutero-Pauline. So the collection could presumably have included one or more of the deutero-Pauline pastoral epistles. Like Philemon, these were addressed to individuals, not churches. Therefore, the presence of the one little personal letter to Philemon in the original collection of Paul's letters is remarkable. It is best explained if someone who had a vital interest in that little personal letter also had a decisive influence in deciding which letters of Paul were to be included in the collection. Who better than Onesimus, the former slave, might that have been? And how might such a former slave have accomplished so important a project had he not achieved sufficient stature in the church so that he could exert his influence in many other churches?

It is a significant fact that on his way to martyrdom in Rome, Ignatius met Onesimus, bishop of Ephesus, in Smyrna. It is no less significant that the young bishop of Smyrna, Polycarp, was their episcopal host. Bishops of other Asian churches were present as well. But Onesimus, Ignatius, and Polycarp would have been the pillars. As far as is known, there had not been a gathering of bishops since the apostolic council in Jerusalem as important as this meeting in Smyrna. After this meeting the canon of scriptures of the anti-Gnostic church would always include (1) the corpus of Paul's letters, including Ephesians, and (2) those gospels which featured the flesh and blood existence of Jesus and the physical reality of his passion.

Hippolytus

A careful examination of the extant writings of Hippolytus indicates that his normative New Testament was not significantly different from that of Irenaeus, who was his teacher. Hippolytus received the fourfold Gospel canon of Matthew, Mark, Luke, and

John. He accepted Acts, thirteen letters of Paul (not including Hebrews), 1 Peter, 1 and 2 John, and the Revelation of John. This makes a total of twenty-two books.[227]

Hippolytus was teaching in Rome when Origen visited the church there around A.D. 215.[228] By that time, Hippolytus had established himself as a learned churchman. Jerome informs us that among the works of Hippolytus was an exhortation, "On the Praise of our Lord and Saviour." It would appear that Jerome had read this sermon carefully, since he writes that in this sermon Hippolytus "indicates that he is speaking in the church in the presence of Origen."[229] Thus, Hippolytus was not only aware of the presence of Origen in the congregation, he took the opportunity to recognize this publicly. Something else that Jerome tells us suggests that this was no chance meeting. We are informed that the wealthy and influential deacon of Alexandria, Ambrosius, had urged Origen to emulate Hippolytus in writing commentaries on the Scriptures, and in this connection had offered him "seven and even more secretaries, and their expenses, and an equal number of copyists." This certainly would have provided a motive for Origen to contact the learned Roman theologian while he was in Rome, and it could possibly have been one of his main reasons for making the trip to Rome.

In any case, Hippolytus is an important witness to the New Testament as understood in Rome in a formative period of Origen's career, and Origen did contact him. Since Hippolytus was a student of Irenaeus, it is natural to suppose that Origen, in emulating Hippolytus in writing commentaries on the Scriptures, would also have been receptive to what Irenaeus and Hippolytus had to say about Christian books that were to be regarded as Scripture. This offers an explanation for the undeniable fact that the New Testament of Origen is very close to that of Irenaeus.[230]

In A.D. 235, Emperor Maximin began a persecution directed against the leaders of the church. Origen perceived the importance of this threat to the faith and made it the occasion for composing his famous "Exhortation to Martyrdom." In writing this treatise, Origen drew heavily on the Old Testament, including 2 Maccabees. As for New Testament books, Origen confined himself largely to the scriptures that were normative for Polycarp, Irenaeus, and Hippolytus.[231]

Hippolytus probably never lived to read Origen's "Exhortation to Martyrdom," nor did he need to. He perished as a martyr very early in Maximin's persecution. And what of Origen? "Origen died at Tyre in A.D. 253 shortly after the persecution of Decius who became emperor in A.D. 249. Although we do not know whether his great desire to be a martyr was realized, we do know that he suffered most severely in the persecution."[232]

Hippolytus's major work was his "Refutation of Heresies," which in part was based on the earlier "Refutation of Heresies" composed by Irenaeus.

All of this evidence from Hippolytus supports the general conclusions to which our analysis of the problem of the development of the New Testament canon has otherwise brought us. *Persecution and martyrdom, along with the threat of heresy and the catholic response to that threat, were significant factors contributing to the formation of the New Testament canon.* The gospel of Jesus Christ itself is the only sufficient cause for the New Testament. But persecution and heresy were major secondary factors, causing the church to form the particular New Testament that has been handed down in the church.

The main connection between the New Testament of Irenaeus in Gaul and the New Testament of Origen in Egypt was the church in Rome. *It was in Rome during the adult life span of Irenaeus, Hippolytus, and Origen that the creative compromises were found that contributed to the Christian Bible of Origen.*

However, we must not overemphasize the importance for Origen of the church in Rome. Origen reminds us of the importance of persecution and martyrdom in Egypt in forming the character of the church in Alexandria. Seven years after the martyrdom of Hippolytus, Origen, looking back forty years to the persecutions that took his father and some of his friends, wrote as follows:

> This was when one really was a believer, when one used to go to martyrdom with courage in the church, when returning from the cemeteries wither we had accompanied the bodies of the martyrs, we came back to our meetings, and the whole church would be assembled there, unbreakable. Then the catechumens were catechized in the midst of the martyrdoms, and in turn, these catechumens overcame tortures and confessed the living God without fear. It was then that we saw prodigies. Then too, the faithful were few in numbers but were really faithful, advancing along "the straight and narrow path leading to life" (Matt. 7:14).[233]

Summary Conclusions

In answer to the question, How did the traditions concerning Jesus come to be enshrined within the New Testament? it should now be apparent that the answer must take into account a complex pattern of development.

The traditions concerning Jesus represented a norm by which it was possible for Christians to identify themselves in an alien world in which they were confused with Jews and atheists. The Gospels of Matthew, Mark, Luke, and John do not falsify the Jesus tradition, but rather preserve and interpret it for the use of the gentile church. The letters of Paul are an essential part of the apostolic and literary constitution of that church. These letters constitute an indispensable norm that enables the student of the New Testament to delineate its development from Jesus to Constantine. They also are an abiding touchstone for those who would be sure of the god of Abraham, for whom Jesus speaks.

The achievement of the apostles (best represented in the letters of Paul, but also illumined by the other New Testament writings) was to bear the faith of Jesus Christ from its Jewish and Palestinian womb into the cosmos which God creates and loves.

The traditions concerning Jesus are our pristine source for understanding that faith and that God.

The role of Christian apology, the combating of heresy, the administrative wisdom of countless early unknown bishops, the concept of "apostolicity," and the courage and commitment of thousands of nameless confessors and martyrs must be taken into account when we think about the development of the New Testament canon.

However, there are certain particular lines of development that have emerged from this study. These lines of development can be identified with certain key figures in church history. In the form of an overall outline, we can sketch at least the following lines of development: (1) from Syria to Asia Minor and Rome with Ignatius, (2) from Asia Minor to Rome with Polycarp, (3) from Asia Minor to Gaul with Irenaeus, (4) from Gaul back to Rome with Irenaeus and Hippolytus, (5) from Rome to Alexandria with Hippolytus and Origen, (6) from Alexandria to Caesarea and Cappadocia with Origen, and (7) from Caesarea and Alexandria to Constantinople with Eusebius and Athanasius. Rome is obviously central to this development. And at each stage we are to recognize that there was a wider and wider acceptance of this developing Roman tradition until, with empire-wide persecution, the tradition itself became empirewide. Therefore, by the time of Eusebius it could probably be said with a great deal of justification: these are the books that are accepted in the great church everywhere.

All of these key church leaders were committed to an ideal of Christian martyrdom that was held at arm's length when not actually rejected by the Gnostics. Most of these leaders suffered and died as martyrs to faith in Jesus Christ as their only Lord and Savior. The faith for which they lived and died was inextricably bound up with their confidence in the divine inspiration of the New Testament scriptures, which sustained and nourished their faith both in life and in death.

Notes

1. Thomas H. Huxley, *Science and Christian Tradition* (New York: Appleton, 1915), p. 270.

2. J. J. Griesbach, "A Demonstration that Mark was Written after Matthew and Luke," in *J. J. Griesbach: Synoptic and Text-Critical Studies, 1776–1976,* Society for New Testament Studies Monographs 34, trans. Bernard Orchard, eds. Bernard Orchard, Thomas R. W. Longstaff (Cambridge: University Press, 1978), p. 111.

3. Basil C. Butler, *The Originality of St. Matthew: A Critique of the Two-Document Hypothesis* (Cambridge: University Press, 1951).

4. For an important treatment of the compositional relationship between Matthew and Luke see Bernard Orchard, *Matthew, Luke and Mark: The Griesbach Solution to the Synoptic Question,* vol. 1 (Manchester: Koinonia, 1976).

5. Alois Grillmeier, *Christ in Christian Tradition,* trans. John Bowden, 2nd ed. rev. (London: Mowbrays, 1975).

6. Hans von Campenhausen, *The Formation of the Christian Bible,* trans. J. A. Baker (Philadelphia: Fortress, 1972).

7. Other examples are discussed in Chapter 6 of William R. Farmer, *The Synoptic Problem: A Critical Review of the Problem of the Literary Relationships Between Matthew, Mark and Luke* (New York: Macmillan, 1964).

8. The plausibility of this suggestion is strengthened by the probability that Isa. 53:7–12 played an important role in the earliest christological reflection of the church.

9. Arthur Jeffrey, "The Canon of the Old Testament," in *The Interpreter's Bible,* vol. 1 (Nashville: Abingdon, 1952), p. 35. The whole of this article is highly recommended.

10. Paul's efforts to follow his practice of accommodation among gentiles in Antioch met with effective resistance and, at least as far west as the churches of Galatia, he encountered very serious difficulties with those who misunderstood his accommodating as "man pleasing."

11. Even Matthew and Luke, which both contain impressive amounts

of tradition formulated in pre-A.D. 70 Palestinian Christian communities, appear to have achieved their present form outside of Palestine.

12. See Van Austin Harvey, *The Historian and the Believer: The Morality of Historical Knowledge and Christian Belief* (New York: Macmillan, 1966).

13. See outline, p. 26, for a definition of this twofold and compound crisis.

14. William R. Farmer, "An Historical Essay on the Humanity of Christ," in *Christian History and Interpretation,* eds. William R. Farmer, C. F. D. Moule, Richard R. Niebuhr (Cambridge: University Press, 1967), pp. 112–15. For a profoundly original and convincing interpretation of Jesus, in no way indentured to the Marcan hypothesis, see Howard Thurman, *Jesus and the Disinherited* (Nashville: Abingdon, 1969).

15. I am indebted to E. P. Sanders for drawing my attention in correspondence to the distinction between the age-old explicit food laws and the relatively more recent dietary restrictions growing out of the extension of the purity code to the laity.

16. Cf. William R. Farmer, "Who are the Tax-Collectors and Sinners in 'The Synoptic Gospel Tradition?'," in *From Faith to Faith,* essays in honor of Donald Miller, ed. Dikran Hadidian (Pittsburgh: Pickwick, 1979).

17. Farmer, "Historical Essay," pp. 112–15.

18. William R. Farmer, "The Dynamic of Christianity, The Question of Development between Jesus and Paul," *Religion and Life* 38, no. 4 (Winter 1969): 570–77. See also Birger Gerhardsson, "Paul and the Jesus Tradition," in *The Origins of the Gospel Traditions* (Philadelphia: Fortress, 1977), pp. 31–41.

19. Cf. Rudolf Bultmann, "Jesus and Paul," in *Existence and Faith,* trans. Schubert M. Ogden (New York: Meridian, 1960), pp. 190–95.

20. Cf. John Knox, *Chapters in a Life of Paul* (New York: Abingdon, 1946). The hypothesis concerning the chronology of Paul's career which this book develops was originally stated a decade earlier in two articles by Knox that appeared in the *Journal of Religion* 16: 341ff. and in the *Journal of Biblical Literature* 58: 15ff. Robert Jewett, *A Chronology of Paul's Life* (Philadelphia: Fortress, 1979) and Gerd Lüdemann, *Paulus der Heidenapostel,* Band I, Studien zur Chronolgie (Göttingen: Vandenhoeck and Ruprecht, 1980) both build on the work of Knox and advance his argument in important but different ways.

21. Farmer, "Dynamic of Christianity," pp. 570–77.

22. Needless to say, both Peter and Paul could have had and probably did have followers and supporters for whom this apostolic con-

currence was less than normative. Cf. C. K. Barrett on Peter being used at Corinth, "Cephas and Corinth," in *Abraham Unser Vater,* Festschrift für Otto Michel, eds. Otto Betz, Martin Hengel, Peter Schmidt (Leiden: Brill, 1963).

23. However, attaching John's name to a gospel, three letters, and an apocalypse may signify that this apostle exercised an influence second only to Peter's and Paul's in the formation of the church that formed the New Testament canon.

24. See H. Chadwick, "St. Peter and St. Paul in Rome: The Problem of the Memoria Apostolorum ad Catacumbas," *Journal of Theological Studies,* n.s. 8 (1957): 31–52.

25. See "Mythological Tradition" below, pp. 77-83.

26. How and under what circumstances Paul did refer to sayings of Jesus is set forth in David Dungan, *The Sayings of Jesus in the Churches of Paul* (Philadelphia: Fortress, 1971). See also Birger Gerhardsson, "Paul and the Jesus Tradition," pp. 33–41. Gerhardsson points out that Paul, on occasion at least, clearly upheld the distinction between that which was said "by the Lord" and that which was said "in the Lord." However, not all early Christians made this distinction.

27. See *The Didache* 11 and *The Apostolic Constitutions* 8.

28. This clearly presupposes an agricultural phenomenon typical of many Palestinian fields. It is impossible to tell by outward appearance the depth of the soil since the limestone, which appears as outcropping here and there, can be as little as an inch or so beneath the surface anywhere in the field.

29. Martin Dibelius, *From Tradition to Gospel* (New York: Scribner's, 1935), pp 152–153; and *Die Forgeschichte des Evangeliums,* 3rd ed. rev. (Tübingen: Mohr-Siebeck, 1959), pp. 150–51. Cf. George A. Kennedy, *The Art of Rhetoric in the Roman World* (Princeton: Princeton University Press, 1972); and idem, *Classical Rhetoric and its Christian and Secular Tradition from Ancient to Modern Times* (Chapel Hill: University of North Carolina Press, 1980).

30. *Institutio Oratoria de Quintilian* 1. 9. 3–6.

31. F. H. Colson, "Quintilian I. 9 and the 'Chria' in Ancient Education," *Classical Review* (November–December 1921): 86–87; *Questiones Progymnasmaticae* (Leipzig: Georgius Reichel, 1909).

32. Note that chreiai were written down in order that they might be committed to memory. The relationship between oral and written tradition is more complex than is usually imagined and deserves more thought than it is usually given. Our difficulties are further compounded when we must reckon with the problematical effects of translation upon the transmission of oral and/or written tradition. Cf. Birger Gerhardsson, *Memory and Manuscript, Oral Tradition and Written Transmis-*

sion in Rabbinic Judaism and Early Christianity, Acta Seminarii Neotestamentici Upsaliensis 22, trans. Eric J. Shape (Uppsala: Gleerup, 1961).

33. See E. R. Goodenough, *Jewish Symbols in the Greco-Roman Period,* vol. 1, *The Archaeological Evidence from Palestine,* Bollingen Series 37 (New York: Pantheon, 1953). See also Wilfred L. Knox, *Some Hellenistic Elements in Primitive Christianity,* 1942 Schweich Lectures (London: H. Milford, 1944), especially pp. 30–31. Even more important are the two works by Saul Lieberman, *Greek in Jewish Palestine* (New York: Jewish Theological Seminary of America, 1942), and *Hellenism in Jewish Palestine* (New York: Jewish Theological Seminary of America, 1950). See also David Daube, "Rabbinic Methods of Interpretation and Hellenistic Rhetoric," *Hebrew Union College Annual* 22 (1949): 239–64. Cf. S. Stein, "The Influence of Symposia Literature on the Literary Form of the Pessah Haggadah," *Journal of Jewish Studies* 8, no. 1 and 2 (1957): 13–44; Morton Smith, "Palestinian Judaism in the First Century," in *Israel: Its Role in Civilization,* ed. Mosche Davis (New York: Harper, 1956), pp. 67–81; Avigdor Tcherikover, *Hellenistic Civilization and the Jews,* trans. S. Applebaum (Philadelphia: Jewish Publication Society of America, 1959); P. Benoit, *Discoveries in the Judean Desert,* vol. 2 (Oxford: Clarendon Press, 1961), pp. 209–10. For a balanced overall judgment, cf. Werner Jaeger, *Early Christianity and Greek Paideia* (Cambridge: University Press, 1961), pp. 5–21. For the early Hellenistic period see Martin Hengel, *Judaism and Hellenism: Studies in their Encounter in Palestine during the Early Hellenistic Period,* trans. John Bowden (Philadelphia: Fortress, 1974).

34. Writing at the end of the first century and in another part of the empire, Tacitus could say: "But now all of these rules and rhetoricians . . . are common property and there is scarcely a bystander in the throng but who, if not fully instructed, has at least been initiated into the rudiments of culture" (*Dialogue* 19).

35. Cf. especially nos. 3a, 9b, 10, 16b, 19, 21, 22, 23, 24, and 27 in Paul Fiebig's *Die Gleichnisreden Jesus* (Tübingen: J. C. B. Mohr, 1912). Daube rightly calls for a thorough inquiry into the debt of Talmudic jurisprudence to Hellenistic rhetoric ("Rabbinic Methods," p. 263). Henry A. Fischel has traced the transformation of cynic chreia forms in rabbinic literature in "Studies in Cynicism and the Ancient Near East: The Transformation of a Chreia," in *Religions in Antiquity: Essays in Memory of E. R. Goodenough,* ed. Jacob Neusner (Leiden: Brill, 1968), pp. 372–411.

36. The relation of the gospel genre to the genre of Hellenistic popular biography is developed by Philip L. Shuler in *A Genre for the Gos-*

pels: The Biographical Character of Matthew (Philadelphia, Fortress Press, 1982). See also Charles H. Talbert, *What Is a Gospel?* (Philadelphia: Fortress, 1977).

37. George Kennedy, "Classical and Christian Source Criticism," in *The Relationships Among the Gospels: An Interdisciplinary Dialogue,* ed. William O. Walker, Jr. (San Antonio: Trinity University Press, 1978), pp. 147–52, has encouraged New Testament scholars to re-examine and take more seriously the external evidence regarding the origin of the Gospels.

38. All citations from Eusebius's *Ecclesiastical History* (hereafter designated *E.H.*) are composed with the aid of K. Lake and J. E. L. Oulton, Loeb Library edition, 2 vols. (New York: Putnam's, 1926–1932) and J. Lawlor and J. E. L. Oulton, 2 vols. (London: SPCK, 1927–1928), with appeal to the original text as printed in the Loeb Library edition when necessary.

39. Eusebius, *E.H.* 3. 39. 3–4.

40. *Ibid.* 3. 39. 15. See Kennedy, "Classical and Christian Source Criticism," p. 147, for a rendering of the Greek that differs in some respects from that given here. Kennedy is interested in showing that Papias was referring to the note-taking that was preliminary to composition, not to the actual composition of Mark's Gospel (p. 148).

41. Eusebius, *E.H.* 3. 39. 16. See J. Kürzinger, "Das Papiaszeugnis und die Eretgestoldt des Matthäusevangeliums," *Biblische Zeitschrift* 4, Neue Folge (January 1960): 19–38. Kürzinger concludes that the Papias report does not mean "Hebrew language," but "a Jewish style." Wayne A. Meeks is unconvinced. Cf. "Hypomnemata from an Untamed Sceptic: A Response to George Kennedy," in Walker, *Relationships Among the Gospels,* p. 165.

42. Clement, *Stromateis* 1. 1. 11; Eusebius, *E.H.* 5. 11. 3–4.

43. Eusebius, *E.H.* 6. 14. 5–7; Clement, *Hypotyposeis* 6.

44. George Kennedy acknowledges that modern scholars have usually understood Clement's testimony this way. Without questioning Marcan priority, Kennedy seeks to comply with his counsel to take the external evidence seriously by suggesting an alternate interpretation. "There is, at least, the possibility that Eusebius had muddied the text of Clement . . ." This is not a good example of how best to take the external evidence seriously. In fact, it is a good example of how not to take it seriously. It is an example of how, in the interests of maintaining belief in Marcan priority, even fine scholars can fall into the trap of explaining away evidence that conflicts with Marcan priority. Neither Meeks, "Hypomnemata," pp. 167–71, nor Reginald H. Fuller, "Classics and the Gospels: The Seminar," in Walker, *Relationships Among the Gospels,* pp. 176–83, in their discussions of Kennedy's treatment of

"The External Evidence," comment on this point in Kennedy's otherwise quite valuable work.

45. "One ought to keep in mind that Clement is a member of the Church of Alexandria, where Mark, the Evangelist, was acclaimed as founder and first bishop (cf. Eusebius, *E.H.* 2. 16. 1.). He, therefore, should have no interest at all to place Mark's Gospel after the other two that contain a genealogy of Jesus, but for a definite and grounded persuasion of historical nature." From a research report by Prof. Giuseppe G. Gamba, Universita' Pontificia Salesiana, Rome, to be published in a forthcoming volume by Mercer University Press.

46. Eusebius, *E.H.* 5. 8. 1–4.

47. Hans von Campenhausen, *The Formation of the Christian Bible* (Philadelphia: Fortress, 1972), p. 195.

48. Ibid.

49. Eusebius, *E.H.* 6. 25. 3–6.

50. Meeks, "Hypomnemata," pp. 170–71, observes that there are grave limits to the probative power of all these reports. He makes two points that bear on the question of sequence: (1) "They are completely uninterested in the 'synoptic problem' " and (2) "Even when these authors speak of the order of the Gospels, it is not certain that it is the *chronological* order with which they are concerned." But the fact that these authors are uninterested in the "synoptic problem" (in the *chronological* order of the Gospels) provides no critical ground for discounting the importance of their evidence. To the contrary, whatever one can infer logically from their testimony that is of relevance for the question of sequence is all the more trustworthy as evidence since it is drawn from the testimony of authors who, on the point at issue, are disinterested witnesses.

51. In all that is written under this heading I am gratefully indebted to Professor Guiseppe Gamba for a written response to a paper I presented at the Cambridge Griesbach Conference, Pembroke College, August 1979. I have drawn from my paper in the preceding section of this book, that is, in the discussion of "External Evidence—Church Fathers." Professor Gamba holds that there is much additional external evidence to support the view that the historical sequence was Matthew, Luke, Mark, John. I have abstracted what follows from his more detailed and more fully documented report. Gamba's full report will be published with other papers from the Cambridge Griesbach Conference in a forthcoming volume by Mercer University Press.

52. Kurt Aland, *Synopsis Quattuor Evangeliorum* (Stuttgart: Württembergische Bibelanstalt, 1964), p. 533. See Jürgen Regul, *Die Antimarcionistischen Evangelienprologe* (Freiburg: Herder, 1969).

53. Aland, *Synopsis,* p. 539.

54. Ibid., pp. 539–47. The key phrase is: "Quam in prioribus viderat," literally, "which he saw in [both of two] preceding [gospels]."

55. Cf. Migne, *Patrologia Latina,* vol. 103, col. 279–86.

56. Cf. Regul, *Antimarcionistischen,* p. 214.

57. Migne, *Patrologia Latina,* vol. 35, col. 2391.

58. See E. Nestle-K. Aland, *Novum Testamentum Graece et Latine,* 22nd ed., (Stuttgart: Württembergische Bibelanstalt, 1963), p. xiv.

59. See Farmer, *Synoptic Problem,* pp. 220–25, 243–46, 248–53, 255–78. See Orchard, *Matthew, Luke and Mark,* pp. 37–68, for compositional reasons to conclude that Luke is secondary to Matthew. For further reasons not to believe in the independence of Matthew and Luke see Austin Farrar, "On Dispensing with 'Q'," in *Studies in the Gospel: Essays in Memory of R. H. Lightfoot,* ed. D. E. Nineham (Oxford: Blackwell, 1957), pp. 55–58, For a penetrating critique of the Q hypothesis see David L. Dungan, "Mark—The Abridgement of Matthew and Luke," in *Jesus and Man's Hope,* vol. 1 (Pittsburg: Pittsburg Theological Seminary, 1970), pp. 74–81. See also Edward C. Hobbs, "A Quarter Century Without 'Q'," *Perkins School of Theology Journal* 33, no. 4 (Summer 1980): 10–19.

60. E. P. Sanders, "Appendix II: Suggested Exceptions to the Priority of Mark," in *The Tendencies of the Synoptic Tradition* (Cambridge: University Press, 1969), pp. 290–93. Sanders gives a brief explanation for each passage and the relevant bibliographical references.

61. F. P. Badham, *St. Mark's Indebtedness to St. Matthew* (New York: Herrick and Co., 1897), p. 1.

62. Ibid., p. 2.

63. Ibid., p. 3.

64. Ibid., p. 4.

65. Ibid., p. 5.

66. Ibid., pp. 6–7.

67. Ibid., p. 7.

68. Ibid., p. 12.

69. Ibid., p. 13.

70. Ibid., p. 14.

71. Ibid.

72. Ibid., p. 16.

73. Ibid.

74. Ibid., p. 17.

75. Ibid.

76. Ibid., p. 18.

77. Ibid., p. 19.

78. Ibid.

79. Ibid.

80. Ibid., p. 20.

81. Ibid.

82. That which follows is taken from more extensive lists given by Badham on pp. 20–34 of his book.

83. Pierson Parker, "A Second Look at The Gospel Before Mark," Society of Biblical Literature *Seminar Papers* 1 (1979): 147–68.

84. See, however, Excursus IV, "The Priority of Mark" by G. M. Styler in C. F. D Moule's *The Birth of the New Testament* (New York: Harper and Row, 1962), pp. 223–32. Styler is answered by Lamar Cope, "The Pivotal Evidence for Marcan Priority is Reversing Itself," in *New Synoptic Studies: Cambridge Gospel Conference and Beyond,* ed. William R. Farmer, and scheduled for publication by Mercer University Press in 1983.

85. For the possibility of dating all the Gospels before A.D. 70 see J. A. T. Robinson, *Redating the New Testament* (Philadelphia: Westminster, 1976), pp. 86–117, 254–311.

86. See William R. Farmer, "The Provenance of Matthew" in *The Teacher's Yoke: Studies in Memory of Henry Trantham,* eds. E. Jerry Vardaman, James Leo Garrett, Jr. (Waco: Baylor University Press, 1964), pp. 109–16.

87. See Krister Stendahl, *The School of St. Matthew* (Philadelphia: Fortress, 1968).

88. H. I. Marrou, *A History of Education in Antiquity,* trans. George Lamb (New York: Sheed and Ward, 1956), pp. 194–96. Italics mine.

89. David Daube, "Rabbinic Methods of Interpretation and Hellenistic Rhetoric," *Hebrew Union College Annual* 22, part 1 (1949): 239–64.

90. See Marrou, *Education in Antiquity,* p. 201, for the complete list.

91. Donald L. Clark, *Rhetoric in Greco-Roman Education* (Westport: Greenwood Press, 1977), p. 196.

92. Ibid., p. 199.

93. Manuscript in Bridwell Library, Southern Methodist University. Shuler has developed this work into a comprehensive study of the genre of the Gospels, *A Genre for the Gospels.* See Talbert, *What Is a Gospel?* for a valuable study which approaches the problem in a different way. See also David Tiede, *The Charismatic Figure as Miracle Worker* (Missoula: Scholars, 1972); Dieter Georgi, "The Records of Jesus in the Light of Ancient Accounts of Revered Men" in Protocol series of *Hermeneutical Studies in Hellenistic and Modern Culture,* no. 4 (1973); and G. N. Stanton, "The Gospels and Ancient Bibliographical Writing" in his *Jesus of Nazareth in New Testament Preaching* (New York: Cam-

bridge University Press, 1975). See also Philip L. Shuler, "The Griesbach Hypothesis and Gospel Genre," *Perkins School of Theology Journal* 32, no. 4 (Summer 1980): 41–49; D. R. Stuart, *Epochs of Greek and Roman Biography* (Berkeley: University of California Press, 1928); and Arnaldo Momigliano, *The Development of Greek Biography* (Cambridge: Harvard University Press, 1971). Peter Agnew points out a congruence between Shuler's findings and those of Talbert, and relates this to David Dungan's work on Mark, "The 'Two-Gospel' Hypothesis and a Biographical Genre for the Gospels," in *New Synoptic Studies: Cambridge Gospel Conference and Beyond,* ed. William R. Farmer, to be published in 1983 by Mercer University Press.

94. See M. J. Suggs, *Wisdom, Christology and Law in Matthew's Gospel* (Cambridge: Harvard University Press, 1970), for a treatment of this subject from the viewpoint of the two-document hypothesis.

95. Cf. *Gospel of Thomas.*

96. Michael Goulder, *Midrash and Lection in Matthew* (London: SPCK, 1974), assuming Matthew's use of Mark, concludes that Matthew has created the poetic form of much of his logia material. This way he precludes a need for Q where Mark's form of the logia is secondary to the form of oral tradition, and where Matthew has preserved the tradition closer to the oral form. Assuming the secondary character of Mark makes it unnecessary to argue that Matthew has created the poetic form of the logia. See especially p. 90.

97. *Appolonius of Tyana* 1. 31.

98. Ibid. 1. 17.

99. As cited by H. A. W. Meyer in *Critical and Exegetical Handbook of the Gospel of Matthew,* 6th ed. rev., trans. Peter Christie (Edinburgh: T. & T. Clark, 1878), p. 155.

100. Cf. Matt. 5:45 and the discussion of Jesus' ethical teachings above, pp. 47–48, and especially "love of enemy," p. 48.

101. Cf. 2 Macc. 7:9, 36–39; 4 Macc. 9:9, 15; 10:21; 12:11–20. Polycarp's confident reply to his persecutors refers to punishment for the impious in general and is appropriately noninflammatory. See *Martyrdom of Polycarp* 11. 2.

102. Cf. Jack Kingsbury, *Matthew: Structure, Christology, Kingdom* (Philadelphia: Fortress, 1975), pp. 40–83.

103. Farmer, *Synoptic Problem,* pp. 220–25. See also Berhard Orchard, *Matthew, Luke, Mark* (Bury, Greater Manchester:Koinonia, 1976).

104. Luke 23:34. These words may not have been in the original text of Luke since some early manuscripts do not contain them. But they are in other early manuscripts, and whenever dated the point remains.

105. See W. R. Farmer, "Notes on a Literary and Form-Critical Analysis of Some of the Synoptic Material Peculiar to Luke," *New Testament Studies* 8 (July 1962): 301–16.

106. Cf. Luke 10:30; 13:1–5. Note also the absence of any reference to the topography of Galilee or to activities associated with life in Galilee.

107. The literature on John is vast. New possibilities for understanding John have been opened up by J. Louis Martyn, *History and Theology in the Fourth Gospel,* rev. ed. (Nashville: Abingdon, 1979). See also Raymond E. Brown, *The Gospel According to John,* 2 vols. (New York: Doubleday, 1966–70); Rudolf Schnackenburg, *The Gospel According to St. John* (New York: Herder and Herder, 1968); Wayne A. Meeks, *The Prophet King: Moses Traditions and the Johannine Christology* (Leiden: Brill, 1967); Peder Borgen, *Bread from Heaven* (Leiden: Brill, 1965).

108. Rudolf Bultmann, *The History of the Synoptic Tradition* (New York: Harper and Row, 1963); Martin Dibelius, *A Fresh Approach to the New Testament and Early Christian Literature* (New York: Scribners, 1936); William R. Farmer, "The Two-Document Hypothesis as a Methodological Criterion in Synoptic Research," *Anglican Theological Review* 48, no. 4 (October 1966): 380–96.

109. Willi Marxsen, *Mark the Evangelist: Studies on the Redaction History of the Gospel,* trans. James Boyce, Donald Tuel, William Polhman with Roy A. Harrisville (Nashville: Abingdon, 1969); James M. Robinson, *The Problem of History in Mark* (London: SCM, 1957). See especially the contributions of the students and associates of Norman Perrin in *The Passion in Mark, Studies on Mark 14—16,* ed. Werner H. Kelber (Philadelphia: Fortress, 1976), who tend to concur that Mark is largely responsible for the composition of his passion narrative. In general, redaction criticism has served to strengthen confidence in the critical grounds for the skeptical conclusions reached by William Wrede in his famous study of the "messianic secret" motif in Mark, *The Messianic Secret,* trans. J. C. G. Greig (Cambridge: J. Clarke, 1971). That is, redaction criticism based on the two-source hypothesis has led critics to the conclusion that the gospel tradition as found in the earliest Gospel is largely the work of the evangelist and not useful for the purposes of establishing the actual public career of Jesus.

110. See Theodore J. Weeden, *Mark-Traditions in Conflict* (Philadelphia: Fortress, 1971); Norman Perrin, "Towards an Interpretation of the Gospel of Mark," in *Christology and a Modern Pilgrimage: A Discussion with Norman Perrin,* ed. Hans Dieter Betz (Claremont: New Testament Colloquium, 1971); Paul J. Achtemeier, *Mark,* Proclamation Commentaries (Philadelphia: Fortress, 1975); Thomas R. W. Longstaff, "Crisis and Christology: The Theology of the Gospel of

Mark," *Perkins School of Theology Journal* (Summer 1980). For additional bibliography see Howard Clark Kee, "Mark's Gospel in Recent Research," *Interpretation* 32, no. 4 (October 1978): 353–68.

111. See Farmer, *Synoptic Problem* and Stoldt, *History and Criticism.*

112. See Stoldt, *History and Criticism,* pp. 259–60.

113. Birger Gerhardsson, *Memory and Manuscript.*

114. A major breakthrough in gospel criticism was made by Roland Mushat Frye with his discovery that: "In terms of conflation, the procedure postulated for Mark in the Griesbach Hypothesis conforms closely to what can be seen wherever I have found a literary work in which conflation is demonstrable beyond a shadow of doubt . . . alteration between or among *Vorlagen,* condensation of overall or total length of the *Vorlagen,* frequent expansion within pericopes, and addition of lively details to provide a fresher and more circumstantial narrative. Here the conformity to . . . the Griesbach explanation . . . is telling evidence in its favor." From "The Synoptic Problems and Analogies in Other Literatures," in Walker, *Relationships Among the Gospels,* p. 285.

115. "The Genre to which Marcion's Antitheses Belonged" in "Reactionary Trends in the Gospel-Producing Activity of the Early Church: Marcion, Tatian, Mark," *L'evangile de Marc. Tradition et redaction,* Bibliotheca Ephemeridum Theologicarum Lovaniensium 33. Louvain (1975): 188–94.

116. Matt. 5:9

117. Matt. 10:34

118. Matt. 5:18–19

119. Matt. 12:8

120. Matt. 7:1

121. Matt. 23:13

122. Matt. 10:5

123. Luke 9:51–52

124. Matt. 28:16–20

125. Luke 24:50

126. That Mark was written for Christians facing or undergoing persecution was argued in 1924 by D. W. Riddle, "The Martyr Motif in the Gospel according to Mark," *Journal of Religion* 4 (1924): 397–410. Ten years later Riddle published "Die Verbolgungslogien in formgeschichtlicher und sogiologischer Beleuchtung," *Zeitschrift für die Neutestamentliche Wissenschaft* 33 (1934): 271–89. Mark 4:19; 8:34–38; 13:9–13 are mentioned by Riddle as passages which presuppose a situation of persecution. K. G. Reploh in *Markus—Lehrer der Gemeinde* (Stuttgart: Verlag Katholisches Bibelwerk, 1969), concludes that Mark's community either expected or was experiencing persecu-

tion. He cites as evidence: Mark 8:35–38; 9:42; 10:30, 35–40 (pp. 428–45). B. M. F. van Iersel reviews the entire question in "The Gospel According to St. Mark—Written for a Persecuted Community?" *Nederlands Theologisch Tijdschrift* 34 (January 1980): 15–36. He concludes with Weeden and N. Perrin that Mark was written to encourage Christians facing persecution. Van Iersel (p. 35) draws attention to Mark 3:28–29; 4:17; 4:35–41; 8:34–39; 9:42–48; 10:29–30; 10:38–39; 13:9–13; 14:27–31; 14:53–72; 15:29–32.

127. These Syrian Christians are referred to by some Chalcedonian theologians as "monophysites."

128. F. E. Peters, *The Harvest of Hellenism* (New York: Simon and Schuster, 1970), p. 65. See also idem, *Alexander the Great and the Unity of Mankind,* Proceedings of the British Academy, vol. 19 (London, 1933), pp. 1–28.

129. See Charles Odahl, "Constantine's Conversion to Christinity," in *Problems in European History,* ed. Harold T. Parker (Durham: Moore Publishing Co., 1979), pp. 1–18. Cf. Samuel Laeuchli, "The Milvian Bridge," in *The Serpent and the Dove: Five Essays on Early Christianity* (Nashville: Abingdon, 1966), pp. 102–50. The most important English historian on Constantine is Norman Baynes, *Constantine the Great and the Christian Church* (London: H. Milford, 1930), and especially "Eusebius and Christian Empire," in *Byzantine Studies and Other Essays* (University of London: The Athlone Press, 1955), pp. 168–72. Constantine's "conversion" is always to be seen against the background of his constancy in following the imperial examples of predecessors such as Diocletian and Elagabalus. See G. H. Halsbergbe, *The Cult of Sol Invictus* (Leiden: Brill, 1972). Other important works on Constantine include Franz J. Dolger, *Sol Solutis: Gebet und Gesang im Christlichen Altertum,* Liturgische Forschungen, vol. 4/5 (Münster: Verlag der Aschendorffschen Verlagsbuckhandlung, 1925), and Lucien Cerfaux et J. Tondriau, *Un Concurrent du Christianisme. Le culte des souverains dans la civilisation greco-romaine* (Tournai: Desclée, 1957). For extensive bibliography on Constantinism in Christian theology, see Raffaele Farina, *L'impero e l'imperatore Christiano in Eusebio di Cesarea. La prima teologia politica del Christianesimo* (Zurich: Pas Verlag, 1966).

130. Eusebius, *E.H.* 7. 15.

131. Eusebius, *Life of Constantine* (hereafter designated *L.C.*) (Cambridge: John Hayes, 1683) 3.1. Cf. W. H. C. Frend, *The Early Church* (London: Hodder and Stoughton, 1965), pp. 128–38. Lactantius reports that during the persecution under Diocletian and Galerius, when the authorities came to the church in Nicomedia, "The books of the Holy Scriptures were searched out and committed to the flames"

(Lactantius, *The Manner in which Persecutors Died* 12).

132. Eusebius, *L.C.* 1. 32.

133. Ibid. 4. 22.

134. Eusebius saw Constantine as a unique authority to whom God made new revelations and was willing to draw a parallel between him and Paul. In addressing the emperor he cited words from Paul's epistle to the Galatians as follows: " . . . God himself 'not by men nor through men' (Gal. 1:1), but by means of the Common Saviour Himself (that is, Jesus Christ), and frequent enlightening visions of His divinity revealed and uncovered . . . (secrets to you)"—*In Praise of Constantine* 11. 1. Within the context of this recognition of Constantine as the recipient of revelation direct from God, mediated only through his Son and not through Scripture or the bishops, one can paraphrase Constantine's words to the bishops and place them on the lips of Paul as follows: "You (Peter, James, and John) are representatives of Christ in those matters transacted within the circle of the circumcised; but in those done outside that circle, I am the representative of Christ constituted by God." For an answer to those who interpret statements about Constantine's divine tutelage as harmless flattery, see H. A. Drake, *In Praise of Constantine: A Historical Study and New Translation of Eusebius' Tricennial Orations* (Berkeley: University of California Press, 1976), p. 173, chap. 11, n. 3. That Drake is right in questioning the view of those who regard such statements as "harmless flattery" is borne out by the work of Charles Odahl. Flattery, perhaps, but hardly harmless. Eusebius was representative of most bishops in accepting and endorsing the revolutionary militarization of the Christian church as a part of the Constantine revolution. See Charles Odahl, "Constantine and the Militarization of Christianity" (Ph.D. diss., University of California, 1976). See especially Norman Baynes, "Eusebius and Christian Empire," in *Byzantine Studies and Other Essays* (London: Athlone Press, 1955), pp. 168–85.

135. Eusebius, *L.C.* 4. 24.

136. Conversely, the Christian church was to be subject to imperial veto in matters previously regarded as its private prerogative. Thus, when the Christians of Antioch wanted Eusebius as their own bishop, Constantine intervened and blocked the move. Cf. Drake, *Praise of Constantine*, p. 7.

137. Eusebius, *L.C.* 4. 27.

138. Ibid. 4. 25.

139. Charles Odahl demonstrates that Constantine made effective use of biblical imagery drawn from Isaiah, Daniel, the Gospel of Luke, and the Revelation of John in his Christian propaganda. See "The Use of Apocalyptic Imagery in Constantine's Christian Propaganda," *Cen-*

terpoint—The Journal of Interdisciplinary Studies, 4 Spring 1982, City University of New York.

140. Stefan Weinstock, "Pax and the 'Ara Pacis'," *Journal of Roman Studies* 50 (1960), concludes that *Pax Augusta* was an unfulfilled dream of the Roman emperors going back to Caesar (p. 52), who as "peacemaker" was connected with Alexander (p. 46). Weinstock notes that *Pax Augusta* had a second root in Roman culture.

141. W. H. C. Frend, *Martyrdom and Persecution in the Early Church: A Study of Conflict from the Maccabees to Donatus* (Oxford: Blackwell, 1965), p. 312, recognizes that the decision of Emperor Caracalla to give the status of Roman citizen to nearly all free men in the empire was patterned after Alexander. Frend sees this as a possible counterpart to Caracalla's "dream of uniting all his subjects under the protection of one divinity" and observes that this "process was not to end until . . . Constantine placed the empire under one divinity—the god of the Christians." The case for a definitive connection between Alexander and Constantine has not been made, but the historical and ideological parallels are inescapable. H. A. Drake begins his analysis of Eusebius by drawing attention to the statue of Constantine the Great in the courtyard of Rome's Palazzo dei Conservatori on the Capitaline Hill. He notes that the eyes are fixed upward. After acknowledging the Christian symbolism of the "upward eyes," Drake writes: "But Constantine also styled himself 'The Great,' and those eyes pull the mind back in time to another figure so styled, Alexander III of Macedone, the young conqueror, famous for images that depict him with a similar gaze." Drake notes that Lysippos' statue of Alexander in this pose is described by Plutarch, *De Alexandri Magni Fortuna aut Virtute* 2. 2. He also notes that Trajan and Alexander the Great figure prominently as leading personalities of the past with whom Constantine's early reign was associated (see Drake, *Praise of Constantine,* p. 136).

142. Eusebius, *L.C.* 4. 2. Kenneth L. Carroll drew attention to this passage in "Toward a Commonly Received New Testament," *Bulletin of the John Rylands Library* 44, no. 2 (March 1962): 341. He saw the commission as helping to speed up the process of arriving at a commonly accepted New Testament in the East.

143. Eusebius, *L.C.* 4. 37.

144. Ibid. Casper Rene Gregory, *Canon and Text of the New Testament* (New York: Scribners, 1924), pp. 35–36, conjectures that the reason Constantine ordered the fifty copies from Eusebius was that he had made inquiries and had learned that Eusebius had in the famous library of Caesarea the finest known and most accurately written copies of the Bible, and that he had access to the best scribes available in that region.

145. I am indebted to Bruce Metzger for drawing my attention to

the substantial uncial manuscript support for placing the catholic epistles before the epistles of Paul. Except for the fourth century Sinaiticus (א), which places Paul's epistles immediately after the four Gospels and places Acts between Paul's epistles and the catholic epistles, all uncials which have both Paul's epistles and the catholic epistles place the latter before Paul's epistles. Cf. B (IV); A. (V); C (V); Ψ (VIII-IX); S^{ap} (VIII-IX); L^{ap} (IX); P^{apr} (IX); K^{ap} (IX). Cf. William H. P. Hatch, *The Principal Uncial Manuscripts of the New Testament* (Chicago: University of Chicago Press, 1939). How this strongly attested tradition for ordering the catholic epistles before Paul's could eventually have been reversed (so that Paul's epistles come before the catholic epistles in our received New Testament) remains at present unexplained.

146. Cf. Gregory, *Canon and Text,* pp. 275–77.

147. Edgar J. Goodspeed, *The Formation of the New Testament* (Chicago: University of Chicago Press, 1926), pp. 131–32.

148. Eusebius, *E.H.* 3. 25. 1–7.

149. Goodspeed, *Formation,* pp. 332–35.

150. See n. 145.

151. See n. 134.

152. See n. 145. All of this accords very well with Constantine's arrangement to have himself buried in the church of the apostles.

153. Constantine faced the challenge of uniting an empire divided by political strife and religious persecution. This created an overriding need for consensus in religious as well as in secular matters. See Drake, *Praise of Constantine,* p. 66.

154. Charles Odahl has shown that the Revelation of John was important in sustaining the faith of Christians facing persecution and that Constantine was inspired by it in creating the controlling images of his new order. "Implicit in the message of the apocalyptic motifs examined here (that is, those drawn by Constantine from biblical sources, especially the Revelation of John) was an invitation to the Christian population to join with their Christian emperor in establishing a new world order" (Odahl, "Use of Apocalyptic Imagery"). This removes all doubt that Constantine himself would have preferred the inclusion of Revelation.

155. Eusebius saw Constantine as the fulfillment of the eschatological promises in Daniel 7 and Rev. 21:2 ("new Jerusalem"). See *L.C.* 3. 3 and *Oration* 3. 2–4.

156. W. W. Tarn, *Alexander the Great* (New York: Cambridge University Press, 1948). See also Ernest Barker, *Alexander to Constantine* (Oxford: Clarendon, 1956). For a critical evaluation of Tarn's view of Alexander, see E. Badian, "Alexander the Great and the Unity of Mankind," Historia 7 (1958): 425–40.

157. Arnold Ehrkardt, "Jesus Christ and Alexander the Great," in

his *The Framework of the New Testament Stories* (New York: Manchester University Press, 1964), p. 42.

158. Rather than Julian, who made conscious appeal to Alexander's example.

159. Drake, *Praise of Constantine,* p. 79, suggests that in place of referring to the "conversion" of Constantine, we should refer to A.D. 312 as the year of the "inspiration" of Constantine, when he apprehended his success in battle as a sign of divine approval of "his mission as the Great mediator, sincerely determined to reunify the empire, without making the mistakes of the persecutors. . . ." On the larger question of whether Constantine's religious feeling was based on a wholehearted commitment to Christianity, Drake (p. 63) observes that Constantine attempted to separate his personal belief from the policy that he would follow as emperor. Belief and policy in Constantine were "compatible but not identical."

160. Constantine expressed his concern for the Christian churches outside the Roman Empire, specifically in Persia, in a letter to the king of Persia. Thus, through personal diplomacy, Constantine was prepared to exercise his "episcopal" concern for the church in parts of the world over which he exercised no direct control. The Pope of Rome eventually took over this "episcopal" function and even today is prepared to exercise it wherever his jurisdictional or spiritual authority is recognized —sometimes at considerable personal cost.

161. " . . . under Constantine, the councils of the church were forced to play a role of unity at all costs. . . . The church *had* to be one." See Laeuchli, "Broken Altar," p. 203.

162. The prevailing quietude on the question of the canon within the Chalcedonian churches, except for a relatively brief period during and following the Reformation, is in keeping with the mind of Constantine in such matters. Constantine urged agreement where it could be reached. Disagreement that was inevitable was to be voluntarily repressed, guarded "in the secret recesses" of the mind. Cf. Drake, *Praise of Constantine,* p. 68.

163. An appendix of unknown date found attached to certain forms of the canons of the Synod of Laodicea (A.D. 363) lists all New Testament books but the Revelation of John in the same order as Athanasius. In A.D. 393, the Synod of Hippo published a list identical with that of Athanasius. The Synod of Carthage (A.D. 397), at which Augustine was present, published the same list arranged as we know it now. That this arrangement was not universally recognized is shown by the fact that Pope Innocent I in A.D. 405 listed Acts next to last, just before Revelation, as did Augustine. Jerome, who accepted the same twenty-seven books, listed Acts after Paul's letters, but before the catholic epistles. Cf. Alexander Souter, *The Text and Canon of the New Testament,* 2nd

ed. rev. by C. S. C. Williams (Naperville: Allenson, 1954), pp. 178–79, and Goodspeed, *Formation,* pp. 126–27; 193–96. Kurt Aland, *The Problem of the New Testament Canon* (Westminster, Md.: Canterbury, 1962), pp. 11–13, traces the development from Athanasius, noting that his compulsory stay in the West during the Arian controversies occasioned Athanasius's recognition of the Revelation of John. Aland notes that in A.D. 417 Pelagius spoke of our twenty-seven book canon "as an established fact for the whole church (Libellus Fidei)." Actually, however, in the West and especially in the East the twenty-seven book canon was a long time in being universally accepted. Augustine appears to have had second thoughts about Hebrews, and the Antiochene school was slow to accept James, 2 and 3 John, 2 Peter, Jude, and the Revelation of John.

164. Irenaeus cites both revelations as scriptural. However, the view that Irenaeus regarded the Shepherd of Hermas as canonical may be questioned on the grounds that the criteria of "apostolicity" was determinative for Irenaeus. See Denis Farkasfalvy, "Theology of Scripture in St. Irenaeus," *Review Benedictine* 78 (1968): 319–33.

165. Adolf von Harnack, *The Origin of the New Testament,* trans. J. R. Wilkinson (London: Williams and Norgate, 1925), pp. 169–78.

166. Eusebius, *E.H.* 6. 25. 3–14. This is the position of Irenaeus. See Denis Farkasfalvy, "Theology of Scripture."

167. Eusebius, *E.H.* 6. 25. 8–10.

168. On all this concerning Origen, see Robert M. Grant, *The Formation of the New Testament* (New York: Harper and Row, 1965), pp. 170–72; and J. Ruwet, "Les 'Antilegomena' dans les oeuvres d'Origene'," *Biblica* 23 (1942): 170–72.

169. Goodspeed, *Formation,* pp. 82–88; Grant, *Formation of the New Testament,* pp. 164–70. For a full discussion of Clement's use of Christian scriptures, see J. Ruwet, "Clement d' Alexandrie, Canon des Ecritures et apocryphes," *Biblica* 29 (1948): 77–99; 240–68; 391–408.

170. The possible significance of this number for Irenaeus's New Testament is recognized by others. Cf. Goodspeed, *Formation,* p. 78, where he says that "it is perhaps significant." Grant, *Formation of the New Testament,* pp. 155-56, stops short of drawing any conclusions, noting that the exact number of twenty-two is not certain.

171. Philemon is nowhere cited in the extant works of Irenaeus. It may be assumed, however, that it was included in the Pauline corpus known to Irenaeus. We know from Tertullian that Philemon was in the ten-letter Pauline corpus of Marcion.

172. See n. 142.

173. Indeed, Origen did more than that. He began the tradition of learned Christian scholars keeping company with the imperial household. In his *Ecclesiastical History,* Eusebius relates that: "Origen's

fame was now universal, so as to reach the ears of the emperor's mother, Mamaea by name, a religious woman if there ever was one. She set great store on securing a sight of the man (Origen), and on testing that understanding of divine things which was the wonder of all. She was then staying at Antiochia, and summoned him to her presence with a military escort. And when he had stayed with her for some time, and shown her very many things that were for the glory of the Lord and the excellence of the divine teaching, he hastened back to his accustomed duties" (*E.H.* 6. 21. 3). This story discloses nicely that Origen was a model for Eusebius not only as a scholar, but as a church statesman who gave his time and energy to the imperial household when it was requested.

174. Eusebius, *E.H.* 6. 12. 3–6.

175. See Frend, *Martyrdom.*

176. Eusebius, *E.H.* 5. preface.

177. Ibid. 5. 4. 1–2.

178. Ibid. 5. 2. 4–5.

179. Ibid. 5. 2. 6–7.

180. Ibid. 5. 2. 8.

181. How particular it is may be seen by comparing it with the scriptures that had a part in the formation of the Christian martyrs of North Africa where the fourfold Gospel and the Pauline corpus are less important, and books like the Similitudes of Enoch, Hermas, and the Apocalypse of Peter are of special influence. Cf. Frend, *Martyrdom,* p. 363.

182. For example, among the catholic epistles the only two books that have a secure place on all New Testament lists, 1 John and 1 Peter, are noted for their support of the example of martyrdom. Cf. 1 Pet. 2:21, "Christ also suffered for you, leaving you an example, that you should follow in his steps"; 1 John 2:6, "He who says he abides in him ought to walk in the same way in which he walked"; 1 John 3:16, "By this we know love, that he laid down his life for us; and we ought to lay down our lives for the brethren."

183. Eusebius, *E.H.* 5. 3. 4.

184. Cf. Frend, *Early Church,* p. 65. "The Gnostic was not a man of martyrdom. Indeed, he deliberately rejected its necessity . . . "

185. Ibid. "There was to be no 'Witness Against the World'." I owe the insight that the anti-Gnostic church which endorsed martyrdom would have needed episcopal leadership and interregional consultation to a paper read by Elaine Pagels at the Yale University Symposium on Gnosticism (1978).

186. Frend, *Early Church,* pp. 128–29.

187. Ibid., pp. 131–32.

188. Ibid., p. 65.

189. The Gnostic Heracleon, disciple of Valentinus, discounted martyrdom, noting that many apostles had not been martyrs. The Gnostic scriptures included books featuring some of these names like Philip. Cf. Frend, *Martyrdom,* pp. 354–55.

190. *Ante-Nicene Christian Library, The Writings of Irenaeus,* vol. 1 (Edinburg: T. & T. Clark, 1868).

191. *Against Heresies* 3. 1. 1.

192. Ibid. 3. 18. 5.

193. Ibid. 3. 18. 6.

194. Von Campenhausen, *Formation of the Christian Bible,* p. 207.

195. My reading of the evidence supports the conclusion of Kenneth L. Carroll that the role of Montanism in the creation of the New Testament was not as decisive as Goodspeed and others have held. I do not agree, however, that Knox has overemphasized the influence of the Marcionite movement. And I see no reason to challenge Knox's judgment, cited by Carroll, that the "New Testament came into existence as a conscious creation between 150 and 175, which was probably the period of Marcion's most vigorous and influential activity." See Kenneth L. Carroll, "The Earliest New Testament," *Bulletin of the John Rylands Library* 38, no. 1 (September 1955): 48–51. I see Luke-Acts as a pre-Marcionite work. Therefore, unlike Knox, I cannot credit Marcion with creating the "Gospel-Apostle" form of the New Testament. But there is no way to be sure that, had Marcion not followed the Gospel-Apostle model of Luke-Acts in forming his New Testament, the church would have done so. As Harnack shows, there were various shapes the New Testament might have assumed. Undoubtedly, then, the fact that Marcion followed one particular model had a decisive influence on the creation of the New Testament of the church precisely because the church responded to Marcion's challenge by developing this model even further.

196. Cf. C. F. Burney, *The Poetry of Our Lord* (New York: Oxford, 1925).

197. For an illustration of the way this process can be understood in connection with specific sayings of Jesus, see William R. Farmer, "Notes on a Literary and Form-Critical Analysis," pp. 301–16.

198. Alfred Resch, *Agrapha: Ausserkanonische Schriftfragmente gesammelt und untersucht* (TU XV, 3–4), 2nd ed. (Leipsig, 1906); Helmut Koester, *Synoptische Uberlieferung bei den apostolischer Vatern* (Berlin: Akademie-Verlag, 1957).

199. Cf. Robert Funk, "The Apostolic Parousia: Form and Significance," in *Christian History and Interpretation: Studies Presented to John Knox,* eds. W. R. Farmer, C. F. D. Moule, R. R. Niebuhr (New York: Cambridge University Press, 1967), pp. 249–68.

199a. Cf. Victor Paul Furnish, *Theology and Ethics of Paul* (Nashville: Abingdon, 1972), p. 222: "Paul's suffering and serving as an apostle are to be regarded as a sort of 'parable' of Christ's own saving death and resurrection."

200. For an up-to-date discussion of Luke-Acts, see the work of Charles Talbert, *Literary Patterns, Theological Themes, and the Genre of Luke-Acts,* Society of Biblical Literature Monograph Series, vol. 20 (Missoula: Scholars, 1974). Talbert succeeds in relating Luke-Acts to Hellenistic biography in the tradition of lives of philosophers joined with lives of their successors. He argues persuasively (p. 135) that the evangelist wanted "to say that the true tradition in his time was located in certain successors of Paul (Acts 20:17–35)."

201. John Knox, "Acts and the Pauline Letter Corpus," in *Studies in Luke-Acts,* eds. Leander E. Keck and J. Louis Martyn (Philadelphia: Fortress, 1980).

202. See above, "The Shape and Content of Mark," p. 165, and "Peter and the Gospel of Mark," p. 168.

203. For the evidence that Mark was written after Matthew and Luke, see especially Farmer, *Synoptic Problem;* Orchard, *Matthew, Luke and Mark;* Stoldt, *History and Criticism;* J. J. Griesbach, "Demonstration." See also David Dungan, "Mark—The Abridgement of Matthew and Luke," in *Jesus and Man's Hope,* ed. Dikran Y. Hadidian (Pittsburg: Perspective, 1970), pp. 51–97; and Thomas R. W. Longstaff, *Evidence of Conflation in Mark? A Study in the Synoptic Problem,* Society of Biblical Literature Dissertation Series 28 (Missoula: Scholars Press, 1977); and Frye, "Synoptic Problems and Analogies," pp. 261–302.

204. John Knox, *Marcion and the New Testament: An Essay in the History of the Canon* (Chicago: University of Chicago Press, 1942), p. 156.

205. Adolf von Harnack, *Marcion: Das Evangelium von Fremden Gott,* 2nd ed. (Leipzig: J. C. Hinricks, 1924), p. 243.

206. Harnack, *Marcion,* p. 21; Frend, *Early Church,* p. 66.

207. Cf. Robert M. Grant, *Gnosticism and Early Christianity* (New York: Columbia University, 1966), p. 122. I am indebted to David Balas for drawing my attention to Grant's discussion of this matter. What I have written was written before reading Grant. Our two accounts represent quite independent historical reconstructions. Needless to say, we could both independently be wrong in our common conjecture that there is some connection between Marcion's purpose in going to Rome and the recent events in Palestine. But if this conjecture is sound, it could serve to ground future investigation of Marcion in the history of his time in new and important ways. David Balas has accepted as quite possible Grant's conjecture of a connection between Marcion's purpose and the bloody suppression of the bar Cochba uprising. Balas concludes

his discussion with this observation: "Finally, the shaken confidence of many Jews in the confirmed goodness, omniscience, and all-powerfulness of Yahweh (incompatible as it seemed with the historical realities of the time) was taken as an admission that the god of the Old Testament was inferior to the all-good and perfect god revealed in Jesus Christ. Paradoxically, it was precisely by having accepted Jewish scriptures and history, at least to a large extent in their contemporary Jewish interpretation, that Marcion arrived at his radical dissociation of the two Testaments!" David Balas, "Marcion Revisited: A 'Post-Harnack' Perspective," in *Texts and Testaments: Critical Essays on the Bible and Early Church Fathers,* ed. Eugene March (San Antonio: Trinity University Press, 1980), p. 99. For the suggestion that R. Akiba carried the news of the coming of the messiah (bar Cochba) as far north as Galatia [and thus to the backyard of Marcion during the very decade that preceded Marcion's decisive move to Rome], see Hugo Mantel, "The Causes of the Bar Kokba Revolt," *The Jewish Quarterly Review* 58 (1968): 289–91.

208. S. G. F. Brandon, *The Fall of Jerusalem and the Christian Church: A Study of the Effects of the Jewish Overthrow of A.D. 70 on Christianity* (London: SPCK, 1957). See especially pp. 8–9 and 214–15.

209. Marcion went about "founding communities in opposition to the great church which had cast him out." Frend, *Early Church,* p. 67.

210. There can be no question about the conceptual kinship between the Gospel-Apostle structure of Luke-Acts and the Gospel-Apostle structure of Marcion's canon. The only question is which has influenced the other.

211. Some will say that neither did Paul succeed, and that only with later Paulinists has he had his day in court.

212. Goodspeed, *Formation of the New Testament,* p. 50.

213. Ibid., pp. 51–52.

214. Cf. Arthur Bellonzoni, *The Sayings of Jesus in the Writing of Justin Martyr* (Leiden: Brill, 1967). Georg Strecker disputes the view that such a gospel harmony was used by Justin in "Eine Evangelienharmonie bei Justin und Pseudoklemens?" *New Testament Studies* 24 (April 1978): 297–316.

215. "To the Smyrnaeans" 1—4 in *Epistles of S. Ignatius, The Apostolic Fathers,* trans. J. B. Lightfoot (London: Macmillan, 1926), pp. 156–57.

216. "To S. Polycarp" 2—3 in *Epistles of S. Ignatius, The Apostolic Fathers,* pp. 160–61.

217. Letter of Smyrnaeans on the Martyrdom of S. Polycarp, 1, 19, in *The Apostolic Fathers,* trans. J. B. Lightfoot (London: Macmillan, 1926), pp. 203 and 209.

218. Gregory, *Canon and Text of the New Testament,* pp. 73–75, goes so far as to refer to Polycarp as the keystone of the arch that supports the history of the church and the New Testament from the time of the apostles to the close of the second century.

219. Lightfoot, *Apostolic Fathers,* pp. 168–73.

220. Ernst Barnikol, *Die Entstehung der Kirche in zweiten Jahrhundert und die Zeit Marcions,* no. 8, Forschungen zur Entstehung der Urchristentums der Neuen Testaments und der Kirche (Keil: W. G. Muhlau, 1933), pp. 25–30.

221. Cf. *The Nag Hammadi Library in English,* trans. members of the Institute for Antiquity and Christianity, ed. James Robinson (New York: Harper and Row, 1977).

222. Cf. Robert Grant, "The New Testament Books in Gnostic Circles," in his *Formation of the New Testament,* pp. 121–30, for the New Testament books used by Basilides and the students of Valentinus.

223. According to Tertullian, Valentinus was thwarted in an attempt to become bishop (*Adversus Valentinianos* 4). Cf. E. H. Pagels, "Gnosticism," in *The Interpreter's Dictionary of the Bible,* supplementary volume, eds. Keith Crim, Lloyd Richard Bailey, Sr., Victor Paul Furnish (Nashville: Abingdon, 1976), p. 366.

224. Frend, *Early Church,* p. 77.

225. Ibid., pp. 70–71. The date of Polycarp's death is disputed. Others would date it a decade earlier.

226. John Knox, building in part on the work of his teacher Edgar Goodspeed and others, has gone further than anyone else in offering a credible account of the collection of Paul's letters. It is a story that involves brilliant historical conjecture combined with precise literary and exegetical analysis of both Paul's letters and the letters of Ignatius. Cf. John Knox, "The Pauline Corpus," in *Marcion and the New Testament* (Chicago: University Press, 1942), pp. 39–76, and *Philemon Among the Letters of Paul,* rev. ed. (Nashville: Abingdon, 1959), pp. 71–108. Students of the problem of the New Testament canon will have noted that I have not followed John Knox in dating the completed work Luke-Acts after Marcion. The reason for this is that Knox presupposes Marcan priority at essential points in reaching this conclusion. Since I remain doubtful about this assumption, I must remain skeptical of Knox's results at this point. For those who accept Marcan priority, however, the critical discussion remains largely where Knox left it in 1942 in *Marcion and the New Testament.* I believe that both E. C. Blackman in *Marcion and His Influence* (Naperville: Allenson, 1959) and Hans von Campenhausen in *The Formation of the Christian Bible* are correct in not following Knox at this point. However, neither has answered Knox's arguments and evidence, and thus their own work,

which presupposes Marcan priority with Knox, is at this point critically less consistent than that of Knox. Others will have noted that I have rested nothing on the Muratorian Canon. The reason for this is that its date and provenance have both been thrown into doubt by Albert C. Sundberg, Jr., in "Canon Muratori: A Fourth-Century List," *Harvard Theological Review* 66 (January 1973): 1–41. Sundberg's conclusions have in part been challenged by Everett Ferguson, "Canon Muratori: Date and Provenance," Eighth International Conference on Patristic Studies (Oxford, Sept. 3–8, 1979).

227. This information on Hippolytus's New Testament canon is drawn from Edgar J. Goodspeed, *A History of Early Christian Literature,* rev. Robert M. Grant (Chicago: University Press, 1966), p. 150.

228. Since Origen was born around A.D. 185 or 186, and since he tells us that he visited Rome when Zephyrinus was bishop (A.D. 198–217), Lightfoot conjectures that Origen's visit would probably have taken place towards the close of Zephryinus's episcopate. See Lightfoot, *Apostolic Fathers,* vol. 2, p. 423.

229. *Lives of Illustrious Men* (61), *Nicene and Post-Nicene Fathers,* vol. 3, p. 375.

230. "A fifth influence on Christian Alexandria was Irenaeus, native of Asia Minor (possibly Smyrna) and bishop of Lyons in the last quarter of the second century." Walter J. Burghardt, "Free like God: Recapturing an Ancient Anthropology," *Theology Digest* 26, no. 4 (Winter 1978): 348. Lightfoot conjectures that Hippolytus heard Irenaeus lecture in Rome during Irenaeus's visit there about A.D. 177. The dependence of Hippolytus upon Irenaeus "is obvious on all hands," according to Lightfoot. Therefore, if the two did not first have contact in Rome, it is probable that Hippolytus had his Christian schooling in the south of Gaul since the extant writings of Hippolytus "contain no indication he was ever in the east," where otherwise he might have had contact with Irenaeus in Asia Minor before Irenaeus migrated to Gaul. See Lightfoot, *Apostolic Fathers,* vol. 2, p. 422.

231. Matthew, Mark, Luke, John, Acts, Paul's letters (including Hebrews), 1 John, 1 Peter, and the Revelation of John.

232. John J. O'Meara in the introduction to Origen, prayer, and the exhortation to martyrdom in *Ancient Christian Writers,* eds. Johannes Quasten, Joseph C. Plumpe (London, 1954), pp. 5–6.

233. *Homilies on Jeremias* 4. 3, quoted in Frend, *Martyrdom,* p. 322.

Addendum: On p. 94, I have substituted "traduced" for "believed" in order to take minimal account of an important discovery concerning Augustine's full position on the relationship between the Gospels made by David Peabody after this book had passed the galley proof stage.

Indexes

SCRIPTURE REFERENCES

SUBJECT-AUTHOR INDEX